Radical Economics

General Editor: SAM AA

Debates between economists are not just technical arguments amongst practitioners but often reflect philosophical and ideological positions which are not always made explicit.

Discontent grew with the prevailing economic orthodoxy as the long period of economic expansion in the advanced capitalist economies came to an end in the 1970s; disenchantment was expressed in open discussion about the 'crisis' in economics and in the rise of various kinds of radical economic theory, often using the general title of 'political economy'.

Many economists have looked for a more fruitful point of departure in the ideas of Marx and the classical economists and also in such contemporary economists as Kalecki and Sraffa. Although it is possible to identify a broad radical stream, it does not mean that there are no significant controversies within this radical approach and, indeed, it would be unhealthy if this were not the case.

Can radical economic theory interpret the world better than the current orthodoxy which it challenges? And can it show also how to change it? This is a challenge which this series proposes to take up, adding to work already being done.

Each book will be a useful contribution to its particular field and should become a text around which the study of economics takes place.

Radical Economics

Published

Amit Bhaduri, *Macroeconomics*
Michael Bleaney, *The Rise and Fall of Keynesian Economics*
Keith Cowling, *Monopoly Capitalism*
Michael Howard, *Profits in Economic Theory*
Paul Hare, *Planning the British Economy*
Malcolm C. Sawyer, *The Economics of Michał Kalecki*

Forthcoming

Terry Byres, *The Political Economy of Poor Nations*
Matthew Edel, *Urban Economics*
David Purdy, *The Theory of Wages*

Macroeconomics

The Dynamics of Commodity Production

AMIT BHADURI

MACMILLAN

First published 1986

Published by
MACMILLAN EDUCATION LTD
Houndmills, Basingstoke, Hampshire RG21 2XS
and London
Companies and representatives
throughout the world

Published in India by
MACMILLAN INDIA LTD
Delhi, Bombay,
Madras, Parna,
Bangalore, Hydrabad,
Lucknow, Trivandrum

Printed in Hong Kong

British Library Cataloguing in Publication Data

Bhaduri, Amit
Macroeconomics: the dynamics of commodity
production. —(Radical economics)
1. Macroeconomics
I. Title II. Series
339   HB172.5
ISBN 0–333–29194–8
ISBN 0–333–29195–6 Pbk

For Madhu

Contents

Preface

Yet another textbook on macroeconomics requires some justification from its author. The climate of opinion among economists recently seems to have shifted in favour of the view that the Keynesian style of economic management does not work in industrial capitalism. This has provided an opportunity for various related doctrines like 'monetarism' and 'supply-side economics' to surface as contending views. They argue that the Keynesian view of economic management is theoretically defective and a better alternative is to rely less on economic intervention by the State and more on the market mechanism. An unaware beginner is likely to be caught in these controversies without realising their basis. Conventional Keynesian policies failed under *changed* political circumstances. And yet, the Keynesian style of economic management over years contributed in no small measure to change those very circumstances. In this sense, the very success of Keynesian economics during the post-war years of capitalist prosperity contained its own seed of destruction.

Unfortunately, the initial success of conventional Keynesianism blinded most of its exponents and practitioners to the inherently radical content of that theory. One has to learn this from Kalecki rather than from Keynes. Taking his clues from Marx, Kalecki not only independently discovered most of the central propositions of the Keynesian theory, but he also set it out with striking clarity to point to a set of problems which conventional Keynesianism had preferred to avoid. Conventional Keynesians remained content with the idea that capitalism could be managed by the State. And, they propagated a view of State-managed capitalism based on co-operation rather than conflict among the contending economic classes. In Kalecki's writings there was no such wishful thinking. He recognised that a view of co-operative capitalism was bound to run into serious problems in the longer run, as economic conflict among the classes begins to surface. He forewarned us about it in his theory of political business cycles. For many years, conventional Keynesianism maintained its 'respectability' by distancing itself from this unavoidable truth of conflicting class interests. So, when 'monetarism' and 'supply-side economics' more or less openly propounded views against the interest of the organised working class, conventional Keynesianism was caught unaware. The terms of the debate had been changed; but conventional Keynesianism had not ventured out of its earlier model of co-operative capitalism.

The changed circumstances undoubtedly call for a thorough reformulation. We must bring into focus the radical content of Keynesianism by concentrating on the *common* macroeconomic tradition of Marx, Kalecki and Keynes. This is what the present textbook attempts to do. It shows how Marx's method of analysis in terms of 'historical categories' (Chapter 1) naturally leads to an analysis of capitalist commodity production under the principle of effective demand (Chapter 2). However, the level of effective demand is determinate only with respect to a given class distribution of income. This shows itself in the relationship between prices and money wages and gives rise to the notion of cost-determined prices at the micro-level of the enterprise, discussed at some length in Chapter 3. Thus, Chapters 1 to 3 provide the core of the analysis of capitalist commodity production on which the rest of the argument of this book is built.

Commodity production takes place under uncertainty and the essential features of a monetary economy cannot be understood without introducing uncertainty. Chapter 4 discusses this problem to contrast the Keynesian view of monetary management against the economics and politics of 'new monetarism'.

The simplification of a 'closed' economy is given up in Chapter 5 to extend the principle of effective demand and some monetary problems to an 'open' economy. This enables us to discuss the double-edged nature of trade relations among nations: they are *rivals* as well as *partners* in trade. The controversies about 'free trade versus protection' as well as the economic basis of imperialism can be better appreciated in this context. The financing of international trade and investment also sets the monetary problems in an international context. These problems are discussed in Chapter 5 against the background of the historical evolution of international financial arrangements and its implications for national economics.

Chapter 6 applies the two fundamental ideas of capitalist macroeconomics – the principle of effective demand and the relation between prices and money wages (explained in Chapters 2 and 3 respectively) – to the problem of business cycles and inflation. The inflationary process is seen to be rooted in the economic conflict among the classes which may ultimately involve the State. Regular business fluctuations emphasise an almost absurd aspect of capitalist commodity production. Investment at any steady pace fails to be sustainable because *useful* investment of today exhausts investment opportunities for tomorrow. Therefore, investment and technological development have to assume a peculiarly destructive role to keep the show of capitalist commodity production going.

Chapter 7 sets out more systematically the conditions needed for capitalist commodity production to proceed on an expanding scale. Not only are these conditions highly stringent, but they may never materialise due to the arbitrary initial conditions inherited from past history. History intervenes to make capitalistic accumulation in a steady state impossible. It needs to be emphasised that, like Voltaire's god, we invent the notion of steady capitalistic accumulation only to realise how different any historical process of accumulation must be in reality.

Chapter 8 discusses the relation between economic policy and political ideology. Perhaps the simplest way to characterise such political ideology is to analyse the notion of the State which is supposed to carry out economic policies. Therefore, Chapter 8 explores the notion of the State in relation to economic policy.

It is suggested that any reader interested in the range of issues discussed here must consider Chapters 1 to 4 essential background reading. The materials covered in the remaining chapters may be read according to particular requirements. The level of mathematics required of a reader has been kept to the minimum level possible without sacrificing expositional clarity. Any reader with high school algebra would be able to follow the entire text. Slightly more advanced mathematical techniques, whenever used in the text (e.g., solving difference equations in Chapter 6), have been derived from the first principle. So the reader should have no difficulty in following the algebra. And even a reader who has virtually no background in mathematics can follow the entire argument because literary exposition precedes formal presentation in each case, supplemented by diagrams whenever necessary. There are also suggestions for further reading at the end of each chapter. I have tried to explain briefly the content of the further reading materials and their level of difficulty in most cases to help the reader to choose.

Most of the materials covered here grew out of my attempts to teach a useful course on the macroeconomics of capitalism in various universities in India, Europe and Mexico. I gratefully recall the criticisms and responses of my students and colleagues, too numerous to be individually mentioned here. Nevertheless, I must mention my special intellectual debt to Joan Robinson, with whom I had the opportunity to discuss over a period of nearly twenty years some of the problems analysed here. She, more than anybody else, convinced me of the radical content of Keynesian economics which we could decipher more easily with the help of Marx and Kalecki. The academic profession of economists has generally been too happy to deliberately underplay it. This textbook would have served its purpose if it prepares the reader to ask those uncomfortable questions about the working of a capitalist economy which the mainstream economic profession would prefer us to forget.

Mexico City Amit Bhaduri
December 1984

1
The Nature of Capitalistic Production

A The Historical Context of Economic Analysis

That society is a collection of individuals is an obviously true but somewhat banal statement. It is a true statement in so far as *all* societies satisfy this definition; and it is also a banal statement, because such a definition does not distinguish sufficiently among different types of societies. A primitive tribal society, a society based on slavery or a modern industrial society are all societies as collections of individuals. Clearly the definition lacks any cutting edge to distinguish among those different types of societies.

This raises a point of fundamental importance regarding the use of definitions or categories in social analysis. A category which is so general (e.g. 'society is a collection of individuals') that it actually fails to take into account important differences among social formations is bound to suffer from the vice of over-generalisation. It is a *general* category which does not pay sufficient attention to *particular* characteristics of the type of society being analysed. However, one can also run into the opposite problem of under-generalisation by using categories that are too particular in social analysis. By using categories that are extremely narrow and totally specific to a particular situation, one may end up with an analysis that admits of no generalisation at all. The 'analysis' then becomes a mere description of a particular situation; and, it is not a 'theory' because it is not generalisable to any other situation.

Meaningful theorisation about society must strive to attain a middle path between vacuous over-generalisation on the one hand and mere description on the other. To go beyond mere description, theory must rely on concepts and categories that are not too narrow and specific to a given situation. Nevertheless, this must not be overdone by relying simply on general categories that are so general that they rob the theory altogether of its descriptive relevance in particular situations. In short, theory must be generalisable within a *specified* context.

To define the domain of operation, i.e., the context of a particular economic or social theory, we must begin by asking ourselves what the purpose of that theory is. Radical economic theorising, in the tradition of Marx, maintains that the ultimate purpose of economic analysis is to understand better changes and developments in social history. Given this purpose, the context of economic theory must be defined in relation to history; and this gives rise to the notion of *historical categories* which combine the tautological aspect of purely logical or universal categories (e.g. 'society is a collection of individuals') with its *particular* historical aspects. The use of such historical categories to conduct logical analysis was the most fundamental contribution of the Marxian method of analysis. It also distinguishes the Marxian mode of theorising from all other technocratic views of economic analysis. For instance, much of contemporary analytical economics starts from the assumption of a Robinson Crusoe economy, i.e., one individual *in isolation* making his economic decisions. It is then assumed that a large number of such isolated individuals or Robinson Crusoes constitute the economy so that simply by magnifying (or aggregating) one individual's decision, one can arrive at conclusions regarding how the economic society as a whole functions. In terms of what has been said before, the fallacy of this approach should be evident: it falls into the trap of operating only in terms of some universal concept of the society namely, society simply as a collection of isolated individuals. But as soon as we drop the assumption of an *isolated* individual, we face the question of how individuals are placed in relation to each other in the economic organisation of a particular society. The answer to this question assumes a particular and not a universal form: a slave is placed in a particular relation *vis-à-vis* his mater; the industrial worker is situated in yet another particular way *vis-à-vis* his employer, while the member of a tribal society is placed in a still different manner *vis-à-vis* the tribal chief. The interplay of the general or the universal concept and the particular or the specific concept now becomes somewhat more concrete to grasp. The universal concept of the society simply as a collection of individuals has to be combined with the more particular concept of how these individuals are placed in the social organisation in relation to each other in a particular type of society.

However, the relationships into which individuals are placed *vis-à-vis* each other in a social organisation can have many aspects. For example, there are relations among individuals through family ties or a more general kinship system; there are also relations among individuals through cultural ties, e.g. the same linguistic or religious groupings. All these various aspects of social grouping generate *social* relations which place individuals in definite relations to each other and also *vis-à-vis* the groups to which they belong or do not belong. For economic analysis, however, it is of fundamental importance to start with one definite complex of relations – the relations which exist among individuals in *the social organisation of production*. We may simply call these the *'relations of production'*, as distinguished from many other types of social and cultural relations mentioned above that may also exist among the individuals in a society.

Since these 'relations of production' are specific to different types of societies, they provide a powerful method of historical classification of societies: a slave economy differs from a modern industrial economy mainly because the relations of production that exist between the slave and his master are different from the production relations that obtain between an industrial worker and his employer. This historical specificity of the relations of production not only provides a criterion for historical classification of societies, but its explicit recognition in social analysis transforms general categories (e.g. 'society is a collection of individuals') into historical categories: categories that combine the general aspects with the particular historical aspects in a meaningful way. Nevertheless, the historical specificity of the relations of production also compels us to recognise that there can be no unified social theory which applies to all types of societies. It is again a common vice of the modern technocratic view of economics to suggest that theory is based only on general concepts and assumptions (like, 'economic rationality') which are relevant to all societies. This view is wrong because it is ahistorical; and, it is ahistorical because it ignores the historical specificity of the production relations. It stands to commonsense that the macroeconomic theory of a tribal or a slave economy must be quite different from that of a modern industrial economy. And yet, a purely technocratic and ahistorical view of economic theory will find it difficult to explain precisely how such differences in economic theory may arise, because it tends to ignore those specific historical circumstances of production that are defined by a particular set of production relations. This is an error into which no radical economic theory in the tradition of Marx must fall. It requires in turn an explicit specification of the historical context of economic theory, a context from which the historical categories for further analysis are to be derived. In the analysis developed throughout this work, our historical context is *industrial capitalism*. So our first task must be to define a historically specific set of production relations which differentiates capitalism from other types of social organisation of production. Such production relations are the distinguishing features of capitalistic production. They also emphasise that capitalism is one of the many historically specific forms of social organisation of production; it is no more than one particular segment in the evolution of human history. And, that segment defines the historical context of the macroeconomic theory developed in the following pages.

B Distinguishing Features of Capitalistic Production

If we look at a number of individual capitalist countries, each one of them would have its own particular features and particular history. The purpose of *economic abstraction* is to try to isolate the more or less overlapping features which are common to all these economies organised fundamentally on the basis of *capitalist relations of production*.

Perhaps the most important characteristic of capitalism is *commodity production*, i.e., production not for the direct use of the producer but for the market. In this sense, any product made by the producer for his own use is *not* a commodity. Therefore, there is an essential social distinction between a 'commodity' and a 'product'. Thus, the bread baked by a baker for the use of his own family is only a product; but the bread that is baked for selling in the market is a commodity. The crucial characteristic of any commodity is therefore not its physical characteristic, but the purpose for which it is made: and, the same bread can either be a product for self-consumption or a commodity produced for some anonymous buyer in the market. Whoever buys the commodity in the market then becomes its owner.

The capitalist economy is predominantly a system of *production of commodities by means of commodities*. Virtually everything is produced for the market, with only a very negligible part of the total production retained for self-consumption by the producer. At the same time, the inputs needed for production of commodities are also bought almost entirely from the market. Thus, the baker buys his wheat and his fuel from the market to bake his bread instead of producing all these items of input himself. This makes him a *buyer* of commodities like wheat and coal on the one hand; but on the other hand, he is also the producer of a commodity, namely bread, which he *sells* in the market. This is precisely what is meant by production of commodities by means of commodities, resulting in an impersonal market where exchange of commodities take place with each producer generally having the *dual role* of both a buyer and a seller of commodities in the market.

However, capitalist production is not just production of commodities by means of commodities. Imagine a *self-employed* artisan who buys his leather from the market and sells his shoes in the market. He owns the equipment with which he works and being strictly self-employed, he does not directly hire the services of any outside labourer for making shoes. This is *simple commodity production* because, although the self-employed artisan may be buying all his material inputs like leather as commodity from the market, there is one crucial 'input' (from his point of view) which he never buys as a commodity from the market namely, the labour service. This makes him a 'simple commodity producer' as a self-employed person, rather than a capitalist producer.

By implication, it is now clear that a capitalist *producer* is not only engaged in commodity production, but also buys labour services along with other material inputs as commodities from the market. Therefore, *capitalist production entails production of commodities by means of commodities, when labour service like any other commodity is also bought and sold in the market.*

Whatever is bought and sold in the market has to have a price. Labour *service*, being a commodity like any other under capitalistic production is also bought and sold in the market at a 'price'. This price is the *wage rate* for labour service. However, the wage rate being the price of labour service rather than the labourer must have a time dimension. Hence, the wage rate is related to the duration of time for which the service of a labourer is bought and sold. Thus, it is wage rate per man-hour, man-week or man-month, as the case may be. In contrast, say for example in a slave economy, the very person of the slave, i.e., the labourer himself is bought and sold in the market. Consequently, the price of the slave has no time dimension. This distinction would be apparent if one thinks in terms of purchasing any durable item, say a car. The price of the car like the price of a slave, is without any time dimension; but hiring the service of a car, like hiring labour service, obviously has a time dimension, with the hiring rate varying according to the duration of hiring of the service in days, weeks or months. In a market economy, we should therefore be careful to distinguish between those prices which are defined as *rates* of *flows* of services, etc. during a unit of time[1] and prices which have no such time dimension as they are simply once-for-all transactions. In the latter case, whoever buys a commodity in the market simply becomes its owner whereas, in the former case the buyer becomes the 'owner' only during the period for which he has paid for the service, at the going rate.

It will now be evident that in a slave economy, the buyer of the slave becomes his owner and may use his slave in whatever manner and with whichever intensity he likes (i.e., the slave has to work with no fixed working hours per day). In contrast, in a capitalist economy, the capitalist is only the owner of the services of the labourer for the given period of time for which he buys it. Under a typical wage contract in a modern industrial economy the services of a worker are bought at a wage rate defined say per man-day, i.e., for so many hours per day. Once the contractual amount of service is performed, the labourer is free to use his own time or even to enter into another wage contract with a separate employer. This freedom a slave cannot enjoy; and formally, this is reflected by the fact that wage is defined as a rate per unit of time. To grasp the historical specificity of such wage–labour contract, it may also be contrasted with a tribal economy, where labour is performed by each ordinary member of a tribe. However, it is usually done not in exchange of a wage rate or price, but according to communal customs and obligations. Thus, unlike either in a slave or in a capitalist economy, neither the person nor the services of the person is a commodity for buying and selling in the labour market. In other words, no market either for the person of labour or labour services exists within the tribal economy.

In the above, we have at least three historically specific illustrations of how the use of labour is made under different production relations. A tribal economy governed by customs has no market either for labour or for labour services; labour is simply not a commodity. In contrast, in a slave economy the very person of the slave, i.e., the labourer himself or herself, is bought and sold in the market as a commodity. And finally, a capitalist economy where labour *service*, rather than the labourer, is a commodity. These illustrations highlight the differences in *social forms of labour*, i.e., the mode of labour use in different types of social organisation. Hence, *wage labour· as the predominant social form of labour* emerges as a historically distinguishing feature of capitalist production.

However, wage labour is a consequence, not a cause, of the specific historical circumstances under which capitalist production is organised. In contrast to our earlier examples of say, a self-employed baker or an artisan, the wage labourer is *not* a 'simple commodity producer'. Because, he neither owns the factory in which he works nor would he ever be able to carry on the process of production with his own limited financial means. Indeed, large-scale factory production and distribution trade (e.g. the supermarket chains) have become the dominant form of business organisation under industrial capitalism. They require access to enormous finance to carry on business activity, whereas a typical industrial worker virtually has no 'entry' into the market for finance. Under capitalist rules of finance, a person's ability to borrow (say, from banks) depends on how much property he already owns; because his own property is the collateral security against which more loan can be raised. Such a criterion of 'creditworthiness' systematically discriminates against persons with little or no property and generally rules out the possibility of an ordinary industrial worker ever being able to finance his own business. Thus, being separated from the means of production with which he works, the worker in a capitalist economy is compelled to sell his labour service as a commodity and the 'rules of finance' like creditworthiness, ensure that most wage labourers will continue to remain separated from their means of production (and subsistence) in terms of both ownership rights and control of the production process. Consequently, *the separation of labour from the means of production* provides the definite historical circumstances as well as the underlying precondition for the existence of wage labour as the predominant social form of labour.

The reverse side of the picture is the *property rights* of the capitalists over the means of production which allow them both to control and to organise production on the basis of wage labour. The manner in which labour service is used in production, i.e., the particular nature of the *labour process* is decided and controlled by the owners of property namely the capitalists, often with the aid of hired managers. And, the hired workers have no option but to largely accept the 'discipline of work' imposed on them as a part of the contract of hiring their labour services. This provides the basis for the social organisation of production of commodities along capitalist lines. And, in that very social organisation of production is embedded the particular *class structure* of capitalism. A class is essentially defined in terms of its relation to the *ownership* and control of the means of production: as a simple first approximation, the owners of the means of production constitute the capitalist class, while those who own nothing but their labour service for sale as a commodity in the market constitute the working class. This particular class structure is still another distinguishing feature of capitalist production, where the economic society is fundamentally divided between owners of the means of production and those who own nothing but their labour service. A little reflection will show that this *particular* class structure does not necessarily obtain under other types of society. Thus, in a society of predominantly self-employed peasants, each cultivating peasant owns the land on which he employs only his labour. The means of production, land and implements in this case, are not separated from the ownership of the working peasant and we cannot meaningfully define a class structure in terms of ownership of the means of production, even if some of the peasants may be richer than others, because they own more fertile or greater area of land. This emphasises the point that ownership of means of production rather than relative wealth and poverty, is the crucial dividing line among classes in an economy. Similarly, a slave society does not have the same *particular* class structure of a capitalist society. One could also think of a tribal society, where the tribe as a collective has communal property right to the land it cultivates. Even when individual members of the tribe have rights to *use* the plots of land allotted to them by the community, they do not have the right to *own* them in the sense of capitalist property. When every member has this right to use a piece of land, no one may be compelled to sell his labour service for a livelihood and such communal property right will tend to exclude the existence of wage labour as the dominant social form of labour. From these illustrations of various historically specific forms of property rights, it is now clear that the dominant social form of labour in each society is a consequence of the nature of property rights that obtains under it.

These property rights in turn, define the class structure of a society and is the very basis on which the relations of production of a society are built. The capitalist relations of production therefore reflect the property rights peculiar to a historically specific form of society called 'capitalism'.

It is also in this context that 'capital' emerges as the central concept: capitalists are capitalists because that particular set of production relations bestows on them the right to own 'capital' and the economy is capitalist because it operates on the basis of the rules set by 'capital'. How do we define 'capital' then?

From our preceding discussion it should be evident that 'capital' is *not* just produced means of production. For, produced means of production is a universal concept applicable to all forms of society; the self-employed artisan under simple commodity production uses his implements as means of production and so does a slave. 'Capital', therefore, has to be a concept more specifically related to the production relations under capitalism. Means of production become 'capital' only when (a) they are also separated from the wage-labourers who work with them, and (b) they provide income namely 'profits' to those who own those means of production, entirely by virtue of that ownership right. Unless these two specific social conditions are also satisfied, produced means of production cannot be said to assume the historical characteristics of 'capital'. In other words, *'capital' is also a* social relation specifically embedded in capitalist relations of production; it cannot be treated simply as a physical concept related to equipments and raw materials that are needed as means of production in *any* type of society. Indeed, the failure to distinguish between 'capital' as means of production and 'capital' as a social relation embodying property rights has caused a great deal of confusion in contemporary economic theory. For example, the 'aggregate production function' in modern economic theory, where output is treated as a technologically determined function of labour and 'capital', treats 'capital' simply as a stock of means of production. But then it jumps to the conclusion that the 'marginal product', i.e., the product obtained from an incremental dose of 'capital' is equal to the rate of profit. However, from what has been said before, it is evident that profit is a form of property income, resulting from the ownership rights to the means of production. This is a social relation. Consequently, 'capital' as means of production is confused with 'capital' as property rights in such marginal productivity doctrine of profit; the resulting confusion shows up in what appears superficially as statistical problems in measuring 'capital'.

The thrust of our argument should now be clear: the universal concept of a 'product' takes the particular social form of a 'commodity' under market exchange. The universal concept of 'labour' takes the particular social form of 'wage labour' under capitalism. Similarly, the universal concept of 'produced means of production' takes the particular social character of 'capital' only under capitalist production relations. This method of combining the general or the universal concept with its specific social form in a given historical context suggests the procedure for making the difficult transition from sterile logical analysis based only on universal concepts to more meaningful social analysis based upon historical categories. Because, only in this way are we able to pay sufficient attention to the particular social context of each general concept and avoid meaningless over-generalisation of ahistorical nature (see preceding Section A). Since the historical specificity of universal concepts in each case is derived from a particular set of production relations, we must proceed to analyse industrial capitalism as a specific historical form by basing our concepts and categories of analysis in those production relations that distinguish capitalism from other social formations. For convenience of ready reference in our future argument, we may list below these distinguishing features of capitalistic production relations:

1. *Production of commodities by means of commodities*, where production takes place for the market and all inputs for production are also purchased from the market. This implies that each individual is both a buyer and a seller in the market, giving rise to circular flows of income (as we shall see in the next section).
2. *Wage labour* is the dominant social form of labour. Labour service is bought and sold like any other commodity in the market at a price or wage rate.
3. The particular *class structure* which broadly divides a capitalist society among those who own (and control) the means of production, namely the capitalists and those who own only their labour service, namely the workers. Their ownership or *property rights* allow the capitalists to control the manner in which labour service is used in commodity production, i.e., the *labour process*. It also defines 'capital' as a social relation based on these particular property rights. Its consequence is 'profits' to the capitalists entirely by virtue of their property rights.

C Accounting Concepts and Conventions in a Capitalist Economy

Although most accountants do not make it explicit, their standard accounting practices are crucially dependent on a set of historical categories that are mostly relevant to capitalist production. This means that those accounting conventions will make little sense unless the historically distinguishing features of capitalist production relations, briefly listed at the end of the last section, are presupposed. And, without some awareness of this historical dimension of accounting concepts, one is likely to fall into the *error of confusing historical categories* in making use of the conventional accounting systems.

To illustrate the nature of this confusion, we could start with the important accounting concept of *value added* by an enterprise or an industry (i.e., a collection of enterprises producing similar products). Suppose, this enterprise or industry produces wooden furniture which it intends to sell in the market and buys all its intermediate inputs or raw materials like wood and chemicals from the market. It is clearly a situation of production of commodities by means of commodities because the enterprise or industry is placed in the market *both* as a seller of furniture and as a buyer of wood and chemicals. This enables us to roughly define the value added by such an enterprise or industry as the value of the output produced by it *minus* the value of its purchased inputs at well-defined market prices.

What needs to be noted in the above definition of value added is the fact that the output as well as *all* the required inputs have clearly defined prices in the market, i.e., it is precisely a situation of production of commodities by means of commodities. When that is not the case, e.g. some raw material like wood is collected from the forest instead of being bought from the market, ambiguities begin to appear in the concept of value added. It is often the convention in economic accounting to *impute market prices*, even when the input in question is not actually bought from the market. However, such a procedure based upon *imputed prices* can be highly misleading in many situations precisely because it may result in the error of category confusion. The reasons for this are not difficult to see. To start with, the procedure of imputing prices makes sense only if the input or product in question has a market, i.e. it has become a commodity. A rather interesting example based upon historical research may be used to illustrate this point.[2] When historians analysed the accounts of large landed estates in Poland of the sixteenth and seventeenth centuries, they found that by imputing the then market prices to all the raw materials, the resulting value added in production of these estates becomes unbelievably small, or even negative in some cases. Its explanation lies in the invalid procedure of imputing market prices to many inputs, which historically had no developed market. A typical example was provided by timber located in areas far removed from waterways which could not be transported and therefore had no possibility of being sold as a commodity in the market. And yet, by imputing a uniform market price to such timber, one meaninglessly exaggerated the cost of raw materials only to arrive at a misleadingly low magnitude of value added.

Such errors of confusing historical categories that arise from imposing accounting concepts and procedures relevant for capitalist production relations to very different types of economic organisation, become all the more glaring when one tries to stretch the concept of 'profit' beyond capitalist production relations. Profit is defined as, value added *minus* the value of labour services. This definition presents no problem so long as labour services are purchased at market wage under capitalist production.[3] However, when that is not the case, as for example in a peasant household using only family labour intensively to cultivate its rather small piece of land, imputation of market wage rates to such family labour services may often result in negative profit. Not surprisingly, for similar reasons, historical research on the accounts of large landed estates in sixteenth and seventeenth century Poland also showed such negative profit, when the then market wages were imputed to all the labour services performed by the serfs of those estates.

It should be clear that one cannot read much significance into such calculations of 'negative profit'; in particular, it does not mean that the peasant households or the large landed feudal estates were actually running at a loss in the sense of being economically unviable over time. At best, it supports a contrafactual statement like, if these peasant households or feudal estates were run as capitalist enterprises (which in fact they were not), they would have been economically unviable. One has to deal with such contrafactual statements very carefully because they can have meaning only when opportunities simultaneously exist for also running them as capitalist enterprises, e.g., the household labour of the peasant farm or serf labour of the feudal estate could find alternative employment as wage labour. Only then the market wage rate could be imagined as the *opportunity cost* of their labour service. But, where such opportunities do not exist for one reason or another, such contrafactual statements based upon imputation of wages to different social forms of labour would become positively misleading as a result of confusion in historical categories.

Leaving aside such confusion in historical categories, standard accounting practices even within the limited context of say, a capitalist enterprise, cannot usually avoid some degree of arbitrariness arising from imputed prices. All markets are not sufficiently developed even in a most advanced capitalist economy so that, it becomes necessary to impute prices. The accounting concept of 'capital consumption' or *depreciation* is an important example illustrating this point. To arrive at an annual figure of *net* (as opposed to gross) value added by an enterprise, the accountant deducts from the annual value of output produced by that enterprise not only the cost of raw materials used but also the 'wear and tear' of fixed equipment and machinery during that year. In principle then, depreciation is an allowance made per unit of time (say, a year) to cover the 'wear and tear' of long-lived machines used during the year in production. If markets for all types of second-hand machinery existed, differentiated according to the age of machines, then market value for depreciation could be found in each case. For example, if a particular machine at the end of its third and fourth year of use costs $30 000 and $28 000 respectively in the market, then depreciation during its fourth year of use could simply be calculated as the corresponding difference in price, i.e. ($30 000 − $28 000) = $2 000 only. Nevertheless, the fact remains that even in the most developed capitalist economy, such age-wise finely differentiated markets with standardised prices for second-hand machinery hardly ever exist. Consequently, the accountant has no option but to follow some 'rule-of-thumb' convention, e.g. the method of straight-line depreciation in which the market price of a brand new machine (say, $50 000) is divided by the supposed lifetime of the machine (say, ten years) to arrive at an annual figure for depreciation allowance, i.e. ($50 000 ÷ 10 years) = $5 000 per year.[4]

It can now be seen that even in the most limited context of a capitalist enterprise, the principle of commercial accounting resting on the assumption that every relevant item of calculation is a commodity with a well-defined market price, is bound to face many problems. Indeed, even the value of output produced by the enterprise is not unambiguous when it sells only a part of that output and retains the rest – intentionally or unintentionally – as *changes in its stock of inventories of finished goods*. Accounting convention requires us to value such increases in inventories at the same price at which the rest of its output was sold. Nevertheless, this increased inventory may be totally unintentional reflecting precisely the fact that it could not have been sold at that price. However, for defining the value added by an enterprise, accounting convention typically has to gloss over such problems arising from inventory changes by simply imputing the going market price to inventory changes.

Given the assumption of well-defined market prices (and by imputing prices as accounting conventions whenever necessary) for *all* the commodities produced and used in production, we can define the value added during a period by a capitalist enterprise or industry j as:

$$\text{Value added } (VA_j) = \text{sales } (V_j) + \text{inventory changes } (A_j)$$
$$- \text{value of total intermediate inputs } (U_j) \qquad (1.1)$$

But total intermediate inputs (U_j) consist of purchased intermediate inputs as raw materials (Z_j) as well as the 'wear and tear' of durable items used in production. When no allowance is made to cover this latter element of depreciation (D_j), we have *gross* value added *including* depreciation as,

$$\text{Gross value added } (GVA_j)$$
$$= \text{Sales } (V_j) + \text{inventory changes } (A_j)$$
$$- \text{Purchase of intermediate raw materials } (Z_j) \qquad (1.2)$$

Hence, *net* value added excluding depreciation is,

$$\text{Net value added } (NVA_j)$$
$$= \text{gross value added } (GVA_j) - \text{depreciation } (D_j) \qquad (1.3)$$

Another point to note in (1.1) and (1.2) in defining value added is that, sales (V_j) plus inventory changes (A_j) measure the value of output produced (X_j) during a period. Hence, increase or *accumulation of inventories* has to be added and decrease or *decumulation of (past) inventories* has to be subtracted from the total sales figure (V_j) of the period to arrive at the value of production (X_j) during that period.

The concept of value added by an enterprise or an industry is very useful because, unlike the value of its total production (X_j), the value added (VA_j) roughly measures the contribution made by that enterprise or industry to the economy. Because the value of total production (X_j) also includes the value of purchased intermediate inputs (Z_j) which were *not* produced by that enterprise or industry j

(e.g. (1.2) can be rewritten as, $VA_j + Z_j = V_j + A_j = X_j$). Consequently, the value of total output (X_j) *overestimates* the economic contribution made by the enterprise or industry j. Such overestimation arises from the *error of double counting*: for example, say industry 'w' which sells its final output 'wood' to industry 'f' producing 'furniture', has in the value added by the wood industry (i.e., VA_w) already counted the value of the wood sold to furniture industry. So we must not count *again* the value of wood in the value of furniture produced. But this is exactly what would happen if we take the total output (X_f) instead of the value added (VA_f) by the furniture industry. Hence, to avoid such error of double counting in measuring the contribution made to the economy by an enterprise or industry, it is essential to take its value added (VA_j) which is net of raw materials purchased and *not* the value of its total output (X_j).

We could now imagine the capitalist economy as consisting of several productive sectors. A 'sector' could be almost anything: an enterprise, an industry, a collection of industries legally defined e.g. the 'public' or the 'private' or the 'corporate' sector or even, a complex and large politico-economic organisation like the 'government'. If we sum up the value added by all the productive sectors in the economy, the total value added avoids double counting to estimate the total economic contribution by all the sectors in the economy. This summation of all the sectoral gross value added defined by (1.2) measures the *gross domestic product* (GDP) by the product method. Since depreciation is not deducted from *gross* value added (see (1.2)) GDP includes depreciation. When depreciation (D_j) is deducted as an input cost from each sector's gross value added, the resulting figures is *net* value added by the sector, as already stated in (1.3); summing over the net value added (NVA_j) of all the sectors, we arrive at *net domestic product* (NDP) which excludes depreciation. The *product method* of macroeconomic accounting can then be represented as,

Gross domestic product (GDP)
$$= \sum_j \text{gross value added } (GVA_j) \qquad (1.4)$$

Or, using (1.3) in (1.4),

$$\text{GDP} = \sum_j \text{net value added } (NVA_j) + \sum_j \text{depreciation } (D_j) \quad (1.5)$$

$$= \text{net domestic product } (NDP) + \text{total depreciation } (D) \quad (1.6)$$

where, the Greek letter, Σ represents summation.

Since gross or net domestic product is nothing but total value added with or without depreciation (see (1.4) and (1.6) above), we could also use the alternative definition of gross value added in (1.2) to estimate gross domestic product (GDP) by another route. This leads to an equivalent but alternative accounting by the *expenditure method*. To see this more explicitly, we use definition (1.2) in (1.4) to obtain,

> Gross domestic product (GDP)
> $= \sum_j$ sales $(V_j) + \sum_j$ inventory changes $(A_j) - \sum_j$ purchase of intermediate raw materials (Z_j)

i.e.,

> GDP = total sales (V) + total inventory changes (A)
> $\quad$ − total purchase of intermediate raw materials (Z)

$$(1.7)$$

Total sales (V) in an *open economy with international trade* equals sales to foreign customers as *exports* as well as sales to domestic customers. However, a part of the total expenditure by domestic customers is on the *import* of goods and only the remaining part is spent on the purchase of *domestically produced goods*. Thus, for total sales of domestically produced say, final consumption goods (V_c), we may write,

> *Final sales* of domestically produced consumption goods (V_c) = export of consumption goods (E_c) + total expenditure by domestic customers on consumption goods (C) − import of consumption goods (M_c)

i.e.,

$$V_c = E_c + (C - M_c) \qquad (1.8)$$

Similarly, for final sales of domestically produced investment goods, we write,

$$V_i = E_i + (I - M_i) \qquad (1.9)$$

where E_i and M_i stand for export and import of final investment goods and I is the total expenditure by domestic customers on investment goods.

Total *sales of raw materials* (V_z) consist of raw materials exported (E_z) and raw materials domestically sold (Z_{ds}), i.e.,

$$V_z = E_z + Z_{ds} \qquad (1.10)$$

On the other hand, total *purchase of raw materials* (Z) is simply, import of raw materials (M_z) plus their domestic purchases (Z_{dp}), i.e.

$$Z = M_z + Z_{dp} \tag{1.11}$$

It should also be added here that all inventory changes (A) being only book-keeping valuation without *actual* market transactions, need not be broken down into final sales and purchases in the manner described by equations (1.8) to (1.11).

Now total sales (V) in the economy must equal sales of final consumption goods (V_c), investment goods (V_i) as well as sales of raw materials (V_z), i.e.

$$\text{Total sales } (V) = V_c + V_i + V_z \tag{1.12}$$

Using now accounting relations (1.8) to (1.12) in the definition of gross domestic product as the sum of gross value added by all sectors in (1.7) and collecting terms we obtain,

$$\begin{aligned} \text{GDP} = C + I + A + (E_c + E_i + E_z) - (M_c + M_i + M_z) \\ + (Z_{ds} - Z_{dp}) \end{aligned} \tag{1.13}$$

Clearly ($E_c + E_i + E_z$) represents the total export (E) and ($M_c + M_i + M_z$) represents the total import (M) of the economy. It now needs to be noted that total domestic sales of raw materials (Z_{ds}) must equal total domestic purchase of raw materials (Z_{dp}) by definition, i.e.

Raw materials domestically sold (Z_{ds})
$$= \text{raw materials domestically purchased } (Z_{dp}) \tag{1.14}$$

Hence, using (1.14) in (1.13), *gross domestic product (GDP) by the expenditure method in an open economy* reduces to:

GDP = consumption expenditure (C) + investment expenditure (I) + inventory change (A) + exports (E) − imports (M) (1.15)

where, all *domestic* purchases and sales of raw materials have cancelled out in aggregate economy-wide accounting.

It follows that evaluation of GDP by the expenditure method of (1.15) requires us to look at only expenditures on *final* goods and excludes expenditure on domestically produced raw materials. However, like so many other accounting concepts, *final* expenditure has to be defined arbitrarily with reference to a *given period of time* (e.g. a year). While the concept of *consumption* by the final consumers is intuitively understandable and can be roughly estimated during a period, the concept of *investment* is considerably trickier. In so far as investment consists of addition to the existing stock of means of production, it has *two* elements: the fixed investment in the form of *new machines* as well as additions to other instruments of production; but it also contains the second element of investment in the form of *addition to* the existing stock of *inventories*, represented as inventory change (A) in (1.15) above. Such inventory change can be treated as *investment in inventories*, which is simply the difference between *closing stock* (i.e. the stock at the end of the period) and the *opening stock* (i.e., the stock at the beginning of the period), i.e., investment in inventories during a period equals the value of closing stock *minus* the value of opening stock.

Some of the problems of arbitrariness involved in the *final* expenditure approach would now be clear. Returning to our earlier example of furniture production, only the *final* expenditure on furniture and no intermediate expenditure, say on the wood required to make furniture, will be included. However, when it comes to expenditure on inventory investment, if the stock of wood held by the furniture industry at the end of the year exceeds its stock at the beginning of the year, then the additional wood must also be included as a part of its final expenditure on inventories. Thus, from the mere physical characteristics of a commodity we cannot say whether it is a 'final' expenditure item or an 'intermediate' expenditure item. It is important to realise that the expenditure approach is *not* based upon such *physical* characteristics of commodities. It was illustrated in the case of inventories by setting a definite time period, which allowed us to define the positions regarding closing and opening stock of each commodity j for estimating inventory changes (A_j) during the period, which then entered as '*final*' expenditure in (1.15).

We have seen above that from the very definition of gross value added given in (1.2), it is possible to arrive at an estimate of GDP by the expenditure method in (1.15) by means of a series of simple substitutions. Consequently, the *product method* of estimating GDP which is simply the summation of gross value added by all productive sectors in (1.4) and the *expenditure method* in (1.15) are *equivalent* in theory. Nevertheless, in practice the product method presents some serious conceptual difficulties in so far as value added by certain 'sectors' is concerned. Since, the value added by a sector presupposes that the value of the output produced by it can be more or less unambiguously measured, a serious conceptual problem is faced in *the valuation of services* provided by either the household or the government sector. In particular, the valuation of services of many public goods like a museum or a park becomes highly problematic. This in turn raises the question of how to evaluate the economic contribution i.e., value added of the government which is the provider of public goods like national defence, law and order, etc. for which no market prices exist. Again, just as in the case of depreciation discussed above (see p. 13), in the absence of market prices for many types of public services, the problem of their valuation must be somewhat arbitrarily settled by accounting conventions. It may also be mentioned here that to avoid such arbitrariness, *macro-accounting procedure in centrally planned* or *socialist economies* deliberately excludes value added by the entire 'service sector' including the government. This results in an estimate of *material production* in the economy excluding services, for which the product method of accounting is better suited.

However, macroeconomic accounting in a capitalist economy includes services and such services produced by sectors like the government and the households are usually evaluated by using another *definition of value added from* the income receipt side. Thus, in place of the product method definition of gross value added (GVA_j) by sector j in (1.2), we could also use a definition which shows how the value added is *distributed* among various types of income like profits, wages and rent (see definition (1.16) that follows). In traditional economic accounting such income categories are often called 'factor incomes' because 'capital', labour and land are assumed to be the three basic 'factors of production' to which corresponding incomes in the form of profit, wage and rent accrue. Although such terminology of 'factor income' is widely accepted in conventional macroeconomic accounting, it can be very misleading in so far as it does not pay sufficient attention to the historically specific production relations of capitalism. To return to our earlier discussion (of Sections A and B above), all types of economy – tribal, self-employed or capitalist – will use land, labour and other produced means of production (called 'capital' in conventional theory) in carrying on production. Nevertheless, labourers receive wage as income against the sale of their labour service as a commodity only in a capitalist economy in which wage-labour has become the predominant social form of labour (see p. 7). Similarly, rent is paid to landlords only because they enjoy private property rights over land. Indeed, one could be hard put to find a category of income called 'rent' in a tribal economy where the entire land is communally owned. Again, profit as income to 'capital' as a 'factor of production' is a meaningless statement, because capitalists are legally entitled to such profit only because capitalist property relations bestow on them the rights to privately own those produced means of production. 'Capital' as we explained earlier (see p. 9) is unavoidably a *social* relation of capitalist production. In a self-employed economy of 'simple commodity production', it would be impossible to separate 'profit' and 'wage' as distinct categories of income. The confusion inherent in treating profit, wage and rent as 'factor incomes' should be apparent now: labour, land and other produced means of production (misleadingly called 'capital' in conventional theory) are needed in production in *all* types of economic formations. And yet, wage, rent and profit emerge as income categories for the corresponding classes of workers, landlords (rentiers) and capitalists only under a specific set of property relations. Therefore, to call such incomes of the various classes 'factor incomes' is to emphasise only the *universal* aspect of production that is based upon land, labour and produced means of production without taking into account its *particular* aspect, i.e., property or production relations that characterise capitalistic production.

Avoiding therefore the vice of over-generalisation implied in terminology such as 'factor income', we decompose gross value added by any sector j (GVA_j) into the types of *class income* relevant to capitalism. Broadly, this yields two types of income for each sector: *income from work* (W_j) against the sale of labour service, consisting of wages and salaries (in the language of internal revenue department in many countries this is called 'earned income'). The other type of income is *income from ownership of property* (O_j) in the form of land as well as produced means of production (the internal revenue department is prone to call it 'unearned income'). This latter category of income from property ownership consists of both rent (Q_j) which arises from landed property rights and profits (R_j) that arises from ownership over other produced means of production. Therefore, we have another definition of gross value added by a sector j in terms of accrual of income to various economic classes, i.e.,

Gross value added (GVA_j) = income from work (W_j) + gross income from ownership of property (GO_j) (1.16)

Further, income from property ownership can be subdivided into rent and profit to yield,

$$\text{Gross income from ownership of property } (GO_j) = \text{rent } (Q_j)$$
$$+ \text{gross profit } (GR_j) \quad (1.17)$$

Since gross value added includes depreciation and inventory change in (1.2) and (1.3), gross profit in (1.17) also has to include these two items,[5] i.e.,

$$\text{Gross profit } (GR_j) = \text{net profits } (NR_j) + \text{depreciation } (D_j)$$
$$+ \text{change in inventory of final goods } (A_j) \quad (1.18)$$

The definition of value added in (1.16) can provide a simple method for evaluating the economic contribution made by a sector. Thus, in conformity with (1.16) and (1.17), *the value added by the government* or any other service sector is evaluated as, wages paid plus profit and rent earned by that sector. However, although correct in a narrow accounting sense, such an estimate of value added by the government is not without problems, e.g., the more the government spends in wages and salaries, the more would be its supposed contribution to the economy! It would naturally have been better to estimate the value added by a sector *both* by the product method (i.e., according to (1.2) above) and by the income method (i.e., according to (1.16) and (1.17) above) whenever possible. Unfortunately, as mentioned earlier, for many services (e.g. banking, insurance, government, etc.) the product method of arriving at value added becomes highly problematic and the income method remains the only option in practice.[6]

As before (see (1.4)), summing up the gross value added of all the sectors defined from the income side in (1.16) and (1.17), we obtain an estimate of gross domestic product (GDP) by the *income method*. Thus, from (1.4), (1.16) and (1.17), GDP is simply the sum of gross profit (GR_j), rent (Q_j) and wage (W_j) of all the individual sectors in the economy, i.e.,

$$\text{Gross domestic product } (GDP) = \sum_j \text{gross profit } (GR_j)$$
$$+ \sum_j \text{rent } (Q_j) + \sum_j (\text{wage } W_j))$$

i.e.,
$$GDP = GR + Q + W \quad (1.19)$$

It can now be seen that there are *three equivalent methods* of estimating the gross domestic product -- GDP can be estimated by the *product method* in (1.4), by the *expenditure method* in (1.15) and by the *income method* in (1.19). However, all the three methods have been used so far only to estimate *domestic* and not *national* product. The conceptual distinction between 'domestic' and 'national' magnitudes in macroeconomic accounting is based on a simple idea: 'domestic' is used as a *geographical or locational concept*. Thus (gross or net) domestic product (GDP or NDP) is the aggregate (gross or net) value added of various productive sectors *located* within the given geographical boundaries of a country. 'National', on the other hand is more of a politico-legal concept: it relates to the aggregate product or income which accrues to the *normal residents* in a country from their economic activity *anywhere* in the world. And that politico-legal concept of 'normal residence' in a country rather than the geographical location of economic activity is the relevant criterion in estimating national product or income.[7] Consider, for example, an American business corporation owning some factories in England. The *domestic* product of England will include the entire value added by those factories because they are located in England. However, for estimating the *national* product of England, we must exclude the various types of incomes in the forms of wages, profits and rents accruing to non-residents (Americans and others) in those factories. For instance, in so far as those Americans are normal residents of the United States, their incomes as profit, wage and rent will be added to the national (but not domestic) product of the United States. On the other hand, normal residents of Britain working elsewhere in the world will be contributing to the national (but not domestic) product of Britain. This defines *net income paid abroad* (*H*) as wage, rent and profit (including interest) paid to non-residents by domestically located firms *minus* total income as wage, rent and profit (including interest) earned by normal residents of the country from foreign sources. In macroeconomic accounting such net income payment abroad is usually called 'net factor payment' on the assumption that, wage, rent and profit are payments to the 'factors of production' land, labour and 'capital', respectively. We have already explained (see pp. 19–20) why such terminology is misleading. Therefore, we prefer to use the more straightforward terminology, *net income payment abroad* (*H*). Gross national product (*GNP*) of a country can now be defined simply as,

Gross national product (*GNP*) = gross domestic product (*GDP*)
− net income payment abroad (*H*)   (1.20)

where net income payment abroad (H) = payments to non-residents as, [Gross profits (GR_{nr}) + wages (W_{nr}) + rent (Q_{nr})] – Earning by residents from foreign sources as, [Gross profits (GR_r) + wages (W_r) + rent (Q_r)], i.e.,

$$H = (GR_{nr} - GR_r) + (W_{nr} - W_r) + (Q_{nr} - Q_r) \qquad (1.21)$$

where the subscripts '*nr*' and '*r*' stand for non-residents and residents respectively.

Similarly, in accordance with (1.6), *net national product* (NNP) is simply obtained as gross national product (GNP) defined by (1.20) *minus* depreciation (D).

At this stage it requires to be pointed out that all our estimates so far are supposed to be made *at market prices*, i.e. prices that include the *indirect taxes net of subsidies* paid by the consumers in the economy. This is most obvious when one arrives at GDP by the expenditure method in (1.15) where all the expenditures are at prices paid by final consumers. Since the alternative estimates of GDP in (1.4) and (1.19) are equivalent, they must also be reckoned at market prices. The problem with market price estimates, is that they tend to mix up income accruing to normal residents from production with income accruing to them from redistribution of income through transfers, like indirect taxes and subsidies. Therefore, it is useful to try to obtain an estimate that distinguishes the income accruing to normal residents of a country due to their participation in production (which is captured by the notion of national income) from the income which may also accrue to them due to redistribution of income through indirect taxes and subsidies. In macroeconomic accounting, this is usually done by first estimating the amount of *net* indirect taxes (IT_n) which equals total collection of indirect taxes *minus* total subsidies paid. By deducting the amount of *net* indirect taxes from corresponding estimates at market prices, we obtain the corresponding estimates *at factor cost*. Thus, *net national product at factor cost* (NNP_{fc}) is simply, net national product at market price (NNP) *minus* net (of subsidies) indirect taxes (IT_n), i.e.,

Net national product at factor cost (NNP_{fc}) = net national product at market prices (NNP) – Net indirect taxes (IT_n)

$$(1.22)$$

Or, substituting the definition of NNP at market prices from (1.6) and (1.20) as, $NNP = GDP - D - H$, we obtain,

Net national product at factor cost (NNP_{fc}) = gross domestic product at market prices (GDP) – total depreciation (D) – net income payment abroad (H) – net indirect taxes (IT_n), i.e.,

$$NNP_{fc} = \text{GDP at market price} - (D + H + IT_n) \tag{1.23}$$

This *net national product at factor cost* in (1.22) or (1.23) *is equivalent to the notion of national income* (NI), which could also be estimated directly as accrual of income to all normal residents in a country due to their participation in production anywhere in the world. The step by step procedure for estimation of national income by adding up all the income of normal residents is simple in principle: by adding all forms of income received by normally resident individuals – wages, interests and dividends (i.e., *distributed* profits of private and public firms) as well as earnings by self-employed persons and non-profitmaking institutions – we arrive at aggregate *personal income* (Y_p) before *direct taxes* (DT). To this personal income (Y_p) if we only add the *undistributed profits of the normally resident private business sector* (UR_p), we obtain *private income*, i.e., income of the private sector before direct taxes as $(Y_p + UR_p)$. Adding to this private income, the *undistributed profit of publicly owned enterprises* (UR_g) and subtracting all income transfers in the form of gifts, grants and benefits (B) which are in the nature of income redistribution and hence *not* received by the general public from their participation in production, we arrive at the 'direct' estimate of national income (NI) as:

National income (NI)
= personal income before tax (Y_p)
+ undistributed profits of private enterprises (UR_p)
+ undistributed profits of public enterprises (UR_g)
– net income transfer from the government to the public (B)
$$\tag{1.24}$$

It can now be seen why net national product at factor cost defined in (1.22) is equivalent to the above direct estimate of national income obtained by (1.24). Equating (1.22) with (1.24), we have

$$NNP_{fc} = (NNP - IT_n) = (Y_p + UR_p) + UR_g - B.$$

Introducing direct taxes (DT) on total private income $(Y_p + UR_p)$ explicitly in the preceding expression and collecting terms, we have,

$$NNP = (Y_p + UR_p - DT) + (DT + IT_n + UR_g - B) \tag{1.25}$$

The meaning of (1.25) is self-evident: it simply says that net national product at market prices (NNP) must equal *private* disposable (i.e., after tax) income ($Y_p + UR_p - DT$) plus *public* income from all direct and indirect taxes and undistributed profits of public enterprises net of subsidies and income transfers, i.e., ($DT + IT_n + UR_g - B$). In other words, the equivalence of net national product at factor cost with national income (i.e., $NI \equiv NNP_{fc}$) is based on an accounting truism that, the net national product at market prices is the sum of private disposable income *plus* public income net of transfers as shown by (1.25).

It needs to be emphasised that the basic usefulness of macroeconomic accounting by alternative but equivalent routes, i.e., product, expenditure or income method, is to exhibit the *circular flows of income* in a capitalist economy: every purchase or expenditure in the expenditure method (see (1.15)) is also a sale in the product method (see (1.4)) which generates income to various classes in the economy the income method (see (1.19)). *Such circularity of flows should warn us against any simple-minded analogy between the income of an individual and that of the capitalist economy as a whole.* Precisely because circular flows interlink expenditure to income through sale, such analogies may turn out to be false. For example, less spending means more saving for an individual that leads to his accumulating more assets in one form or another. However, for the society *as a whole*, more savings, i.e., less expenditure by individuals, reduce overall expenditure and sales, which in turn reduce incomes of all concerned through the circular flows of expenditure and income. Thus, the *macroeconomic* relations governing a capitalist economy can turn out to be quite different from the *microeconomic* relations that remain valid at the level of an individual.

The intellectual challenge of understanding the macroeconomics of capitalism arises precisely here. And, macroeconomic accounting exhibiting the *circular* flows becomes an indispensable tool for this purpose.

Notes to Chapter 1

1. For example, like the wage *rate*, there is also interest *rate* say, per quarter, half year or annual, which defines the cost of borrowing money for a specified period of time. Similarly, the profit *rate* also has a time dimension. Note, however, that unlike the wage rate which is measured in

units of money per unit of time, the interest and the profit rate are pure numbers per unit of time.

2. These historical examples of the Polish economy are drawn from the interesting work by W. Kula (1976), *An Economic Theory of the Feudal System.*

3. Consequently, the value added of a self-employed enterprise which does not purchase labour service cannot be split between 'profit' and 'wages' without making further arbitrary assumptions.

4. Even then, one has to choose between the historical cost of a machine and its replacement cost at the current market price. If prices are changing and/or technical change in the design of the machine is taking place through time, the replacement cost need not bear any relation to the historical cost. At the same time, technical change also brings in the question of obsolescence, i.e., the length of the service life, as opposed to the physical life of a machine.

5. Gross profit of an enterprise is its operating surplus (sales) minus variable costs. However, in the 'manufacturing account' of a firm or enterprise, operating surplus must also include inventories of finished goods. Thus, gross profit = sales + (closing account of inventories of finished goods − opening account of inventories of finished goods) − (wages paid and raw materials used in production).

6. Hence, there is usually no possibility of double-checking the estimate of value added for such sectors.

7. The legal criteria for 'normal residence' varies from country to country. As opposed to being a 'national' of a country, a 'normal resident' usually is a category for internal revenue purposes. Typically, he has less political rights (e.g. he may have no voting right) and is liable to be taxed in most countries. Since, concepts such as GNP, national income, etc. relate to normal residents, the use of the term 'national' is somewhat misleading in this context.

Further Reading

Marx's (1904) celebrated introduction to *A Contribution to the Critique of Political Economy* remains the classic for materials covered in Sections A and B of this chapter. Kula's (1976) *An Economic Theory of the Feudal System* is useful reading for appreciating how the historical context makes a difference to economic analysis. Marglin's (1974) essay, '*What do the bosses do*' and Braverman's (1974) *Labour and Monopoly Capital* would help the reader to understand the control of labour process under modern capitalism.

There are many good books on national accounting. Van Arkadie's (1969), *Economic Accounting and Development Planning* provides an elementary, but comprehensive view of accounting at the level of the firm, of the industry and of the economy. Although simpler national accounting procedures, discussed in Section C, uses concepts of value added, incomes and final expenditures by sectors, underlying these are the interindustrial transactions. Transaction tables are constructed to show purchases and sales by each industry simultaneously. Leontief's (1953) *Studies in the Structure of the American*

Economy is the modern classic in this area. Stone's (1961) *Input–Output and National Accounts* as well as *Input–Output Tables and Analysis* (1973) published by the United Nations Organization are more advanced readings, exhibiting the connections between national accounts and input output analysis, built from such transaction tables.

2
The Principle of Effective Demand

A Saving-Investment Balance and Realisation of Profits: a Two-Department Scheme

Commodities, by definition, are produced for the market. Therefore, *how much* commodities to produce (or *which* commodities to produce) are primarily decided in a capitalist economy by what 'the market will take'. In an aggregative sense, the *size* of the market then determines the *level* (i.e. 'how much') of commodity production. The principle of effective demand provides the theory by which the size of the market is determined in a capitalist economy in the *short period*.

The term 'short period' has a specific analytical connotation: it is not a length of calendar time, i.e., so many days or months, but a certain period of time analytically defined by Marshall with respect to the supply conditions in an economy. Very roughly, the short period may be imagined to be that length of calendar time within which the level of *potential* supply of commodities in an economy remains unchanged. Since capital goods usually take considerable length of time to be constructed, installed and put into operation, expansion of capacities to increase potential supply is also time-consuming. Hence it is reasonable to assume that *within the short period the stock of capital goods is given*. This means that installed capacities are roughly given in the short period, whereas the maximum *degree of capacity utilisation* (or what engineers often call 'rated' capacities) on the existing capital stock define the *potential* supply of commodities in the short period. However, this also requires that sufficient labour force is available to operate those installed capacities at the maximum level of utilisation.

Ignoring complications such as import of raw materials, availability of skilled labour or limited non-renewable resources, there are two major constraints – existing capacities and available labour – that would broadly define the *short period potential output* of a sector j $(\overline{X}_j)$.

In symbols, this can be written as,

$$\overline{X}_j = \text{Minimum of } (q_j\overline{N}_j x_j\overline{L}_j) \equiv \text{Min } (q_j\overline{N}_j x_j\overline{L}_j) \qquad (2.1)$$

where, q_j is the capacity-output per machine and $\overline{N}_j =$ the given number of machines in the short period in sector j; hence, $q_j\overline{N}_j$ represents the *full-capacity* output of sector j. Similarly, assuming output per worker to be constant at x_j (irrespective of the degree of capacity utilisation) and $\overline{L}_j =$ the (maximum) available number of workers in sector j, $x_j\overline{L}_j$ represents the *full-employment* output of sector j. The short period potential output $\overline{X}_j$ is the minimum of the full-capacity $(q_j\overline{N}_j)$ and the full-employment $(x_j\overline{L}_j)$ output shown in (2.1).

The logic of commodity production leads us to an important question. How do we know that the size of the market would be such as to ensure that the actual level of output in any sector j (X_j) will coincide with the *potential* level of output $(\overline{X}_j)$ that is producible by sector j in the short period in accordance with (2.1). For whatever reason if the *potential* level of output $(\overline{X}_j)$ exceeds the actual output level (X_j), i.e.,

$$X_j < \overline{X}_j \qquad (2.2)$$

then, from (2.1), it will mean that,

$$X_j < \text{Min } (q_j\overline{N}_j' x_j\overline{L}_j) \qquad (2.3)$$

However, the fact that actual output (X_j) is lower than *both* full-capacity $(q_j\overline{N}_j)$ and full employment output $(x_j\overline{L}_j)$ in (2.3) must also imply that *excess capacity* and *unemployment* of labour *coexist* simultaneously. In other words, condition (2.3) describes a situation where under-utilisation of existing capacities and unemployment of labour appear *simultaneously* in a capitalist economy. How can such a situation arise?

In order to analyse this important problem of coexistence of excess capacity and unemployment, we must have a theory of how the size of the market gets determined. Because, it is the *limited* size of the market which can account for actual output (X_j) being lower than the potential output ($\bar{X}_j$). *The theory of effective demand* proposed by Keynes as well as the problem of realisation of profit formulated by Marx and developed into a theory of profit by Kalecki precisely deal with this issue. All these three important trends of thought revolve around the central issue of why no such synchronisation between the size of the market and the potential level of output need take place in the capitalist economy.

To discuss the essence of this problem it will be convenient to start with two simplifying assumptions namely, (a) there is negligible participation of the government in economic activity and, (b) no engagement of the country in foreign trade.

For the purposes of subsequent analysis this *free enterprise* capitalist economy *closed* to foreign trade may be imagined to consist of only *two departments* or *sectors* – Department I producing investment goods and Department II producing consumption goods. To abstract from the problem of raw materials at this stage, we may assume that each department is *vertically integrated*. This means that all required raw materials needed for the production of either the final consumption good in Department II or final investment good in Department I is produced by the respective department.

There are some essential distinctions between consumption good and investment good, which make this two departmental scheme of analysis, originally proposed by Marx, exceedingly fruitful. First, investment expenditure on long-lived capital equipment involves uncertain expectations regarding the future, simply because, these investment goods are going to be used over a number of years in the future. In contrast, consumption expenditure is primarily related to current needs; in this sense, consumption expenditure is less influenced by future uncertainties. Since investment decision must involve an uncertain future, it is far more difficult to judge the economic motives and expectations that govern the expenditure level on investment goods. In contrast, these complications are less serious in the case of consumption goods. Therefore, as a simplifying device – it only demarcates the zone of our ignorance – we *assume that the level of investment expenditure is autonomously given, within the short period* under consideration.

A second crucial difference between consumption and investment goods follows from their obvious physical characteristics. Investment goods, say machines, are by definition non-consumable. Consequently, workers engaged in the production of investment goods in Department I cannot be physically supported out of their own production; instead they have to be supported out of the production of consumption goods in Department II. Thus, some *surplus has to be produced by workers in the consumption sector over their own consumption in order to support workers in the investment sector.* In addition, whatever the capitalists consume must also be provided from the output of the consumption sector.

This physical distinction between consumption and investment goods leads to a *fundamental condition for macroeconomic balance between the two departments.* Assuming workers consume all their wages and save nothing, the balancing condition emerges as:

Output of consumption sector (Department II)
    − Wage bill of consumption sector (Department II)
    = Surplus of consumption goods (Department II),

which supports everybody else's consumption in the economy. Hence surplus consumption good = wage bill of investment sector (Department I) + consumption by capitalists (of Departments I and II). In symbols,

$$C - W_{II} = S_{II} = W_I + C_P \tag{2.4}$$

or,

$$(S_{II} - C_P) = W_I \tag{2.5}$$

where C is the output of *final* consumption goods, which is the same as the value added (see Chapter 1, Section C for definition) by the consumption sector or Department II; W_{II} is the wage bill of the consumption sector or Department II; S_{II} is the surplus of consumption goods over the wage bill of Department II (i.e., consumption sector); W_I is the wage bill of investment sector or Department I and C_P is the consumption by the entire capitalist class operating in both Departments I and II.

It is instructive to visualise this crucial balance condition (2.5) in terms of a 'box diagram' of the sort shown in Figure 2.1.

The balancing condition (2.5) simply means that the investment sector generates a wage bill, $W_I = ABEF$, which exactly matches the surplus of consumption goods $(S_{II} - C_P) = IJKL$, that remains after paying, (a) the wage bill in the consumption sector, $W_{II} = GHMN$ and, (b) the consumption by the entire capitalist class, $C_P = HILM$.

What is the significance of calling this the crucial condition for balance in a capitalist economy? It is a fundamental condition for

Figure 2.1   *Shaded areas ABEF and IJKL are equal.*

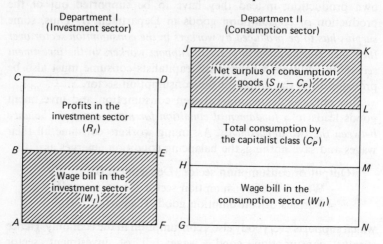

balance in so far as it shows that the *autonomous* expenditure decisions in the investment sector in the form of payment of wages to workers in that sector (i.e., *ABEF* in Figure 2.1) exactly matches the remaining 'surplus' (i.e., *IJKL* in Figure 2.1) after capitalists' consumption (C_P), which was algebraically described by (2.5). That condition (2.5) can now be seen to mean that the *size of the market generated by the wage bill of the investment sector is just large enough to dispose of the entire surplus of consumption goods*. However, if autonomous investment expenditure was smaller and consequently, the investment sector was somewhat smaller in size, with a smaller wage bill than *ABEF*, then part of the surplus of the consumption sector could not be disposed of. This would have resulted in *unplanned accumulation of inventories* ($+A$) of consumption goods. In a reverse case, the size of the investment sector could be too large with the wage bill of the investment sector larger than *ABEF* in Figure 2.1. In that case, the market created by that wage bill could not be met from the surplus of consumption goods. This might in turn lead to *unplanned decumulation of inventories* ($-A$) of final consumption goods, if they were already held in stock. This implies an *accounting identity* which is always satisfied in the form:

Surplus of consumption goods net of capitalists' consumption

$(S_{II} - C_P)$ – wage bill of investment sector (W_I)
= unplanned changes, i.e., accumulation $(+)$ or decumulation
$(-)$ of inventories of final consumption goods $(\pm A)$

i.e.,

$$(S_{II} - C_P) \equiv W_I \pm A \qquad (2.6)$$

The difference between the balancing or an equilibrium condition like (2.5) and the statistical identity (2.6) is obvious by comparison. The equilibrium relationship (2.5) simply implies that there are no unexpected or *unplanned* changes in inventories, i.e. $A = 0$ in (2.6). On the other hand, a statistical identity of the form of (2.6) means that expectations regarding the sale of consumption goods are *not* satisfied and A in (2.6) has some non-zero value. However, unexpected or unplanned accumulation of inventories (i.e. $A > 0$) would simply mean that the capitalists in Department II are unable to satisfy their plans regarding the volume of sales of consumption goods. As a result, a part of their output of consumption good remains unsold in the form unplanned inventory accumulation. An inadequate size of the market resulting from insufficient wage bill of the investment sector could then cause such failure of expectations regarding sales of consumption goods by the capitalists. The important point to note is that *irrespective of whether economic expectations* regarding sales of consumption goods *are fulfilled or not, the statistical identity* (2.6) *holds.* But an equilibrium condition like (2.5) is altogether different. Because, equilibrium obtained through the balancing condition (2.5) implies that sales expectations of the capitalists are precisely satisfied. Consequently in (2.5) there is no change in the unplanned stock of inventories and $A = 0$. In other words, the statistical identity (2.6) is *always* true irrespective of whether expectations of the sellers of consumption goods are satisfied or not; in contrast, the equilibrium relation (2.5) is true *only when* those expectations are satisfied.[1]

Since unplanned accumulation of inventories would mean that firms in the consumption sector cannot sell the volume of consumption goods they expected to sell, part of the surplus of Department II, i.e., S_{II} would fail to satisfy the 'commodity character' of production. Consumption goods are produced as commodity for the market but the market is not large enough to absorb the entire amount of surplus. This, in turn, means that the entire *surplus* of consumption goods cannot be *realised into* profit. Instead, unplanned accumulation of inventories implies that firms producing consumption goods are forced to hold part of their production as inventories that they were unable to sell. Thus, the commodities which were produced and planned to be sold but could not be sold due to lack of market become unplanned inventory accumulation to create a corresponding discrepancy between the *expected* profit of the capitalists and the *realised* profit.[2] Marxist writers describe this as the *realisation problem* of surplus into profit, which was reinstated at the centre of macroeconomic theory through the concept of 'effective demand' by Keynes.

In equilibrium, where such unplanned accumulation of inventories is zero, there is no divergence between the level of planned or expected profit on the one hand and the level of profit actually realised on the other. The total surplus of consumption goods generated by Department II is then fully realised into profit. The total surplus, simply as the excess of production over the wage bill of Department II (represented by the area of the rectangle *HMKJ* i Figure 2.1) is realised as profit by finding a market both through capitalists' consumption (C_P) (represented by *HMLI* in Figure 2.1) and through the wage bill of the workers in the investment sector (w_I) (represented by area *ABEF*, which is equal to *IJKL* in Figure 2.1). This indeed, is the economic meaning of the balance condition (2.4): it shows how the entire surplus S_{II} of Department II is being realised into profits R_{II}, of that Department i.e.,

$$S_{II} = W_I + C_P = R_{II} \tag{2.7}$$

where R_{II} is the profit of the consumption sector (Department II) Equation (2.7) explicitly shows the profit realisation condition of the consumption sector. It shows how the conversion of surplus consumption goods (S_{II}) into profit (R_{II}) of that sector becomes possible through market created by the wage bill of the investment sector (W_I) and the total consumption by the capitalists (C_P).

A formally equivalent condition to (2.7) can be obtained by adding the *realised* profit of Department I,[3] i.e., R_I (represented by rectangle *BCDE* in Figure 2.1) on both sides of (2.7) which yields,

$$R_I + W_I + C_P = R_I + R_{II} = R$$

However, $(R_I + W_I)$ is, by definition, the value added of the investment sector (I) which is also the final expenditure on investment goods, i.e. $R_I + W_I = I$[4]. Further, $R = R_I + R_{II}$, represents the total profit realised in the economy. Therefore, the preceding equation can be rewritten as:

Investment (I) + capitalists, consumption (C_P)
= total profit (R) (2.8)

or, by rearranging terms,

Investment (I) = total profit (R) −
capitalists' consumption (C_P) (2.9)

However, by our assumption made earlier, workers consume their entire wage income and capitalists are the only savers in the economy. Since profits are the total income of the capitalists, deducting capitalists' consumption from their total income, i.e. $(R - C_P)$ we obtain capitalists' saving which is also the total saving of the economy (S) (because, capitalists are the only savers by assumption made earlier). So the preceding equation takes the more familiar form:

Investment (I) = savings (S) (2.10)

Preceding conditions (2.8) to (2.10) describe the same basic macroeconomic balance of the economy in different ways. However, it needs emphasis that they all are derived from the underlying profit realisation equation (2.7) of the consumption sector.

The realisation of profit as an equilibrium condition can be contrasted with the corresponding accounting identity for profits in (2.6). By adding profit of Department I, i.e. R_I on both sides of (2.6) we obtain,

$$R_I + S_{II} - C_P \equiv (W_I + R_I) \pm A \equiv I + A, \qquad (2.11)$$

where $W_I + R_I = I$, by definition.

On the extreme left-hand side of (2.11) we have an *accounting definition of savings* which includes unplanned inventory change, because S_{II} is total surplus of the consumption sector, whether or not realised into profit. Similarly, on the extreme right-hand side of (2.11), the *accounting definition of investment* includes expenditure on final investment goods (I) as well as on inventory change $(+A)$. If we use such accounting or *ex post* definitions of savings and investment, then they would be always equal. Because they treat unplanned inventory accumulation $(+A)$ both as part of 'profit' and as part of investment, on the extreme left and right-hand sides of (2.11). However, this should not be confused with the equilibrium condition (2.10). Investment equals savings in the equilibrium configuration of (2.10) precisely when unplanned inventory change $(+A)$ is zero. Hence, neither the definition of investment nor that of savings include unplanned inventory change in equilibrium. This distinguishes planned or *ex ante* (e.g. in (2.10)) as opposed to accounting or *ex post* (e.g., in (2.11)) equality between investment and savings. It is only the planned or *ex ante* equality which can be seen to define the condition of macroeconomic equilibrium. Being planned or *ex ante* magnitudes, they would naturally exclude all possibilities of *unplanned* changes in inventories shown by (2.11). Consequently, equilibrium means the exact matching of plans of sales with those of purchases so that, unplanned inventory change must be zero at equilibrium.

B Restoring Balance through Quantity- and Price-Adjustment: The Multiplier Analysis

The basic condition of macroeconomic balance elaborated in the preceding section, emphasises a central point of paramount importance: whether stated as a profit realisation equation (in (2.7) or (2.8)) or equivalently, as saving-investment balance condition (in (2.9) or (2.10)), it shows how the total surplus of consumption goods, represented by the area of the rectangle *HJKM* in Figure 2.1 is realised into profit through the market created by capitalists' consumption, represented by the area of the rectangle *HILM* and by consumption of workers in the investment sector represented by the area of the rectangle *ABEF* (i.e., wage bill of Department I). In other words, this macroeconomic balance ensures that the surplus of consumption goods finds a market just large enough to be sold as commodities.

A macroeconomic imbalance would arise if the market for selling surplus consumption goods is too small (or large) resulting in unplanned accumulation (or decumulation) of inventories of final consumption goods. Such an *imbalance* between the level of *commodity production* and the *size of the market* arises because *investment decisions are autonomous in the short period*. Thus, for an arbitrarily given level of investment expenditure, the size of the wage bill of the investment sector (i.e. rectangle *ABEF* in Figure 2.1) may turn out to be either too large or too small in relation to the surplus produced by the consumption sector. This could be clearly visualised by considering a 'disturbance' of the initial balance between the two departments through an autonomous increase in investment expenditure. On the original position of balance, as shown in our earlier Figure 2.1 (where surplus consumption goods, *HMKJ* = capitalists' consumption,

HMLI + wage bill of investment sector, *ABEF*), we superimpose some arbitrary increase in the expenditure on final investment goods. This is shown in Figure 2.2, where the original size of the 'investment box' represented by the same rectangle *ACDF* in Figure 2.1, is increased arbitrarily by dotted lines, constituting another rectangle of size *AQSC*. As can be seen from Figure 2.2, this immediately results in an expansion of the wage bill of Department I (ΔW_I), represented by the shaded area of the rectangle, *ABRQ*, i.e., $\Delta W_I = ABRQ$.

The *autonomous* expansion in the wage bill of the investment sector (shaded area *ABRQ* in Figure 2.2) means in effect an autonomous increase in the size of the market for consumption goods. How the consumption sector would respond to this increase in its market size is the central problem to be analysed.

There are two distinct routes, either through *adjustment in the quantity* of consumption goods produced or through *adjustment in the price* of consumption goods, so that the consumption sector could respond to such an increase in the size of its market.[5] If there is unutilised capacity in the consumption sector as well as unemployed

Figure 2.2 *Multiplier based on quantity adjustment for restoring macro-economic balance. Areas ABEF and IJKL are equal, as in Figure 2.1, showing initial macroeconomic balance. Shaded areas ABRQ, and KLUT are equal, showing final macroeconomic balance.*

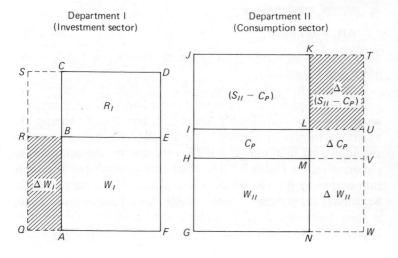

persons, as postulated, for example, in our earlier relation (2.3), it is reasonable to suppose that the quantity of consumption goods produced will tend to expand in response to its increased market; quantity adjustment will then take place by drawing on existing unutilised capacity and unemployment. Thus, with the expansion of demand, *quantity adjustment* would ordinarily predominate in situations of economic depression or recession. On the other hand, with more or less full employment or full capacity utilisation, significant expansion in output is not feasible in the short period. Consequently, *price adjustment* is likely to be more important in response to increased demand in situations of full capacity utilisation or full employment.

However, even if quantity adjustment is made possible in the short period through the coexistence of unutilised capacity and unemployment on a significant scale, the *extent* of quantity adjustment in the consumption sector would be limited to restoring balance. Thus, the output of the consumption sector will expand only up to the point where, the surplus of the consumption sector, net of capitalists' consumption, exactly matches the additional wage bill of the investment sector. In terms of Figure 2.2, this means that the additional wage bill of the investment sector, represented by the area of the shaded rectangle *ABRQ* has to exactly equal the *additional* surplus net of capitalists' consumption in the consumption sector, represented by the shaded rectangle *KLUT*. Algebraically, this corresponds to the earlier condition for balance (2.5), which can now be rewritten for *incremental* magnitudes as,

$$\Delta W_I = \Delta S_{II} - \Delta C_P \qquad (2.12)$$

where ΔW_I = area *ABRQ*, ΔS_{II} = area *MVTK*, and ΔC_P = area *MVUL* in Figure 2.2.

It should, however, be noted that in order to generate this additional surplus *KLUT*, the total expansion of the consumption sector has to be considerably *larger* than area *KLUT*; because the additional surplus represented by the area *KLUT*, is only *a fraction* of the additional total output *NWTK* produced by the consumption sector, as seen in Figure 2.2. Therefore only by expanding consumption output by *NWTK*, which is *several times* the expansion in the wage bill of the investment sector *ABRQ*, that the consumption sector is able to generate enough surplus net of capitalists' consumption (area *KLUT*) to match that additional wage bill *ABRQ* in Figure 2.2.

This several-fold increase in the demand for consumption goods (*NWTK*) resulting from an initial increase in demand from the wage bill of the investment sector (*ABRQ*), means that the demand for consumption goods ultimately gets 'multiplied' several times the initial autonomous increase in demand. The name '*multiplier analysis*' was given to emphasise this fact.

According to the multiplier analysis, expansion of output in the consumption sector takes place until it generates just enough surplus net of capitalists' consumption represented by rectangle *IUTJ* in Figure 2.2 to match the wage bill of the investment sector represented by *QFER* in the same figure, to attain a new position of macro-economic balance between the two departments. Because investment decisions and consequently the wage bill of the investment sector are treated as autonomous, the *adjusting variable is the surplus of the consumption sector*. In other words, *investment governs savings* (surplus). The Marxist writers often stress the same point by emphasising that Department I is the 'leading' sector to which Department II has to adjust under commodity production. This leading role of the investment sector stems from its being the creator of market for consumption goods. And, since commodity production, by definition, is only for the market, investment as the determinant of the size of the market for surplus consumption goods governs the level of commodity production in the consumption sector. Thus, the Keynesian proposition of investment governing savings is only a technical statement emphasising the commodity producing character of a capitalist economy.

The nature of quantity adjustment underlying the multiplier analysis can also be presented in algebraic terms.

Let h_i, h_c = share of profit in the value added of the investment and the consumption sectors, respectively. Thus, profit in the investment sector or Department $I (R_I)$ is,

$$R_I = h_i I \tag{2.13}$$

where I is the value added by the investment sector, i.e., the *final* expenditure on investment goods.

Similarly, profit of the consumption sector or Department II (R_{II}) is,

$$R_{II} = h_c C \tag{2.14}$$

where C is the value added by the consumption sector, i.e. the *final* expenditure on consumption goods.[6] We assume that no wage and a constant fraction, $s_p(1 > s_p > 0)$ of profit is saved; hence, $(1 - s_p)$ is the (marginal as well as average) propensity to consume by the capitalists out of their profit; consequently, total capitalists' consumption out of profit is given as,

$$C_p = (1 - s_p)(R_I + R_{II}) = (1 - s_p).(h_i I + h_c C) \tag{2.15}$$

Using (2.13), (2.14) and (2.15) in the basic condition for macroeconomic balance (2.8) or (2.9), we obtain on simplification,

$$I = s_p(h_i I + h_c . C) \tag{2.16}$$

As expected, investment on the left-hand side equals savings on the right-hand side of (2.16) in correspondence with (2.10).

The macroeconomic balance equation (2.16) could be rewritten as,

$$(1 - s_p h_i)I = s_p h_c C \tag{2.17}$$

which has an interesting economic interpretation. For every unit of value added by the investment sector, the corresponding *wage* income $(1 - h_i)$ is entirely consumed; further, out of the *profit* income h_i, $(1 - s_p)h_i$ is consumed. Hence, *the demand for consumption goods per unit of value added by the investment sector* is represented by the coefficient: $(1 - h_i) + (1 - s_p)h_i = (1 - s_p h_i)$, which appears on the left-hand side of (2.17). Similarly, total demand for consumption goods generated per unit of value added by the consumption sector is $(1 - s_p h_c)$; hence *surplus generated by the consumption sector per unit of its value added* is simply the coefficient: $1 - (1 - s_p h_c) = s_p h_c$, which appears on the right-hand side of (2.17). Thus, the left-hand side of equation (2.17) merely exhibits the demand for consumption goods generated by the investment sector which must balance the surplus generated by the consumption sector which is represented on the right-hand side of the same equation.

To elaborate the multiplier analysis through quantity adjustment, we assume that the distribution of value added between profit and wages remain unaltered in either sector, i.e. h_i and h_c are constants; in addition $s_p(1 > s_p > 0)$ is also assumed to remain constant throughout the analysis. With h_i, h_c and s_p assumed constants, the extent of expansion in the output of the consumption sector required to restore macroeconomic balance as a result of an arbitrary increase ΔI in final investment expenditure is given from (2.17) as,

$$\Delta C = \frac{(1 - s_p h_i)}{s_p h_c} \Delta I \tag{2.18}$$

The above can be interpreted in terms of our earlier Figure 2.2; if the increment in investment ΔI in (2.18) is represented by the rectangle area $AQSC$, then the required increment in the output of the consumption sector ΔC that will restore back macroeconomic balance is a rectangle of area $NKTW$ which is determined by formula (2.18).

It may be recalled that by adding up the value added of both the sectors (i.e., $C + I$) we obtain the estimate of the gross domestic product (GDP) in the economy. This estimate also coincides with the estimate of national income (Y) if we ignore depreciation in a strictly free-enterprise economy closed to foreign trade.[7] This yields national income, $Y =$ domestic product $= C + I$ or

$$\Delta Y = \Delta C + \Delta I$$

Using condition (2.18) in the above definition of increment in national income we obtain the multiplier formula as,

$$\frac{\Delta Y}{\Delta I} = \frac{1 + s_p(h_c - h_i)}{s_p h_c} \tag{2.19}$$

Formula (2.19) represents the traditional multiplier in the context of our two department analysis. It shows the extent by which national income (ΔY) will increase due to an autonomous increase in final investment expenditure (ΔI). When both the sectors have the *same* share of profit in value added, i.e., $h_c = h_i$, (2.19) reduces to a simpler form,

$$\frac{\Delta Y}{\Delta I} = \frac{1}{s_p h}, \; h_c = h_i = h \tag{2.20}$$

Since s_p is the constant (marginal as well as average) propensity to save out of profit, h is the share of profit in national income and no wage is saved, $s_p h = s_p(R/Y)$ represents the (average and marginal) propensity to save in the economy. Hence, (2.20) exhibits the *multiplier formula in a one-sector model as the inverse of the (marginal) propensity to save.*

The multiplier formula (2.19) set in a two department scheme, shows that the value of the multiplier, $\Delta Y/\Delta I$ would be *lower* for a *higher* share of profit in *either* department (i.e., h_i or h_c higher). However, the underlying argument is somewhat different in the two cases. A higher h_i reduces the value of the multiplier by *lowering the demand* generated per unit of value added by the investment sector; whereas a higher h_c reduces the same multiplier value through *increasing the surplus* generated per unit of value added by the consumption sector (see (2.17)). Thus, the value of the multiplier may get reduced through two alternative economic routes – a lower demand for consumption goods per unit of investment (as h_i is increased) or through higher surplus generated per unit of expansion in the consumption sector (as h_c is increased). The distinction between these two routes becomes obscure in the simpler, one sector version of the multiplier given in (2.20).

It will be noted that the ultimately required quantity adjustment in the consumption sector (ΔC) in response to an arbitrary increase in investment (ΔI) is stated as the condition of macroeconomic balance for the incremental magnitudes in (2.18). This is called a *'comparative static'* representation. It shows the *final position* of macroeconomic balance resulting from higher investment after all the required quantity adjustment has been completed in the consumption sector to restore balance. However, it would be useful to have some idea about how this *quantity adjustment can take place in successive rounds* through time until the final position of balance depicted in (2.18) is reached. In other words, we need to examine how the demand for consumption goods increases step by step due to a once-for-all increase in investment (ΔI). As we already saw in equation (2.17), every unit of value added of the investment sector leads to increase in demand for consumption goods by $(1 - s_p h_i)$. Hence, at the very *initial round*, the resulting increase in the demand for consumption goods will be,

$$\Delta C_0 = (1 - s_p h_i)\Delta I,$$

where ΔC_0 represents the initial or 0th round increase in demand for consumption goods. This leads to quantity adjustment, i.e., increase in output of the consumption sector by ΔC_0. Consequently, wage and profit of the consumption sector would also increase. And out of that increased wage and profit of the consumption sector, further demand for consumption goods is generated in the *first round* (ΔC_1). This can be written as,

$$\Delta C_1 = \underbrace{(1-h_c)\Delta C_0}_{} + \underbrace{(1-s_p)h_c\Delta C_0}_{} = (1-s_ph_c)\Delta C_0$$

Consumption out of increased wages in the consumption sector from 0th round

Consumption out of increased profits of the consumption sector from 0th round

The quantity-adjustment by ΔC_1 in the consumption sector in the first round leads in turn to further demand for consumption goods in the next round,

$$\Delta C_2 = (1-h_c)\Delta C_1 + (1-s_p)h_c\Delta C_1 = (1-s_ph_c)\Delta C_1;$$

or, by substituting for the expression for ΔC_1 in terms of ΔC_0 from above,

$$\Delta C_2 = (1-s_ph_c)^2 \cdot \Delta C_0$$

Again, at the next round, the expansion in the demand for consumption goods will be,

$$\Delta C_3 = (1-s_ph_c)^3\Delta C_0$$

and, in general, for the nth round,

$$\Delta C_n = (1-s_ph_c)^n\Delta C_0$$

The total expansion in the consumption sector can then be obtained by summing all the rounds of a convergent, infinite geometric series in the form:

$$\Delta C = (\Delta C_0 + \Delta C_1 + \Delta C_2 + \ldots)$$
$$= [1 + (1-s_ph_c) + (1-s_ph_c)^2 + \ldots]\Delta C_0$$

which sums to[8]

$$\Delta C = \left[\frac{1}{1-(1-s_ph_c)}\right](1-s_ph_i)\Delta I, \quad \text{for } 1 > (1-s_ph_c) > 0$$

$$= \frac{(1-s_ph_i)}{s_ph_c}\Delta I, \tag{2.16}$$

which is exactly the same as (2.16) above.

Undoubtedly there are substantial difficulties in visualising the above geometric series as an actual process through time. For example, the time lag between income receipts and expenditure varies from group to group. Thus, the lag between income and expenditure can be only two calendar months in a particular round, while it can take say a year in the next round. Thus, the elements of the geometric series cannot in general be assumed as uniformly spaced in time. As a result we cannot exactly say how long it takes in calendar time for this process of demand creation to more or less approximate to its ultimate value given by summing the series. Similarly, our analysis maintains its simple character only by assuming that uniform consumption propensities exist for all groups of capitalists and for all groups of workers. When consumption propensities as well as expenditure lags vary from group to group, one would require a more elaborate computational scheme using disaggregate information on consumption propensities and expenditure lags for the different groups. However, despite such computational difficulties, the basic idea of successive rounds of demand triggered off by an autonomous increase in investment remains one of the most powerful ideas in macroeconomic theory.

So long as the multiplier anaysis is based on *quantity adjustment*, the expansion in the consumption sector in response to increased demand from the investment sector takes place in physical quantities. Thus more consumption goods are produced to generate enough surplus and restore balance between the two sectors. Nevertheless such quantity adjustment is not feasible in a situation of full employment or full capacity utilisation in the consumption sector (see equation (2.1) above). Under these conditions, the multiplier mechanism must be based on price and not on quantity adjustments. Referring back to our previous Figure 2.2, we must now clearly distinguish between nominal magnitudes and physical quantities. Let *GN* in Figure 2.2 represent the number of workers employed at the level of full capacity utilisation in the consumption sector. If *GJ* represents the nominal or money *value* of final output (i.e. value added) per worker in the consumption sector, then writing explicitly, final output per worker in the consumption sector,

$$GJ \text{ (in Figure 2.2)} = x_c P_c$$

where x_c is the physical output per worker in the consumption sector and P_c is the price level of consumption goods.

Similarly, productivity per worker in the investment sector *in nominal terms* is shown in Figure 2.2 as AC, i.e.,

$$AC = x_i P_i$$

where x_i is the physical output per worker in the investment sector and P_i is the price level of investment goods.

To analyse the working of the multiplier based on price rather than quantity adjustment, we assume that *physical* productivity per worker in either sector (i.e., x_i or x_c) remains constant. This means that all changes in the productivity levels (i.e., x_i and x_c) that may accrue either due to technological change or due to changes in the degree of capacity utilisation are ignored in the short period to which our analysis applies. With physical productivity levels x_i and x_c assumed constant, for any given level of employment say at GN in Figure 2.2, determined by full utilisation of installed capacity in the consumption sector, the entire burden of adjustment to restore macroeconomic balance caused by an autonomous increase in investment must fall on prices as consumption goods ouput is fixed by assumption. How this may happen in this particular case is shown in Figure 2.3 below.

Suppose, the investment sector has excess capacity and the labour force in the economy is not fully employed. Consequently, it is possible to have a greater level of employment in the investment sector without withdrawing labour from the consumption sector. Such an autonomous increase in real investment is shown by the dotted rectangle $AQSC$ in Figure 2.3, where AQ represents the *additional* number of workers employed in the investment sector and $QS\ (= AC)$ shows constant productivity per worker in the investment sector. In order to meet the *additional* (money) wage bill $ABRQ$ of the investment sector, the consumption sector would now have to generate a larger surplus ($S_{II} - C_p$) that would match that additional wage bill $ABRQ$. However, by our assumption the consumption sector is already working at full capacity and it employs GN amount of labour at constant labour productivity in money terms, $GJ = x_c P_c$.

A *multiplier theory based on price adjustment* would require the price level P_c of consumption goods to rise for generating the additional surplus. This is shown in Figure 2.3 by *vertical* and *not horizontal* (in contrast to Figure 2.2) expansion from the original size of the consumption sector from $GNKJ$ and $GNTU$. Note that this expansion takes place only in nominal terms as labour productivity in the consumption sector rises in money value from GJ to GU. A higher price level for consumption goods, assuming the *money* wage rate to

Figure 2.3   *Multiplier based on price adjustment for restoring macro-economic balance. As in Figures 2.1 and 2.2, areas ABEF and IJKL are equal, showing* initial *macroeconomic balance. Money wage GH and employment GN in the consumption sector are assumed* fixed *throughout. Nominal labour productivity in the consumption sector increases from initial GJ to GU as the price level of consumption goods increases. In the* final *macroeconomic balance shaded areas EFQR and UVWT are equal.*

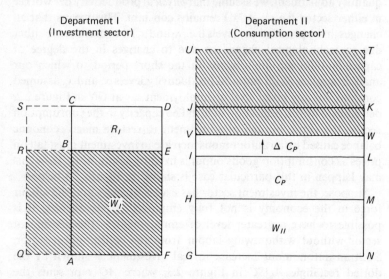

be constant at *GH* in the consumption sector, must also imply that the *share of wages* $(1 - h_c)$ in the consumption sector falls from the ratio *GH/GJ* to *GH/GU*. Conversely, the share of profit h_c in the consumption sector rises from *JH/GJ* to *UH/GU*, leading to higher profits earned by the capitalists. As profits expand both in the consumption sector from *HMKJ* to *HMTU* and in the investment sector from *BCDE* to *REDS* in Figure 2.3, capitalists consume more out of their higher profit in a proportional manner by virtue of relation (2.15) postulated earlier.[9] This additional consumption ΔC_p by the capitalists due to a higher share of profit in the consumption sector is shown in Figure 2.3 by an upward shift of the line *IL* to *VW* so that, *ILWV* represents the *additional* consumption out of the higher profits earned by the capitalists. With *GNMH* representing the wage bill W_{II} of the consumption sector at the constant *money* wage rate *GH*, and

HMWV representing capitalists' new level of consumption, the surplus $(S_{II} - C_p)$ of the consumption sector net of capitalists' consumption at the increased price level of *consumption goods* becomes the rectangle *UVWT* in Figure 2.3. When this total net surplus of the consumption sector *UVWT* equals the total wage bill *EFQR* of the investment sector, the basic macroeconomic balance between the two departments given by earlier condition (2.5) is restored again. However, the restoring mechanism depends exclusively on increase in the price level of consumption goods (by *JU*) with a constant *money* wage rate *GH*.

A higher price level of consumption goods (by *JU*) at a constant *money* wage rate *GH* in Figure 2.3 entails a correspondingly lower *real* wage rate in terms of consumption goods. Consequently the multiplier mechanism based on price adjustment forces a reduction of the real wage rate in terms of consumption goods to generate the required level of surplus. And, so long as the per cent rise in the price level of consumption goods ($\Delta P/P_c \times 100$) exceeds the per cent rise in the *money* wage rate ($\Delta w/w \times 100$), the *real* wage rate in terms of consumption goods becomes flexible downwards to allow for such an adjustment mechanism. Therefore, even without any possibility of quantity adjustment in the consumption sector, there exists an alternative version of the multiplier theory: it is based on adjustment between consumption goods' prices and *money* wages leading to a reduction in the *real* wage rate in terms of consumption goods.

A more general algebraic analysis of the multiplier mechanism based upon such price adjustment in the context of our two-department scheme can now be developed. With L_i, L_c = number of workers employed in the investment and in the consumption sector respectively, and x_i and x_c the labour productivity levels in physical terms and, P_i and P_c = the respective price levels in the two sectors, we have from definition

$$I = P_i x_i L_i \tag{2.21}$$

and

$$C = P_c x_c L_c \tag{2.22}$$

Further, the *money* wage rate in a sector is by definition, the share of wage in the value of final output per worker, i.e.,

$$w_i = (1 - h_i) P_i x_i$$

and,
$$w_c = (1 - h_c)P_c x_c$$

where w_i and w_c are the money wage rates in the investment sector and in the consumption sector respectively.

The preceding relations can be rewritten as,

$$P_i = \frac{w_i}{(1 - h_i)x_i} \tag{2.23}$$

and,

$$P_c = \frac{w_c}{(1 - h_c)x_c} \tag{2.24}$$

showing that the price level in a sector (P_i or P_c) is proportional to the money wage rate (w_i or w_c), so long as physical labour productivity (x_i or x_c) and the distributional parameter (h_i or h_c) remains constant in that sector.[10]

Using (2.21) to (2.24) in the basic condition for macroeconomic balance (2.17), we obtain on simplification:

$$\frac{L_c}{L_i} = \frac{(1 - h_c)}{(1 - h_i)} \cdot \frac{(1 - s_p h_i)}{s_p h_c} \cdot \left(\frac{w_i}{w_c}\right) \tag{2.25}$$

Condition (2.25) shows that the employment in the two sectors must be in a certain *proportion*, if the surplus of the consumption sector is to be exactly realised into profit without any unplanned accumulation or decumulation of inventories of consumption goods.

The proportionality of employment between the two sectors, depicted by condition (2.25) is of crucial importance in analysing the *general multiplier mechanism*, both under quantity- and under price-adjustments. In so far as quantity adjustment is concerned, it now explicitly shows the *employment multiplier*, i.e., the additional employment in the consumption sector (ΔL_c) that would be required to support an autonomous increase in employment in the investment section (ΔL_i), when all the money wages and prices remain constant (implying h_i and h_c as well as w_i and w_c are constant in (2.25)). In this case, (2.25) yields,

$$\Delta L_c = \frac{(1 - h_c)}{(1 - h_i)} \cdot \frac{(1 - s_p h_i)}{s_p h_c} \cdot \left(\frac{w_i}{w_c}\right) \cdot \Delta L_i \tag{2.26}$$

Thus, corresponding to the quantity-adjustment multiplier described earlier, for an autonomous increase in employment in the investment sector by $QA = \Delta L_i$ in Figure 2.2, the *required* expansion of employment in the consumption sector has to be $NW = \Delta L_c$ in the same Figure 2.2, which can now be solved from (2.26) above.

However, in the case of the multiplier based on price adjustment such expansion in the level of employment and output of the consumption sector is not feasible by assumption (as in Figure 2.3). Consequently, distributional parameters like h_i and h_c or the relative wage structure (w_i/w_c) must vary on the right-hand side of (2.25) in response to an autonomously increased employment in the investment sector (ΔL_i). In other words, the proportionality between the employment levels of the two sectors, given by the right-hand side of (2.25), must become *flexible* through suitable changes in the parameter values (like h_i, h_c, w_i and w_c) when the multiplier mechanism is based on price adjustment.

Since a variety of such adjustments in the parameter values are possible under alternative assumptions, several types of multiplier mechanism based on price adjustment can be described. However, the essential point is already emphasised by Figure 2.3 – the *real* wage in terms of consumption goods has to be depressed to generate enough surplus to accommodate a higher level of investment in terms of higher employment in the investment sector (L_i). Thus, an increase in the *share* of *real* investment in the economy means that the proportional L_c/L_i falls as L_i increases. And, the essential point is to consider how the parameters on the right-hand side of (2.25) change by depressing real wage rate so as to restore back the equality shown in (2.25).

The argument can be formally pursued by taking logarithmic differences on both sides of (2.25) to obtain,[11]

$$\left(\frac{\Delta L_i}{L_i} - \frac{\Delta L_c}{L_c}\right) = \frac{1}{h_c} \cdot \left(\frac{\Delta h_c}{1 - h_c}\right) - \frac{(1 - s_p)}{(1 - s_p h_i)}\left(\frac{\Delta h_i}{1 - h_i}\right)$$
$$+ \left(\frac{\Delta w_c}{w_c} - \frac{\Delta w_i}{w_i}\right) \qquad (2.27)$$

However, under the assumption of constant physical labour productivity x_i and x_c in the short period, logarithmic differentiation of (2.23) and (2.24) yields,

$$\left. \begin{aligned} \frac{\Delta h_i}{(1 - h_i)} &= \left(\frac{\Delta P_i}{P_i} - \frac{\Delta w_i}{w_i}\right) \\ \text{and} \\ \frac{\Delta h_c}{(1 - h_c)} &= \left(\frac{\Delta P_c}{P_c} - \frac{\Delta w_c}{w_c}\right) \end{aligned} \right\} \qquad (2.28)$$

Substituting (2.28) in (2.27), we obtain a general representation of the *multiplier analysis based the price-wage adjustment in both the sectors* in the form:

$$\frac{\Delta L_i}{L_i} - \frac{\Delta L_c}{L_c} = \frac{1}{h_c}\left(\frac{\Delta P_c}{P_c} - \frac{\Delta w_c}{w_c}\right) - \frac{(1-s_p)}{(1-s_p h_i)}\left(\frac{\Delta P_i}{P_i} - \frac{\Delta w_i}{w_i}\right)$$
$$+ \left(\frac{\Delta w_c}{w_c} - \frac{\Delta w_i}{w_i}\right) \tag{2.29}$$

The general equation (2.29) exhibiting the multiplier mechanism based on price-wage adjustment can be used to discuss various *special cases*. For instance, in conformity with Figure 2.3, if we assume money wages to be constant in both the sectors (i.e., $\Delta w_i = \Delta w_c = 0$), constant full capacity level of employment in the consumption sector (i.e. $\Delta L_c = 0$) and a constant price level for investment goods (i.e., $\Delta P_i = 0$), then (2.29) reduces to,

$$\frac{\Delta P_c}{P_c} = h_c\left(\frac{\Delta L_i}{L_i}\right) \tag{2.29a}$$

Thus, in Figure 2.3, the proportional increase in the price level of consumption goods, i.e.

$$\frac{\Delta P_c}{P_c} = \frac{UJ}{GJ}$$

required to restore macroeconomic balance must equal

$$\frac{JH}{GJ} \cdot \frac{AQ}{AF}$$

where $JH/GJ = h_c$ and $AQ/AF = \Delta L_i/L_i$, to satisfy (2.29a). To elaborate with an arithmetical illustration, if $h_c = 0.3$ initially, then a 10 per cent increase in investment (i.e. $\Delta L_i/L_i = 0.1$) requires the price level of consumption goods to increase, i.e., the real wage rate in terms of consumption goods to decrease by 3 per cent according to formula (2.29a).

Alternatively, as another special case not so far discussed, we could assume that *relative* prices as well as relative *money* wages remain constant implying, all prices rise in a uniform proportion, i.e.

$$\frac{\Delta P_i}{P_i} = \frac{\Delta P_c}{P_c} = \frac{\Delta P}{P}$$

and, so do all money wage rates, i.e.,

$$\frac{\Delta w_i}{w_i} = \frac{\Delta w_c}{w_c} = \frac{\Delta w}{w}$$

If the level of employment in the consumption sector is constrained by full capacity and $\Delta L_c = 0$, (2.29) under the above assumption of constant *relative* prices and money wage rates simplifies to,

$$\left(\frac{\Delta P}{P} - \frac{\Delta w}{w}\right) = \left(\frac{\Delta L_i}{L_i}\right) \cdot \left[\frac{h_c(1 - s_p h_i)}{(1 - h_c) + s_p(h_c - h_i)}\right] \qquad (2.29b)$$

With the values of the parameters $h_i = 0.25$, $h_c = 0.30$, $s_p = 0.60$, a 10 per cent increase in the employment of the investment sector will now require almost 3.5 per cent decrease in the *real* wage rate in accordance with (2.29b). However, a 3.5 per cent decrease in *real* wage rate may require much larger increase the price level if money wage rate also increases in the meantime. Thus, 20 per cent increase in money wages would require 23.5 per cent increase in the price level to restore balance according to (2.29b).

It should be noted that both in (2.29a) and in (2.29b) quantity adjustment in the consumption sector was assumed to be restricted by full utilisation of capacity in that sector. Alternatively, one could also analyse the working of the multiplier based on price adjustment by assuming full employment of the labour force. However, strict full employment would require labour to be withdrawn from the consumption sector, *reducing* the level of consumption output in order to increase employment in the investment sector. This would imply quantity adjustment *in reverse* in the consumption sector, as the withdrawal of labour would reduce the level of consumption goods output. Consequently, the extent of price rise of consumption goods and the fall in the real wage rate in terms of consumption goods must be greater under the postulate of full employment. However, such an assumption of withdrawal of labour from the consumption sector, even when demand for its output is expanded (because, L_i is higher) does not conform to typical situations and need not be pursued in greater detail here.[12]

Having seen how quantities (see (2.26)) or prices and money wages (see (2.29)) adjust under the multiplier mechanism in the more general two department scheme, we are now in a position to consider an important special case to summarise the analysis. This corresponds to the case where both sectors have uniform values of the parameters, i.e.

$h_i = h_c = h$ (uniform share of profit)

$w_i = w_c = w$ (uniform money wage rate) and

$P_i x_i = P_c x_c = Px$ (uniform labour productivity)

Under these assumptions, the basic condition for macroeconomic balance, represented by the proportionality of employment between the two sectors in (2.25) reduces to the simpler form,

$$\frac{L_c}{L_i} = \frac{(1 - s_p h)}{s_p h}$$

or,

$$\frac{L_i}{(L_c + L_i)} = \frac{L_i}{L} = s_p h = \frac{I}{Y} \tag{2.30}$$

because $I = xPL_i$ and $Y = xPL$ in this case. The nature of quantity- or price-adjustment under the multiplier mechanism that would be required to achieve macroeconomic balance, depicted by (2.30), is captured by means of the simple Figure 2.4.

In Figure 2.4, at some initial, base-year price P, output is measured on the horizontal and investment on the vertical axis. In accordance with (2.30), the slope of the ray OBE passing through the origin, measures the marginal and average propensity to save, i.e. $\tan \theta = s_p h$. At the initial (base year) investment level $I_0 = AB = PxL_i^0$, the economy is operating below the full employment output level $PxL_f = OF$. Consequently, any increase in investment, say from AB to EF, leads to a corresponding quantity adjustment, resulting in additional output $AF = \Delta Y$, which can be calculated from the quantity-adjustment multiplier formula (2.20). However, investment beyond the full-employment level, e.g. $I_1 = JF = pxL_i^1$, cannot lead to further increase in output, measured at the base year price level, P. In such a case, the distribution of income has to change in favour of profit to raise the value of the parameter h. This increases $\tan \theta$ and rotates the line OE anti-clockwise, until at OJ macroeconomic balance between investment and saving is restored again through increased share of profit, h. This rotation of the original savings-line

Figure 2.4 *Restoration of macroeconomic balance through quantity and price-adjustment. Slope of the savings line OE, i.e.* tan *EOF = $s_p h$ from (2.30). Anti-clockwise rotation of the savings line from OE to OJ shows redistribution in favour of profit as h increases to make the slope larger from EOF to JOF.*

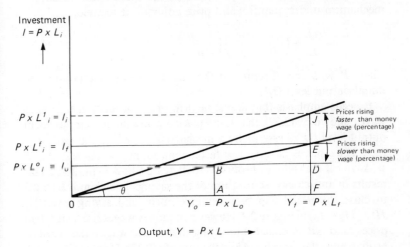

from OE to OJ geometrically represents the price-adjustment multiplier.

The extent of rotation of the savings line from its initial position OBE required for the restoration of macroeconomic balance can be computed from equation (2.30). Logarithmic differentiation of that equation yields,

$$\frac{\Delta L_i}{L_i} = \frac{\Delta L}{L} + \frac{\Delta h}{h} \tag{2.31}$$

where the first term, $\Delta L/L = AF/AO$ shows quantity adjustment, while the second term, $\Delta h/h = \tan EOJ/EOF$ shows price adjustment induced by the multiplier mechanism as the level of investment is autonomously raised from I_0 to I_1, i.e., by a proportion $\Delta L_i/L_i = JD/DF$, from its initial level DF in Figure 2.4.

Further, in view of (2.28), in this special case (of $w_i = w_c = w$; $h_c = h_i = h$; and $P_i x_i = P_c x_c = Px$) we have,

$$\frac{\Delta h}{(1-h)} = \left(\frac{\Delta P}{P} - \frac{\Delta w}{w} \right)$$

or,

$$\frac{\Delta h}{h} = \left(\frac{\Delta P}{P} - \frac{\Delta w}{w}\right)\left(\frac{1-h}{h}\right) \tag{2.32}$$

Thus, (2.31) and (2.32) may be combined to show the multiplier mechanism under quantity and price adjustment to yield,

$$\frac{\Delta L_i}{L_i} = \frac{\Delta L}{L} + \left(\frac{\Delta P}{P} - \frac{\Delta w}{w}\right)\left(\frac{1-h}{h}\right) \tag{2.33}$$

where P, w, h and L represent the initial values (corresponding to initial output level OA).

It needs emphasis that adjustment in prices in relation to money wages, shown by (2.32), that takes place beyond the full employment output level OF is essentially a mechanism to reduce the *real* wage rate. Thus, prices have to rise faster than money wages (i.e., $\Delta P/P > \Delta w/w$), if the share of profit h is to increase ($\Delta h > 0$) in (2.32). This results in anti-clockwise rotation of the savings line from OE to OJ to close the initial gap between investment and saving given by $JD = (I_1 - I_0)$ in Figure 2.4. However, if money wages rise faster than prices (and $\Delta P/P < \Delta w/w$) implying higher *real* wages, the share of profit h must decrease (i.e. $\Delta h < 0$) to satisfy (2.32). This in turn means that the savings line OE rotates clockwise and the initial gap between investment and saving JD *increases* over time in Figure 2.4. In other words, unless the *real* wage rate can be sufficiently depressed, the free enterprise capitalist economy is left without any viable mechanism to restore the macroeconomic balance between investment and saving at full employment.

C Significance of the Principle of Effective Demand

The basic idea underlying the principle of effective demand is simple: since commodities are necessarily produced for a market, the size of the market must *regulate* the level of commodity production. This regulating role of the market is embodied in the proposition that investment *governs* saving, because it is the wage bill of the investment sector that creates the market for 'surplus' consumers' goods to be sold and realised into profit. This basic insight is further formalised by the *multiplier analysis*. Treating investment as the autonomous or *independent variable* in the short period, the analysis shows how a higher level of investment is matched by a correspondingly higher level of saving. That additional saving to match the additional investment is generated in the economy either through a higher level of production (i.e. quantity-adjustment) or through a redistribution of income among the economic classes (i.e., price-adjustment). In the latter case the price level of consumers' goods has to rise at a higher percentage rate than the *money* wage rate so that, the *real* wage rate is depressed sufficiently in terms of consumers' goods to generate the required additional saving. And, since saving adjusts to the independently given level of investment, either through quantity- or through price-wage adjustment in the manner described above, the rate of saving is to be treated as the passive or *dependent variable* in the multiplier analysis.

The two central routes of quantity- or price-adjustment through which the multiplier mechanism allows investment to *govern* saving are exhibited in a convenient, short-hand manner in Figure 2.4 of the previous section. However, the very simplicity of Figure 2.4 could be somewhat misleading, as it resembles an all-purpose, one-commodity model – a commodity which could both be consumed and invested. This obscures the underlying 'physical picture' on which the multiplier argument is based. In particular, such a one-commodity model obscures the obvious fact that, by its definition investment goods consist of *non-consumables*; hence, any expansion in the level of employment in the investment sector results in an expansion in the wage bill of Department I (investment sector) which can only be met by generating additional surplus of *consumables* that are produced by Department II (consumption sector). Consequently, *additional* '*saving*' or surplus has to be, generated in terms of consumables or wage-goods so that, more workers can be supported in the investment sector.

The fact that saving has to be generated in terms of consumables to sustain workers engaged in producing non-consumable investment goods, has a deeper implication. By the very nature of capitalism, capitalists enjoy the power to decide how much to invest, i.e., the level of employment in the investment sector. But the corresponding saving in wage-goods has to be generated to match this independent decision of the capitalists. Under the traditional multiplier analysis based on quantity-adjustment, this places no additional burden on the workers when more saving in terms of wage goods is generated out of a greater production of wage-goods, made possible by the existence of unemployment and excess capacity in the consumption, i.e., the wage-goods sector. However, in case the multiplier operates through price adjustment, the burden of sustaining the additional investment falls on the workers; they are *forced* to generate the matching additional saving in terms of consumables through a reduction in their *real* wage rate in terms of wage-goods. In this later case although the capitalists have the unilateral power to decide how much to invest, the workers are obliged to generate the matching amount of additional saving through a reduction in their *real* wage rate. And yet, the national income statistics would simply report it as higher investment financed by higher saving out of higher profit earned by the capitalists!

The physical distinction, departmentalised into production of consumables (or, more exactly, wage-goods) and non-consumables also enables us to see how the essential *principle of effective demand is readily extendable* to several other situations. So long as we maintain the working hypothesis of one sector exclusively producing wage-goods, all other sectors in the economy must be linked to it through *a fundamental principle of macroeconomic balance* (as explained in Section A of this chapter): *the surplus over the wage bill in the wage-goods sector must sustain consumption by workers elsewhere in the economy.* Thus, whether it is a *'luxury' consumption sector* producing exclusively for capitalists or an *export sector* producing for foreigners, the workers employed in all such sectors would have to be supported out of the surplus generated by the wage-goods sector. Consequently, *an autonomous increase in the wage bill of any one of the non-wage-goods sector would bring into operation the multiplier mechanism* by creating additional demand for wage goods. However, whether the resulting mechanism would be based on quantity-adjustment or on price-adjustment (or a combination of both) in the wage-goods sector depends on further specification of the problem, in a manner summarised by means of the preceding Figure 2.4. In principle then, a wide *variety of multipliers* can be associated with different types of *autonomous* increases in expenditures on non-wage-goods. There would be a multiplier associated with increased 'luxury' consumption by capitalists; a multiplier associated with increase in expenditure on armaments or government's spending in general; similarly, a multiplier mechanism would also be associated with an autonomous increase in export, called the *foreign trade multiplier.*[13]

The preceding argument that even an autonomous increase in 'luxury' consumption by a landlord or capitalist class can expand the market for wage-goods could be used in defence of 'conspicuous consumption' by a leisure class (as Malthus, in effect, had argued over the 'glut controversy' with Ricardo). Similarly, it could be validly argued that increased armament expenditure helps to counter the immediate problem of insufficient effective demand in a capitalist economy. If all this sounds rather absurd, the source of such absurdity is to be found in the very logic of commodity production itself: every autonomous increase in expenditure on workers' non-consumables becomes justified, so long as it creates a market for commodities! Keynes' argument that even a public work programme consisting entirely of digging holes to fill them up again can be used to reduce unemployment dramatised this very point.

The fuller implication of the argument that every autonomous increase in the demand for wage-goods would create its own additional supply through the multiplier mechanism based either on quantity- or on price-adjustment, can perhaps be better understood by reversing it. Thus, an imagined expansion in the output of the consumption goods sector itself (say, in Figure 2.2) results in additional surplus in terms of consumables. However, under commodity production, there is no guarantee whatsoever that this additional surplus would be either consumed by the capitalist class or invested, i.e., paid in wage bill to employ more workers in the investment sector. In other words, the surplus of commodities in Department II would not necessarily find a market where it can be realised into profit if the autonomous expenditure on non-consumables happens to be too small. Once this is seen, it is easy to understand what was essentially wrong with the usual formulation of *Say's law* which maintained that 'supply creates its own demand'. The additional supply or surplus of the consumption sector need not, under conditions of commodity production, create its own demand which originates in autonomous investment. From this point of view, Say's law fails to recognise the basic character of commodity production where demand originating in the investment sector regulates the level of supply coming from the consumption sector. Hence, it is by *inverting Say's law*, and letting autonomous increase in the demand for consumption goods create its own additional supply, that we are able to understand the economic law which rules commodity production in a capitalist economy.

In this reversal of Say's law lies the deeper ideological impact of the principle of effective demand. Because, it also implies an *inversion of causation between the micro-level at which an individual* (or a 'household') *operates and the macro-level at which the capitalist economy as a whole operates.* For an individual without the possibility of borrowing or running down assets, his income governs expenditure during a given period. Consequently, an individual's investment decisions will be broadly limited by his saving. By arguing that causation runs in precisely the opposite direction for the capitalist economy *as a whole*, where aggregate demand (expenditure) governs aggregate supply (income), the principle of effective demand succeeded in breaking the old analogy between the individual and the society.

However, such an analogy is deeply rooted in the liberal ideological tradition which has been accustomed to look upon the society as a mere collection of individuals. Such a tradition presupposes that by suitably magnifying (or aggregating) the behaviours of individuals, one could arrive at laws governing capitalist commodity production. The principle of effective demand teaches us that this is misleading. Indeed, the Victorian virtue of thrift at the level of an individual household could turn into a *social* vice under the logic of commodity production in times of economic depression. Yet another example based upon this false analogy was the 'Treasury View' propounded to counter policies of increased public investment during the 1930s:

> There was heavy unemployment in England even before the world slump set in. In 1929, Lloyd George was campaigning for a programme of public works. In reply, British officials propounded the 'Treasury View' that if the Government borrowed, say, a hundred million pounds to set men to work on road building and so forth, *foreign investment would be reduced by an equal sum* and no overall increase in employment would occur.[14]

The 'Treasury View' implicitly accepted the analogy between the individual and the society by assuming that if the government spends more in one direction (e.g. road-building), then it would be forced to spend less in another direction (e.g. foreign investment). Because it wrongly assumed that total income and saving are *given* for the economy, just as it is given in the case of an individual. In a similar way, it is argued even today that a higher level of public investment or government budget deficit will 'crowd out' private investment by an equal amount. A real contribution of the principle of effective demand was to point out exactly why such arguments based on an explicit or implicit analogy between the individual household and the capitalist economy, can turn out to be thoroughly misleading in understanding the logic of commodity production.

Notes on Chapter 2

1. More formally, an equilibrium condition is like the solution to an equation which is true only for a *particular* value of the variable e.g., $x + 3 = 7$ holds only if, $x = 4$. Similarly, (2.5) is an equilibrium condition because it holds only when there is no unplanned change in the level of inventories, i.e., $A = 0$. In contrast, (2.6) is true for *all* values of A; hence it is an identity. In passing, the reader may also note that there may be systems with multiple equilibria just as an equation can have multiple solutions e.g., $x^2 - 6x + 8 = (x - 4)(x - 2) = 0$, has two solutions at $x = 4$ and $x = 2$.
2. In the accountants' definition of profit, accumulation of inventories evaluated at imputed market prices is treated as part of gross profit; see definition (1.18) of Chapter 1. However, such a definition avoids the realisation problem, which is usually of central importance to the firms in maintaining comfortable 'cash-flow' positions.
3. The question of how profit is realised in the investment sector (R_I) is left open in our discussion. Since investment expenditure is treated as autonomous, we may assume that it is just sufficient so as not to lead to any unplanned change in the level of inventories of final investment goods, i.e., there is no realisation problem of selling investment goods in the market. This simplifying assumption will be dropped only when an explicit demand function for investment goods is introduced in Chapters 6 or 7.
4. See definitions (1.16) and (1.17) of gross value added in Chapter 1 (rent has been excluded from our present analysis for simplicity). The total income received by the investment sector as profit (R_I) and wage (W_I) must add up to the total *final* expenditure on investment goods (net of raw material cost, etc.), by the circular flow of national income mentioned at the end of Chapter 1.
5. There could also be decumulation of inventories held from earlier periods. Nevertheless such inventory decumulation could not be a general method of adjustment because it requires us to assume that past history was such that it allowed a sufficient level of inventory to be held. This need not be the case and we simplify the analysis by assuming that there are no inventories held from the past.
6. See previous note 4 of this chapter explaining why the *final* expenditure on a sector equals the value added by that sector.
7. In a free-enterprise economy with no economic role for the government, there are no indirect taxes or subsides; hence, estimates at market prices and at factor cost must coincide (see relation (1.22) of Chapter 1). Further in a strictly closed economy, there is neither any income earned nor paid

abroad (see relation (1.20) of Chapter 1); nor is there any export or import (see (1.15) of Chapter 1). Hence, gross domestic product = net national product at factor cost $\equiv$ national income, under the simplifying assumptions made above.

8. $1 + a + a^2 + \ldots + a^n$ is a geometric series. If $1 > a > 0$, each higher-ordered term becomes smaller and the series is convergent. The sum of the series is easily obtained as, $S = 1 + a + a^2 + a^3 \ldots + a^n$. or, multiplying both sides by 'a', $aS = a + a^2 + a^3 \ldots + a^{n+1}$. Now, deducting aS from S and cancelling all the possible terms, $S - aS = (1-a)S = 1 - a^{n+1}$; or, $S = (1 - a^{n+1})/(1-a)$. However, for large n, a^{n+1} is small if $1 > a > 0$ and can be ignored to yield, $S = 1/1 - a$. This formula for summing a convergent, geometric series is used in the text where, $a = (1 - s_p h_c)$.

9. For the sake of expositional simplicity, we ignore the problem of realisation of surplus into profits and conduct the analysis (in comparative static terms) as if, all surplus has been realised into profit.

10. The full implication of this proposition is discussed in Chapter 3.

11. The derivation of equations (2.27) to (2.29) involves the use of logarithms and calculus and may be skipped by the less mathematical reader. He should concentrate on Figure 2.4 which explains the argument geometrically.

12. It shows the weakness of the assumption of strict full employment. However, with such strict full employment of labour, $L_i + L_c = L_f$ is a constant so that, $\Delta L_i = -\Delta L_c$; when this is substituted and the algebra is simplified, the right-hand side of (2.29) becomes $(L_f/L_c) \cdot (\Delta L_i/L_i)$ where, $L_f/L_c = (L_i + L_c)/L_c = 1 + (L_i/L_c)$, can be calculated from (2.25) for the initial situation (before additional labour ΔL_i is employed in the investment sector). This procedure enables us to calculate the extent of decrease in *real* wage for given percentage increase in employment in the investment sector $(\Delta L_i/L_i)$ under conditions of full employment.

13. Analysed in greater detail in Chapter 5, Section A.

14. Quoted from Joan Robinson (1965), 'Kalecki and Keynes', *Collected Economic Papers*, vol. 3, p. 92.

Further Reading

Kalecki's (1971) essay (no. 7) 'The determinants of profits' as well as his essay (no. 13), 'The problem of effective demand with Tugan-Baranovski and Rosa Luxemburg' in his *Selected Essay on the Dynamics of the Capitalist Economy* provide modern discussions on the problem of realisation of profit.

Kahn's (1972) article 'The relation of home investment to unemployment' in his *Selected Essays in Employment and Growth* first formulated the multiplier analysis in 1931. Samuelson's 'The simple mathematics of income determination', in *Income, Employment and Public Policy* (1948) shows how to extend the multiplier analysis, particularly taking into account government budget. Similarly, Lange's 'On the theory of the multiplier' in his *Papers in Economics and Sociology* (Lange, 1970) discusses possible extensions of the multiplier analysis in a mathematically slightly more advanced manner. It contains, in particular, interesting discussions of the 'foreign trade multiplier' (to which we return in Chapter 5, Section A) and of the multiplier in a more dynamic setting. Goodwin's 'The multiplier as a matrix' (Goodwin, 1949) provides an interesting extension, but requires some background in linear algebra.

The price-adjustment multiplier was formulated in Kaldor's (1960) 'Alternative theories of distribution' reprinted in his *Essays on Value and Distribution*. Joan Robinson's (1965) article 'Kalecki and Keynes' in her *Collected Economic Papers*, Vol. 3 provides a highly readable account of the connection between the theories of profit realisation and of effective demand, independently formulated by the two authors. Indeed, this chapter shows how these two formulations can be integrated in the Marxian two department scheme under quantity- and price-adjustment.

3

The Relation Between Prices and Money Wages

A Money and Real Wages: The Wage-Unit and the Wage-Cut Controversy

The working of the multiplier mechanism based on the principle of effective demand set out in the last chapter involved quantity- or price-adjustment. However, which type of adjustment would predominate as a result of an increase in effective demand depends on the supply conditions in the economy. It is easy to see that quantity-adjustment dominates when supply is elastic; conversely, price-adjustments dominate if supply is inelastic. The basic idea, representing the two polar opposite cases of either strict quantity- or price-adjustment, are shown in Figure 3.1.

With totally (or infinitely) elastic conditions of supply, represented by the *horizontal* supply line $P_1 S_1$, a rise in demand from D_1 to D_2 as a result of higher demand caused by investment, leads only to quantity-adjustment from OQ_1 to OQ_2 at constant supply price OP_1. Thus while quantity supplied increases by $Q_1 Q_2$, the price level remains constant at OP_1, i.e. totally insensitive to variation in the level of demand. In the opposite case of totally inelastic supply conditions, represented by the *vertical* supply curve $Q_1 C$, the same increase in demand from D_1 to D_2 shows itself entirely through adjustment in prices from OP_1 to OP_2, while the quantity supplied remains constant at OQ_1. The former case of an infinitely elastic supply represented by the supply curve $P_1 S_1$ corresponds to a situation of *cost-determined price*. Because, suppliers or firms are shown as willing to supply virtually an indefinite amount so long as the price OP_1 covers their costs. Consequently, variation in demand, e.g. from D_1 to D_2 has no

Figure 3.1 *Quantity- and price-adjustment under different supply conditions. Two diametrically opposite supply conditions, represented by a perfectly elastic, horizontal supply curve P_1S_1 and a perfectly inelastic, vertical supply curve Q_1C.*

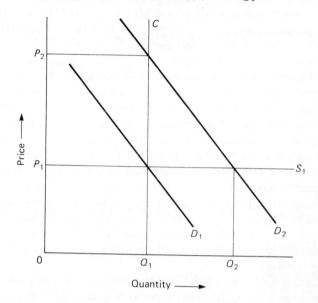

influence on the price level at OP_1. Conversely, the latter case of totally inelastic supply represented by the vertical supply curve Q_1C points to a situation of *demand-determined price*. Because variation in demand from D_1 to D_2 is all important in this case for explaining variation in price from OP_1 to OP_2.

However, prices are to some extent cost-determined even in the conventional textbook theory of perfect competition, where the rising segment of the marginal cost curve represents the short-period supply curve for the firm. Thus, for every parametrically given price level which the perfectly competitive firm cannot influence, a firm equates price (i.e. marginal revenue) with marginal cost (MC) to set the profit-maximising level of output. An essential distinction between this representation of the supply behaviour of the competitive firm and cost-determined constant price which remains insensitive to variation in demand, such as represented by the horizontal supply curve P_1S_1 in Figure 3.1, arises from the assumption of (roughly) *constant* marginal cost in the latter case. However, it should also be noted that with such constant marginal cost, under perfect competition there is no *determinate* profit-maximising level of output of the firm: if the given competitive price exceeds marginal cost ($p > MC$), firms should be expanding their profit-maximising output *indefinitely*. Conversely, if price is less than marginal cost ($p < MC$), firms should be contracting their output *indefinitely*. The assumption of constant marginal cost resulting in a horizontal supply curve such as P_1S_1 in Figure 3.1 then becomes incompatible with the assumption of any determinate equilibrium under perfect competition. Nevertheless, this assumption of constant marginal cost is not only convenient but also realistic in describing the fundamentals of the multiplier based on *quantity adjustment*. Because, it shows how variations in demand from D_1 to D_2 in Figure 3.1 caused by say variation in the level of investment, leads only to an increased quantity by Q_1Q_2 with no influence on the level of price OP_1. Unlike, in the case described by the perfectly competitive model, the *scale* of output produced, namely OQ_1 or OQ_2 in Figure 3.1, is determined solely by the level of effective demand shown by the *position* of the demand curve D_1 or D_2 in Figure 3.1. In other words the assumption of cost-determined constant prices permits the level of demand to determine the scale of output leaving prices constant.

In retrospect, one of the major novelties associated with the macroeconomic analysis pioneered by Kalecki and Keynes arose precisely from recognising the possibility that quantities could be the *dominant* adjusting variables while prices remained more or less cost-determined constants during the short period. This ran counter to the Marshallian view. Marshall had distinguished his short from the long period basically in terms of the degree of flexibility in supply conditions: the shorter the period, the less flexible (elastic) is supply and consequently, the greater is the extent of adjustment in prices rather than in quantities. Prices were therefore reckoned to be the dominant adjusting variables in the short period analysis by Marshall.[1]

This traditional point of view was reversed by Keynes on the basis of what now appears a commonsense observation: with unemployment and under-utilised capacity coexisting on a significant scale at times of economic depression, quantities produced are likely to respond far more rapidly than prices to a higher level of effective demand. In other words, the *speed of adjustment* of quantities would tend to be higher than that of prices, at least as a typical feature of economic depression. This *reversal in the ordering of the speeds of adjustment* – quantities adjusting more rapidly than prices in the short period – was a novel feature distinguishing the Keynesian short-period analysis from the Marshallian tradition. And this meant assuming a highly elastic (aggregate) supply function in the short-period as an important feature of the capitalist economy in depression.

Naturally, if prices are assumed to be strictly cost-determined and therefore insensitive to variations in the level of demand (like the supply curve P_1S_1 in Figure 3.1), the multiplier mechanism can operate entirely in real terms through quantity-adjustment. A higher level of effective demand in such a regime of strictly cost-determined prices leads exclusively to higher output (by $Q_1 Q_2$ in Figure 3.1) and employment, in line with the traditional quantity-adjustment multiplier discussed earlier in Chapter 2. But this raises a further question. *If the level of effective demand determines quantities rather than prices, then what determines the level of prices in the short period?* Or, in terms of previous Figure 3.1, if the variation in demand from D_1 to D_2 leads only to quantity adjustment from OQ_1 to OQ_2 with no influence on the level of price at OP_1, then what determines the price level at OP_1 in the first place? The clue to answering this question lies naturally in specifying the 'costs' which would determine the *levels* of such cost-determined price at OP_1, i.e., the position of the horizontal supply curve in Figure 3.1.

One of the basic postulates of Keynes–Kalecki type of macroeconomics is to proceed on the *empirical* assumption that the cost of labour, i.e. level of the *money* wage rate is by far the most important element determining the cost of production in manufacturing business. Therefore, *the level of money wage rate exerts a decisive influence on the level of costs which in turn determines the level of prices in the short run.* Indeed, as a first approximation for macroeconomic analysis, the general price level may often be assumed to be more or less proportional to the money wage rate; the higher is that historically given money wage rate, the higher is the corresponding general level of prices. This, in essence, provides the basic skeleton of short period macroeconomic analysis of a capitalist economy based on *two fundamental principles*.

(i) Quantities are determined by the level of aggregate demand;
(ii) The general price level is determined by the historically given level of the *money* wage rate.

This is a drastic conceptual departure both from the Marshallian 'partial equilibrium' as well as from the Walrasian 'general equilibrium' tradition, where forces of demand and supply interact to determine quantities and prices *simultaneously* in one or many markets. Instead, a fruitful separation is suggested here: quantities, by and large, are demand-determined through the level of effective demand, while prices tend to be cost-determined through the historically given level of money wage rate in a capitalist economy.

A scheme of analysis based on the above separation finds its clearest expression in Keynes' use of a *'wage-unit' measure* for all relevant macroeconomic variables in the *General Theory*.[2] If prices are cost-determined, varying in proportion to the money wage rate, then by dividing the nominal, i.e., money value of a variable by the money wage rate, a measure of the underlying physical quantities can be obtained. Thus, using notations of Chapter 2, if C is the nominal money value of consumption goods, X_c is the physical quantity of final consumption goods, P_c is the price level of consumption goods, and w_c is the money wage level of the consumption sector, then the wage-unit measure of consumption goods is given as

$$C_w = \frac{\text{Money or nominal value of final consumption goods } (C)}{\text{Money wage rate } (w_c)}$$

$$= \frac{X_c P_c}{w_c} \tag{3.1}$$

Thus, so long as prices vary in proportion to the money wage rate, the ratio (P_c/w_c) remains constant in (3.1) and consumption measured in wage-unit as C_w also provides a measure which is strictly proportional to the physical volume (X_c) of consumption goods. In other words, a more or less proportional link between prices and money wages – e.g., a 10 per cent change in the money wage rate leading roughly to a 10 per cent change in the price level – permits the wage-unit measure to be effectively used for isolating quantity or volume changes from the more superficial changes in the nominal or money values of the relevant variables. Note also that this wage-unit device to isolate volume from nominal change provides a framework which does *not* need to assume constant prices and money wages. Indeed, it is a common misunderstanding of the argument in the *General Theory* (likely to be enhanced even by our earlier Figure 3.1) to suppose that it is based on the postulate of constant prices and money wages. Had such an assumption actually been made, measurements in wage-units would have been totally redundant. Clearly, there is no need to distinguish between changes in nominal (money) values and real magnitudes if prices remain constant! Precisely because such changes in prices and money wage rates had not been ruled out, Keynes in the *General Theory* found it necessary to devise the wage-unit to measure all the relevant variables, including the stock of money. Adjustments in quantities could then be captured through the wage-unit measure, while the nominal levels of prices and money wages remained free to change in a more or less proportional manner as described by relation (3.1). It may not be out of place to mention here that both prices and money wages fell during the depression of the 1930s which formed the background of the *General Theory*. However, the fall in money wages and prices was much less, compared to the massive reduction in the volume of output and employment which the wage-unit tried to capture.

The more or less proportional relation between the general price level and the *money* wage rate presumed in the wage-unit measure would naturally imply that the *real* wage rate is highly inflexible even when the *money* wage rate is flexible. In order to understand how the *real* wage rate could remain constant while money wage varied, we need to begin with the commonsense observation that both *wage* contracts and wage bargains are necessarily made in the generalised purchasing power of money and not in terms of individual commodities. However, this leaves the capitalists and the managers of the firms generally with the option to raise their prices of individual commodities as the labour cost per unit of output rises due to an increase in the money wage rate. In each industry j, one could therefore imagine that the price level P_j is set in relation to the money wage rate w_j ruling in that industry. This implies a wage rate in terms of the product of that particular industry, i.e., a *product* wage rate w_j/P_j. Thus, there would be a product wage rate exclusively in terms of food, in terms of clothes, in terms of machines, etc. for each industry. In general, in accordance with earlier relations (2.23) and (2.24) of Chapter 2, the wage rate of an industry in terms of its own product can be written in the form,

$$\text{Product wage rate in industry } j = \frac{w_j}{P_j} = x_j(1 - h_j) \qquad (3.2)$$

where w_j is the *money* wage rate in industry j, P_j is the price of commodity j (we assume each industry j produces a single or 'composite' commodity j), x_j is the physical labour productivity in industry j, and h_j is the share of profit in value added by industry j.

It is evident from the extreme right-hand side of (3.2) that the product wage rate is in *physical* units of product j. It is a fraction $(1 - h_j)$ of the physical productivity of labour (x_j) in that industry. Consequently, the validity of the wage-unit measure in any industry j can be seen to depend on the degree of constancy of the inverse of the product wage rate (i.e., P_j/w_j) in that industry. For instance, the right-hand side of (3.1) requires the inverse of the product wage in terms of consumption goods, i.e., P_c/w_c to be constant. However, the inverse of the product wage rate in any industry j also measures the amount of 'labour commanded' per unit of output of that industry j. For example, if the price of a commodity $P_j = \$500$ and the going money wage rate in that industry is $w_j = \$100$ then 5 units of labour can be said to be commanded per unit of output of industry j. In other words, the wage-unit is a measure of *labour commanded per unit of output*. At the same time, the inverse of labour productivity, i.e., $1/x_j$ in (3.2), measures the amount of (direct) *labour used per unit of output*. Hence, the difference between labour commanded and labour used per unit of output is a measure of the '*surplus labour*' *expropriated per unit of output*. This is given for a unit of output in industry j as,

$$\text{Labour commanded} \left(\frac{P_j}{w_j}\right) - \text{labour used}\left(\frac{1}{x_j}\right),$$

which from (3.2) reduces to,

$$\left(\frac{P_j}{w_j}\right) - \left(\frac{1}{x_j}\right) = \frac{1}{x_j}\left(\frac{h_j}{1 - h_j}\right)$$

$$= \frac{1}{x_j}(h_j + h_j^2 + \ldots) \qquad h_j < 1 \qquad (3.3)$$

Equation (3.3) clearly exhibits that, given labour productivity (x_j), the surplus labour expropriated per unit of output is greater the higher is the share of profit (h_j) in the value added of an industry.

The significance of the proportionality postulate between prices and money wages which leaves the real wage rate constant can now be seen from a different angle. From equation (3.2), such proportionality would hold if, (i) labour productivity x_j is constant in the short period, and (ii) the share of profit h_j is also constant. In terms of equation (3.3), this implies that the amount of *surplus* labour expropriated per unit of output *j* also remains constant so long as price is proportional to money wage in an industry *j*.

Except for accounting purposes, the concept of industry-wise *product* wage rate is not very useful in macroeconomic analysis. Because, workers in general, are only concerned with how much their *money* wage rate can buy of those *particular* commodities which typically enter their budget. Thus, the product wage in terms of particular wage-goods or a composite basket of wage-goods corresponds to the idea of a *real* wage rate that concerns the workers. To illustrate the point, the product wage rate in terms of 'machinery' or investment-goods is irrelevant from the workers' point of view. Nevertheless, the product wage rate in terms of 'bread' or 'shoe' that goes into defining the *real* wage rate would concern the workers as it influences their standard of living. This emphasises again why neither wage contract nor wage bargain can take place in terms of the individual product of an industry. And, even if we could imagine such wage bargain in terms of a few selected wage-goods which define the *real* wage rate, there would be many other product wage rates that would be considered irrelevant by the workers in their wage bargain. For each individual capitalist, however, the product wage rate in his industry entails a measure of *potential profit* in terms of surplus labour per unit of output (see (3.3)). This potential surplus is a reflection of the price policy for that product in relation to the ruling wage cost in that industry. However, unless the commodity can actually be sold in the market at that price, the potential profit embodied in the surplus labour is not *realised*. In other words, by setting prices high in relation to the money wage rate, an individual capitalist can only ensure higher *potential* profit per unit of output, but he cannot ensure that such profit would actually be realised in money through sale of that commodity in the market.

This simple proposition goes to the heart of one of the central contradictions under which capitalistic commodity production takes place. Although by setting his price higher, an individual capitalist can depress the product wage rate and raise his potential surplus or profit per unit of output, no individual capitalist has the power to ensure the realisation of that potential into actual profit. The realisation of potential into actual (money) profit depends on the *general* state of the market which is not governed by the decision of any *single* capitalist. Instead, it is the outcome of expenditure decisions by the capitalist class *as a whole*. This was indeed a central point about the profit realisation equation (2.8) given in Chapter 2. Further, although it may seem at first sight that an individual capitalist can influence the state of the *particular* market for his product by varying his price, this would seldom be the case in reality. For instance, at the given money wage rate, if an individual capitalist increases his price to depress the *product* wage rate and thereby increase *potential* surplus per unit of output, his rival capitalist firms in the same industry may not follow suit. This will lead to a shrinking share of the market for this particular capitalist who increases only his *potential* surplus but now faces an additional problem in realising that surplus into profit.

This crucial asymmetry between potential and realised profit under capitalistic commodity production needs to be emphasised. An *individual* capitalist can influence only the potential level of profit through his price policy, but the *aggregate* market outcome will ultimately decide how much of that potential can be actually realised. And, precisely this asymmetry makes the microeconomic foundation of macroeconomics such a problematic area of analysis under capitalism. The micro decision by an individual capitalist regarding his *potential* profit per unit of output through setting his individual price policy may have an altogether different outcome in terms of realised profits. Because realisation depends on the macro level of demand over which an individual capitalist has neither control nor adequate information.

In the context of the above analysis focusing on the relation between potential and realised profit, it is now easy to see why the pre-Keynesian idea of stimulating employment by cutting the money wage rate is based on faulty reasoning. The orthodox belief ran in terms of a commensense analogy: for any commodity say tomatoes, a reduction in its price would increase the level of its demand. By analogy, it was argued that a reduction in the price of labour, i.e., the (money) wage rate would stimulate the demand for labour in situations of serious unemployment.

The fallacy of this reasoning stems from treating labour on par with any other commodity. To begin with, a reduction in the *money* wage rate can be expected to have repercussions on the general price level through a corresponding reduction in the cost of production in a regime of cost-determined prices. Consequently, as both prices and money wages are reduced, the *net* effect on the *real* wage rate may become indeterminate. For instance, if the percentage reduction in price happens to be larger than that in *money* wage, then the *real* wage rate is actually increased while the *money* wage rate is reduced. Only in the opposite case of percentage reduction in price being smaller than that in the money wage rate, both the money *and* the real wage rate move in the same direction. However, if the assumption underlying the wage-unit measure holds, then price and money wage are reduced by the *same* proportion, so that the *real* wage rate remains constant while the *money* wage rate is reduced. And, once it is recalled that wage contracts (and wage bargains) can only be made in *money* terms, the ambiguity of the orthodox position becomes evident, because it cannot ensure that by cutting the *money* wage rate, the *real* wage rate is also simultaneously reduced. That would depend on how strongly the general price level responds to any given reduction in the money wage rate, particularly in situations of severe economic depression.

Nevertheless, unless the *real* and the individual *product* wage rates are simultaneously reduced as a consequence of cutting the *money* wage rate, the *derived demand for labour* as a commodity used in the production of other commodities, has no reason to increase even under orthodox economic reasoning. For instance, profit-maximising firms of neoclassical theory would equate the marginal product of labour (i.e., the product obtained from employing an additional unit of labour at the margin) to the *product* wage rate in any particular industry. On profit-maximising assumption, they would employ more labour only if the product wage rate is lower. However, as we have already seen, a policy of cutting the *money* wage rate does not by any means ensure that the *product* wage rates are also necessarily reduced simultaneously.

But the fallacy of orthodox reasoning in the context of this *wage-cut controversy* goes even deeper. Consider the most favourable case for orthodox theory where all prices remain constant (i.e., a regime of *fixed* prices) despite reduction in the *money* wage rate. In such a hypothetical situation, by assumption, the *real* and each individual *product* wage rate are also reduced simultaneously as a result of the reduction in the *money* wage rate. However, the economy is now likely to face an even more serious *problem of effective demand* elaborated in Chapter 2. Returning to Figure 2.2 of that chapter, a reduction in the real wage rate in terms of consumption goods, would mean a *higher potential surplus* of consumption goods (represented by the rectangle *HJKM* in the initial situation in Figure 2.2) that seeks realisation into profit. At the same time, a lower real wage in terms of consumption goods also entails a lower real wage bill of the investment section $W_I (= ABEF$ in Figure 2.2) for any autonomously given level of investment in the short period. Thus, any reduction in the *real* (and money) wage rate increases the level of surplus of consumption goods seeking realisation into profits, whereas it decreases the market for consumption goods generated by the wage bill of the investment sector.[3] As a result, the discrepancy between the level of *potential* surplus (profit) and *realised* profit increases, showing itself in terms of unplanned accumulation of inventories of finished consumption goods. Such a depressed state of effective demand caused by a reduction in the real (and money) wage rate is likely to further aggravate, rather than alleviate the problem of unemployment.

To sum up, the orthodox view that a reduction in the money (and real) wage rate would stimulate employment is logically unacceptable, because it fails to take into account *two major* types of *feedbacks following from wage cut* in a capitalist economy. First, is the feedback from *money* wage to the level of prices on which the wage-unit measure was based. Secondly, there occurs a feedback from variation in the *real* wage rate to the level of effective demand on which the multiplier analysis of Chapter 2 is based. Both these feedbacks can also be briefly summarised in terms of Figure 2.4 of Chapter 2. As shown by Figure 2.4, if the feedback from money wage to price is weak (i.e., prices rise *slower* than money wages in percentage terms), the overall savings propensity $s_p h$ given by the slope of the ray OBE, decreases as the *real* wage rate increases. Consequently, the level of effective demand created by the multiplier mechanism is higher in this case (see equation (2.20) of Chapter 2 in particular). On the other hand, if the feedback from money wage to price is strong (i.e. prices rise *faster* than money wages in percentage terms), the savings propensity increases as the *real* wage rate decreases, making the level of effective demand created through the multiplier lower in this case. The borderline case assumed in the wage-unit measure leaves the *real* wage altogether inflexible as money wage and price rise in strictly the same proportion. With no change in the *real* wage rate, the savings propensity depicted by the slope of the ray OBE in Figure 2.4 also remains unaltered. Consequently, the value of the multiplier in creating effective demand does not change either.

However, such strong feedback from money wage to price, the borderline case of which is represented by the wage-unit measure, points to a deeper macroeconomic problem underlying capitalistic commodity production. When the *real* wage rate is inflexible downwards under such strong feedback from money wage to price, any gap between investment (expenditure) and savings (income) cannot be closed by the market mechanism at full employment (see Figure 2.4, Chapter 2 where this gap is represented by *EJ*). This failure of the market mechanism to bridge the gap (*EJ* in Figure 2.4) between investment and saving at full employment under the downward inflexibility of the *real* wage rates is often described by apologists of capitalism as 'workers' indiscipline'. What, in effect, it means is the ability of the trade unions to maintain or even raise their *real* wage rate at full employment. However, when the market can no longer 'discipline' the workers to accept the *real* wage rate that would generate enough saving to match the level of investment that has been *unilaterally* decided by the capitalists, the market economy is left without any self-regulating mechanism to balance aggregate demand with aggregate supply of wage goods at full employment. Strictly cost-determined prices presumed by the wage-unit measure imply such as inflexible *real* wage rate and become *incompatible* with the principle of effective demand that investment *governs* saving when the capitalist economy operates at full employment. But this logical incompatibility only manifests the contradiction that a capitalist economy must face in trying to maintain full employment.

B Pricing of Industrial Commodities

The basic distinction between *demand-determined* and *cost-determined* prices made in the last section (see Figure 3.1) is useful for emphasising intrinsic differences in the conditions of supply in different lines of production. The production of many *unprocessed raw materials*, such as agricultural and mining products, tends to be typically inelastic in supply in the short period. With inelastic supply, variations in demand tend to transmit themselves rather easily and rapidly to prices. Thus, prices tend to rise and fall with the state of demand for most of these unprocessed raw materials. These demand-determined prices have the major characteristic of being *flexible in response to demand in the short period*.

There is a good deal of empirical evidence on this short-period flexibility of unprocessed raw material prices. Although sudden shifts in supply caused by change in weather conditions naturally dominate the price movements of crops, there are also unmistakable traces of the influence of variations in demand on such price movements. Thus, 'with the exception of 1958, U.S. wholesale prices of domestically produced food crops fell (absolutely) in every recession year since World War II'.[4] Similarly, the prices of many *mining products* also vary in accordance with the state of demand. For instance, it has been estimated that the price of non-ferrous metal increases by as much as 3 to 6 per cent for every 1 per cent increase in the level of world industrial production (relative to the trend).[5] Evidence has also accumulated at the international level to suggest that the export prices of unprocessed primary products respond systematically to the level of world industrial activity. Thus, during years of high industrial activity in the industrialised countries, the less developed countries exporting primary products tend to obtain favourable prices for their exports. On the other hand, during years of economic recession in the industrialised world, export prices for those primary products are perceptibly depressed. The prices of primary products thus exhibit a pro-cyclical pattern in general.

This flexible response of unprocessed raw material prices to variations in demand stands in contrast to the (especially downward) inflexibility of a whole range of prices of industrially manufactured goods. The prices for this latter group of commodities tend to be far less sensitive to variations in demand. For these commodities, the 'shock' of unexpected variation in demand is mostly absorbed by unplanned changes in inventory levels of the finished goods, leaving the prices inflexible at least during the short period. Thus, an unexpected fall (rise) in demand causes unplanned accumulation (decumulation) in the level of inventories, but prices are not immediately revised.

This brings us to an important point, contrary to textbook teaching in the neoclassical tradition. In a modern industrial economy with the manufacturing industries dominating production, the immediate signals of whether there is excess demand or excess supply are sent out, not by changes in the level of prices but by changes in the level of inventories. With cost- rather than demand-determined price as the dominant practice of manufacturing business, such changes in inventories leading perhaps to corresponding changes in the level of production at the next round, become the main adjustment variable to deal with fluctuations in demand. And, these prices adjust sluggishly to variations in demand, but respond rapidly to changes in costs. In short, a change in the general price level is perhaps a better indicator (or signal) of changing cost conditions than of changing demand conditions in a modern industrial economy.

However, this sensitivity of the prices of manufactured goods to variation in costs raises a further issue: *which elements of cost* actually enter in the determination of such prices? Broadly speaking, there have been two contesting views based on numerous empirical enquiries over the last forty years or so. Some have claimed that *full-cost pricing* is the basic mode of price formation in manufacturing business. This means *all* costs, i.e. the *variable cost* of labour and raw materials as well as the *fixed overhead cost* of machinery (and interest cost of borrowing finance) enter into the calculation of firms in setting their prices. Thus, firms calculate their *total unit cost*, i.e., variable and fixed cost per unit of output, and set prices by allowing for a profit margin on that unit *total* cost. The other view stresses, in contrast, the short-period nature of price formation. In the short period, fixed overhead cost of capital equipment and of borrowed finance are *given* data in the sense that they are irreversible decisions that have already been made in the past. Consequently, firms take fixed cost as given data and formulate their short period price policy by focusing attention primarily on the *variable* cost per unit of output. With wage and raw material as the two most important elements of variable costs, the *unit prime cost* is defined as wage and raw material cost per unit of output. In the short period, according to this view of direct cost pricing, firms set their prices by allowing for some profit margin over the unit prime cost.

The distinction between full-cost and prime-cost pricing method therefore depends on the nature of *cost-norms* used by firms. However, since the former full-cost method includes also the cost of fixed capital per unit of output, measuring such items of fixed cost becomes especially problematic. For instance, the cost of any fixed equipment may be set either at its historical cost, i.e. original purchase price or at its current replacement price in the market. More serious, however, is the problem of the level of output at which the unit total cost is to be calculated. Since average *fixed* cost would decrease with higher levels of output, the total unit cost (consisting of both unit variable and unit fixed cost) become highly sensitive to the level of output at which that average is calculated. Consequently, the unit *total* cost required as the norm for full-cost pricing can only be estimated at a *specified* level of output. However, since prices are set before and not after sales, firms require to specify beforehand the output level on the basis of which such average fixed cost can be estimated. Frequently, level of output specified at some 'normal' degree of capacity utilisation serves that purpose. All elements of fixed cost (e.g., cost of machines, interest payment on borrowed finance or even managerial salaries) are then averaged with reference to this level of output at 'normal' capacity. And, full-cost pricing, defined at the level of such 'normal' capacity output, is often described as the method of *normal cost pricing*.

It is to be noted that many of the problems of full-cost pricing, e.g., whether machines are to be valued at historical or replacement cost or how to define the level of 'normal' capacity, arise because unit *fixed* cost also enters the calculation. These problems could be largely avoided if *fixed* costs were excluded from the cost-norms of firms. This provides an operational justification for direct cost pricing which *includes* wage and raw material costs (i.e., prime costs), but *excludes* all overhead and fixed costs. And, in so far as prime cost varies roughly in proportion with the level of output (e.g., doubling or having output level also doubles or halves prime costs), the average prime cost per unit of output or *unit* prime cost remains constant. Consequently, there arises no need to define any 'normal' capacity level for measuring average prime cost.

However, unit prime cost can be constant only if technological conditions permit both raw material required per unit of output as well as labour required per unit of output to be constant.[6] Such technological conditions are often satisfied because modern manufacturing business typically operates under *excess capacity* where some reserve in capacity is maintained even at times of reasonably high industrial activity. Both raw material and labour requirement per unit of output remains roughly constant so long as the firm operates under such excess capacity. Only at output levels beyond capacity do the variable costs of the firms begin to rise rather sharply, as an attempt is made to squeeze out higher levels of output through such measures as additional shifts of work, overtime, decreasing maintenance and repair time, etc. This results in something like an inverted L-shaped variable cost curve, shown in Figure 3.2. It is to be noted that our previous Figure 3.1 could actually be derived from cost curves represented by Figure 3.2. So long as the unit prime cost remains constant at *OB* in Figure 3.2, the cost-determined *supply price* also remains constant at OP_1 in Figure 3.1. This is reproduced again in

Figure 3.2 as the cost-determined supply curve P_1S_1, where suppliers are shown willing to sell up to normal capacity output OC at that constant price OP_1. Note also that the vertical difference between the price OP_1 and the unit prime cost OB, i.e., BP_1 in Figure 3.2 shows the *mark up on unit prime cost* in setting price. This mark up implying a profit margin BP_1 per unit of output is assumed to remain constant up to normal capacity level of output OC, as shown by a constant vertical distance between the unit prime cost curve BD and the supply curve P_1S_1 up to normal capacity output at OC in Figure 3.2.

If the cost of labour were the *only* item of unit prime (variable) cost, then our earlier equation (3.2) of this chapter could be used to find the *profit margin* per unit of output BP_1 in Figure 3.2. Because (3.2) can be rewritten as the price equation for an enterprise or industry j in terms of its wage cost per unit of output, i.e.,

$$P_j = \frac{w_j}{x_j(1-h_j)} \tag{3.4}$$

Figure 3.2 *Behaviour of cost with respect to output in manufacturing enterprise. OC = normal capacity output AVC (Average Variable Cost) = unit prime cost which remains constant at OB up to normal capacity output OC. MC (Marginal Cost) = cost of producing an additional unit of output. P_1S_1 = supply curve shown only up to normal capacity output OC; hence OP_1 = price and BP_1 = profit margin.*

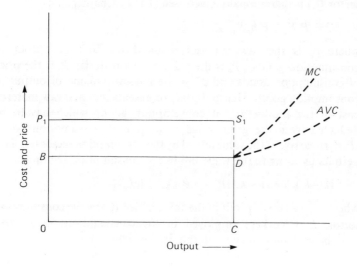

where $1/x_j$ = labour required per unit of output of j; hence, w_j/x_j = wage cost (which is also prime cost) per unit of output of j.

The profit margin per unit of output (BP_1 in Figure 3.2) is given as the difference between price (P_j) and unit prime cost (w_j/x_j). From (3.4),

$$BP_1 \text{ as the profit margin per unit of output } j = \frac{w_j}{x_j(1-h_j)} - \frac{w_j}{x_j}$$

$$= \left(\frac{h_j}{1-h_j}\right) \cdot \frac{w_j}{x_j} \quad (3.5)$$

As the share of profit in value added (h_j) increases the profit margin must also increase in (3.5).

Using wage as the *only* prime cost, a price equation like (3.4) shows the strict proportionality between price (P_j) and the money wage rate (w_j), so long as labour productivity (x_j) and the share of profit (h_j) remain constant. This essential property of the wage-unit measure, discussed in Section A of this chapter, continues to hold even if raw materials enter as a further element of unit prime cost, but only if those raw materials are *processed* within the manufacturing sector and thus follow the practice of mark up pricing.

Explicit introduction of raw materials into our analysis would require us to distinguish between the *gross* value of output and the *value added* by a sector. Thus, the value added by the consumption sector (C) is definitionally given (see (1.1) of Chapter 1) as,

$$C = P_c X_c - P_z b_c X_c$$

where b_c is the raw material required per unit of output of consumption goods,[7] P_z is the price of raw material, P_c is the price of consumption goods and X_c is the physical volume of output of consumption goods. Hence, $P_z b_c X_c$ represents the total raw material cost in the production of consumption goods which has to be deducted from the gross value of output of consumption goods ($P_c X_c$) to arrive at the value added by the consumption sector (C). This permits us to write the wage bill in the consumption sector as,

$$(1-h_c)C = (1-h_c)(P_c - b_c P_z)X_c = wL_c$$

where h_c = share of profit in the value added (C) by the consumption sector, L_c = workers employed in the consumption sector, and w = the *uniform* money wage rate in the economy.

The above relation immediately reduces to,

$$(1 - h_c)(P_c - b_c P_z)x_c = w, \qquad \text{where } x_c = \frac{X_c}{L_c}$$

so that,

$$P_c = \frac{w}{x_c(1 - h_c)} + b_c P_z \qquad (3.6)$$

Comparing equations (3.4) with (3.6), it is evident that the price of consumption goods (P_c) depends on the mark up factor, $1/1 - h_c$ on unit wage cost for producing consumption goods, i.e., w/x_c *plus* the raw material cost per unit of consumption goods (i.e., $b_c P_z$).

However, raw materials are also required in producing raw materials so that the *value added* by the raw material sector (Z) is obtained in the same way as,

$$Z = P_z X_z - P_z b_z X_z$$

where b_z = raw material needed per unit of production of raw material $(1 > b_z > 0)$[8], X_z = physical volume of output of raw materials. Therefore, $P_z b_z X_z$ represents the total raw material cost in producing raw materials, which has to be deducted from the gross value of output of raw materials $(P_z X_z)$ to arrive at the value added by the raw material sector (Z). As before, writing the wage bill of the raw material sector, we obtain,

$$(1 - h_z)Z = (1 - h_z)(1 - b_z)P_z X_z = wL_z$$

where h_z = share of profit in the value added (Z) by the raw material sector.

The above equation simplifies to yield the price of raw material (p_z) as,

$$P_z = \frac{w}{x_z(1 - b_z)(1 - h_z)}, \qquad \text{where } x_z = \frac{X_z}{L_z} \qquad (3.7)$$

Note that the crucial aspect of the price equation (3.7) for raw materials is the proportionality of raw material price (p_z) to the money wage rate w, so long as other parameters $(x_z, h_z$ and $b_z)$ remain constant. And this proportionality obtains *only* under the assumption that raw materials are *processed* within the domestic manufacturing sector, making raw material price (P_z) also cost- rather than demand-determined.

Substituting (3.7) in (3.6) and simplifying, we obtain the price of consumption goods as,

$$P_c = \left[\frac{1}{x_c(1-h_c)} + \frac{b_c}{x_z(1-b_z)(1-h_z)} \right] \cdot w \tag{3.8}$$

Thus, so long as the parameters within the square-bracketed term on the right-hand side of (3.8) remain constant, the price of consumption goods (P_c) is proportional to the money wage rate (w), *despite* explicit introduction of raw materials into the analysis. This proves our earlier contention that the proportional relation between price and money wage rate is not disturbed (as demonstrated by (3.8)) so long as raw materials are also processed, having cost-determined prices (as shown by (3.7)). However, since that proportionality holds *only if* the raw materials themselves are also processed and priced on a mark up basis on their unit prime cost (as in (3.7)), the validity of the wage-unit measure depends on the extent to which *processed* raw materials with such cost-determined prices are quantitatively more significant in a modern industrial economy than *unprocessed* raw materials having typically demand-determined prices.

It should be noted that the proportionality between price and wage in (3.8) despite the existence of raw materials is possible only because all prime costs are reducible to direct and indirect labour cost. Thus, $1/x_c$ represents labour *directly* used per unit of production of consumption goods. However, labour is also *indirectly* required to produce the raw material (b_c) that goes into the production of each unit of consumption goods. Thus, $1/x_z$ being labour used per unit of raw material, b_c/x_z is the labour required to produce b_c amount of raw material. However, since raw material is required to produce raw material (see (3.7)), a further amount of labour, $b_z b_c/x_z$ is required to produce that b_c amount of raw material in the first round. That amount of raw material in turn, requires,

$$\frac{b_z(b_z b_c)}{x_z} = \frac{b_z^2 b_c}{x_z}$$

amount of labour in the next round and so on, until the convergent, infinite geometric series,

$$\left(\frac{b_c}{x_z} + \frac{b_c b_z}{x_z} + \frac{b_c b_z^2}{x_z} + \ldots \right)$$

sums up to $b_c/x_z(1-b_z)$, yielding the total direct and indirect labour required in the production of raw material per unit of consumption good. This is precisely the expression which appears in (3.8) along with direct labour $(1/x_c)$ required in the production of a unit of consumption goods. And, these direct $(1/x_c)$ and indirect $(b_c/x_z(1 - b_z))$ labour costs are marked up by their respective profit margins $1/(1 - h_c)$ and $1/(1 - h_z)$ (see (3.4) and (3.5)) to arrive ultimately at the price equation for consumption goods in (3.8). This interpretation of a price equation like (3.8) makes its clear that the proportionality between price and money wage becomes possible only when *all* prime costs are ultimately reducible as labour costs.

The overwhelming *empirical* evidence in favour of cost-determined prices in any modern industrial economy makes the theoretical *dichotomy* proposed by Keynes and Kalecki highly relevant for macro-economic analysis. As mentioned earlier (see p. 65), according to this dichotomy, quantity-adjustments are mostly governed by the level of demand, while prices generally adjust to cost conditions. Further, since *money* wage rate is usually the most important element of cost in the economy, prices tend to be determined largely in relation to the historically given money wage rate in an industrial economy.[9] The logical extreme case of this is exhibited by the proportionality between price and money wage discussed above.

Nevertheless, the empirical evidence for cost-determined price becomes hard to justify in terms of orthodox notion of 'economic rationality'. For instance, even if marginal (and average variable) cost remains constant up to normal capacity output as presumed in Figure 3.2, it would be 'rational' for the profit-maximising firm to equate marginal revenue (MR) with (constant) marginal cost (MC) to set its optimal level of output and price. However, as Figure 3.3 shows, the optimal level of price would then increase from OP_1 to OP_2 as demand shifts from D_1 to D_2. Consequently, profit margin per unit of output (see (3.5)) would also increase from BP_1 to BP_2 in response to increased demand. This contradicts the postulate of cost-determined price with an *invariant* profit margin, such as BP_1, shown in our earlier Figure 3.2.

However, at least part of this theoretical difficulty of interpreting the evidence of *constant* mark up in pricing can be resolved by recognising that firms generally operate in an *uncertain business environment* for setting their prices. It is an attribute of such uncertain environment that all information does not have the same status in terms of reliability; nor can they be reduced to the same status by

Figure 3.3 *Implication of orthodox economic rationality in setting price under constant marginal and average variable cost. OB = constant unit prime cost = marginal cost (MC) = average variable cost (AVC) Dotted lines MR_1 and MR_2 are the marginal revenue curves, corresponding to demand (average revenue) curves D_1 and D_2 respectively. OQ_1 and OQ_2 are profit-maximising output levels and P_1 and P_2 are the prices at levels of demand D_1 and D_2 respectively. Hence, profit margin per unit of output increases from BP_1 to BP_2 as demand shifts from D_1 to D_2.*

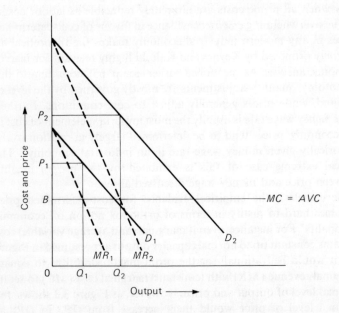

actuarial 'expected value' calculation, e.g., by weighting the possible outcomes of a relevant variable by its respective probabilities because, such probabilities themselves are unknown. Thus, a useful distinction could be made in the present context between '*hard*' *information* about which firms feel reasonably confident and '*soft*' *information* in which they have little confidence. And, firms would generally tend to rely more on 'hard' information in devising their decision-rules under uncertainty. Since information regarding production costs are usually far more reliably known to each firm as a micro-unit than information regarding variations in the level of demand for the commodity it produces – i.e., information regarding cost is 'hard' but information on demand is 'soft' at the level of an individual firm – it is natural for the firm to follow a procedure for setting price that is more sensitive to cost than to demand. It must also be pointed out that, this very 'softness' of information regarding demand conditions makes variation of profit margin in response to fluctuating demand, as exhibited by Figure 3.3, an unlikely procedure for setting price under uncertainty. And, the best that a firm can typically hope to achieve under these uncertain circumstances is to follow *procedural rationality* of having a fixed margin of profit on unit (prime) cost in setting its price. So long as such price leads to a more or less *satisfactory* outcome in terms of profits, the profit margin is maintained at its previous level. The margin may be adjusted rather cautiously, only if the firm becomes reasonably convinced that demand conditions have actually changed. But to be reasonably convinced of changed demand conditions takes time for an individual firm, because the 'soft' information on demand only gradually turns into 'harder' information over time. Thus, the profit margin responds sluggishly to changing demand conditions.

Although placing more weight on 'hard' rather than on 'soft' information in setting price could basically be a matter of convention, such convention is often justified in terms of *bounded rationality*. For instance, even if it were possible for firms under certain circumstances to convert 'soft' into 'hard' information, such conversion may either be too time-consuming and/or too expensive in terms of the processing of all the available data.[10] Under these circumstances, firms may actually be rational, at least in a limited sense, in not taking into account the 'soft' information in making their decisions and follow a *procedure* of limited (or bounded) rationality by concentrating mostly on the available 'hard' information.

This procedural rationality need *not* lead to an optimal outcome. It is rational only in terms of *procedure* but not necessarily rational in terms of outcome.[11] But so long as the procedure leads to a reasonably *'satisfying'* outcome, that procedure need not be abandoned. This contrasts sharply with the textbook version of economic rationality. For example, the profit maximisation procedure by which a firm equates its marginal cost with marginal revenue, is rational *both* in terms of procedure and in terms of outcome (i.e. maximum profit). However, this conventional view of 'economic rationality' which does not distinguish between the procedure and the outcome is based on an illegitimate oversimplification, namely all types of information are *equally* reliable even under uncertainty. Thus, the firm is supposed to place as much weight on the relatively 'soft' information on demand (i.e., marginal revenue) as it does on the 'hard' information regarding cost (i.e. marginal cost; see Figure 3.3). In contrast, *procedural* rationality, illustrated in the present context by the mark up pricing rule, recognises that all information is *not* of the same status. Therefore, it sets procedures for decision-making that are rational only in so far as the more reliable (and perhaps, more easily available) set of information is concerned. The wisespread practice of cost-determined prices seem to bear out the validity of such a view of procedural rationality.

Notes to Chapter 3

1. Similarly, the Walrasian preoccupation with price adjustment in a 'pure exchange economy' rules out by assumption the very possibility of quantity adjustment that forms the core of modern macroeconomic analysis since Keynes.
2. See J. M. Keynes (1936), *The General Theory of Employment, Interest and Money*, Chapter 4, entitled 'The Choice of Units'.
3. The observant reader might wonder whether capitalists' consumption out of increased profits can provide a larger market for consumption goods. However, this is most unlikely, particularly because the increased 'profit' is *potential* rather than actual in the consumption sector.
4. Arthur M. Okun (1981), *Prices and Quantities: A Macroeconomic Analysis*, p. 136.
5. Estimated by Richard N. Cooper and Robert Z. Lawrence (1975), 'The 1972–75 Commodity Boom', p. 691.
6. Theoretically, one can also think of compensating variations between the two elements of variable cost, on account of labour and of raw material, which neutralise one another. But this special case is not very relevant here.
7. For simplicity (of not working with many simultaneous equations), we assume one *homogeneous* raw material which is domestically processed.
8. The coefficient b_z must be a (positive) fraction less than unity to make production of raw material economically viable, i.e., *less* than one unit of raw material must be needed to produce a unit of raw material.
9. Broad estimates for the American economy in the early 1970s suggest that wage accounts for nearly 70 per cent of unit prime cost in the manufacturing industries.
10. For example, each move in a chess game could be optimally calculated by processing information on all possible counter-movers. However, such processing of information, even for a large computer, would be so vast as to be virtually impracticable in terms of time and resources. The

computer is therefore instructed to play chess by devising mc ves on the basis of processing more limited information, i.e., on simpler (rational) *procedures.* The reader should note the distinction between 'soft' information that 'in principle' could be made 'hard' (e.g., in the chess game) and 'soft' information which by its very nature cannot become 'hard'.

11. As Max Weber, the celebrated sociologist had noted large bureaucracies are 'rational'. However, as we now see, their rationality is *procedural*; such large organisations need not be 'rational' in terms of optimal *outcome.*

Further Reading

Chapters 4 ('The choice of units') and 19 ('Changes in money wages') of Keynes' (1936) *General Theory* as well as the summary of Kalecki's (1971) views presented in the essay (no. 5) 'Costs and prices' in his *Selected Essays on the Dynamics of the Capitalist Economy* provide the basis of Section A. In another essay (no. 14) (Kalecki, 1971) 'Class struggle and the distribution of national income' in the same volume of *Selected Essays*, Kalecki extends the analysis of the relation between prices and money wages in a three department scheme, involving a luxury consumption sector; also, he explicitly takes into account oligopolistic market structures. The relation between money and real wages was discussed especially in the context of the 'wage-cut-controversy' in a series of articles by Reynolds ('Relations between wage rates, costs and prices'), Lerner ('The relation between wage policies and price policies'), Tarshis ('Changes in real and money wages') and Dunlop ('Wage policies of trade unions'). These articles are still worth reading and are reprinted in the American Economic Association volume (1951), *Readings in the Theory of Income Distribution.* The influence of wage bargain in money terms on real wage was also discussed by Marx (1969) in *Wages, Price and Profit.* It is especially interesting, as it departs from the Keynes–Kalecki view of a proportional relation between price and money wage.

The article by Hall and Hitch (1939), 'Price theory and business behaviour' stimulated much of the modern discussion on mark-up/full cost pricing. The monograph by Coutts, Godley and Nordhaus (1978), *Industrial Pricing in the United Kingdom*, especially Chapters 1–4, is good empirical reading. Okun's (1981) *Prices and Quantities*, Chapter 4 as well as Gordon's article (1981), 'Output fluctuations and gradual price adjustment' provide up-to-date surveys of various reformulations of cost-determined prices. Scherer (1970) in *Industrial Market Structure and Economic Performance* Chapter 5 presents a fairly exhaustive but advanced account of theories underlying mark-up pricing. Simon's (1979) 'Rational decision-making in business organizations' presents a case for bounded and procedural rationality under uncertainty and serious data processing problems.

4

The Social Device of Money

A Characteristics of a Monetary Economy

The role and scope of operation of money in a modern industrial economy are far too wide-ranging and complex to be encapsuled in definitions. Money as a social institution has gradually evolved through the ages and its various characteristics and functions have undergone continuous change during its long course of evolution.

Perhaps the oldest and simplest role of money has been as *a unit of account*. But the fact that in a modern industrial economy everybody uses the same unit of account and all important economic contracts (e.g., the wage contract) are made in the *uniform* accounting unit of money, lends money an exceptional significance in its role as an accounting unit. Since participants in the economic system are willing to accept a uniform social convention for accounting in terms of money, money becomes *the* unit of account or 'measuring rod' for the system. This, in turn, results in the role of money as the *medium of exchange* for all economic transactions, simply because of its common acceptability to everybody.

The economic organisation of the modern nation-state also legalises its common acceptability at least within a country. For money is the *legal tender* of the monetary authority or the Central Bank of a modern State. It is legalised by the monetary authority as the medium of payment which cannot legally be refused in settlement of debts and claims. And, so long as confidence in the political authority of the State is not in question, there is no reason for individuals not to accept money as the medium of exchange for all payments and receipts.

The use of a uniform legal tender, called 'money', presupposes *confidence* in the authority of the State. One of the central puzzles of defining 'money' stems precisely from this fact: so long as the required confidence exists, not only between the State or its monetary authority and the individual, but also among some individual participants themselves, personal promises to settle debt (e.g. in the form of personal bank cheques, promissory notes, etc.) can also play at least in a limited way, the role of money. Thus, cheques can be 're-endorsed' and promissory notes can circulate in multilateral settlements of debt, to blur the distinction between such 'special money' created on personal trust among a group of transactors and 'money' that a Central Bank issues on the basis of the legal and political authority of the State.

It is not only extremely convenient but almost imperative for everyone to accept a generalised medium of exchange, if specialisation in production is not to be hindered on account of inadequate facilities for exchange. The convenience of everyone accepting the same medium for exchange is self-evident in an economy where *exchange is more or less completely generalised, but production is highly specialised.* Indeed, it is difficult to imagine how division of labour and specialisation in production can proceed beyond a point without this social institution of money. Consider, for example, the capitalist owner and his workers in a shoefactory. The workers cannot reckon their wages exclusively in terms of shoes, because they have to buy other consumables like food, clothing and housing. Their wage income must entitle them as consumers to *generalised purchasing power* in the form of money over the whole range of commodities that they may wish to consume, necessitating wage-contract in money. Likewise, our capitalist has to buy his diverse range of inputs like leather, chemicals and machines for producing shoes; at the same time he also has to pay wages in the generalised purchasing power of money. But all this would be impossible unless his profit also entitles him to generalised purchasing power of money. The crucial distinction between 'surplus product' of shoes in the present context and its *realisation* into profit in terms of money, discussed at length in Chapters 2 and 3, would have been meaningless, if, for example, the unplanned inventories of shoes were accepted as generalised purchasing power by everybody. Thus, every particular surplus product (e.g. 'shoes') needs to be realised into money profit because, *only* money is accepted in settlement of debt by every buyer and seller in the economy. The fact that nearly all contracts and transactions are made in money requires sales to be realised in money. Consequently, the problem of *realisation of surplus into profit* is essentially a problem of the monetary economy.

An academic economist's traditional preoccupation with the *barter economy* tends to obscure this crucial problem of realisation of profit through sales in a monetary economy. By definition, a barter system is devoid of the concept of a generalised purchasing power. At the most, a barter system has a mere unit of account or a numéraire commodity. However, this accounting unit must not be confused with generalised purchasing power in terms of which producers 'realise' their sales and profits. Under barter exchange the shoe producer offers his excess of shoes over personal consumption to say, the wheat grower for obtaining wheat in exchange of his shoes. Such barter exchange can be visualised if there is a *double coincidence of demand*: the shoe maker demands wheat and the wheat grower demands shoes, but neither needs a generalised purchasing power, called 'money' against their sales as an *intermediate step* in conducting such exchanges. An essential distinction between the barter and the monetary economy lies precisely in this *universal* intermediate step. Because, in a monetary economy no exchange is possible in the market without going through the crucial intermediate step of money. Thus, our shoe factory owner sells his shoes in the market *for money* and not directly for any other commodity in exchange. Indeed, capitalist commodity production has never been organised on the basis of such double or multiple coincidence of demand described by a barter system. The capitalist shoe factory owner neither knows nor does he care about what the buyers of shoes have to offer in the market in exchange. Similarly, the buyers' demand for shoes becomes effective in the market only when they have money and not other commodities to offer in exchange.

The general intermediation of money in exchange means that each decision to sell is only for money and the ability to buy any commodity is only with money. This simple fact *breaks the link of simultaneity between sale and purchase*, which would otherwise have been ensured by the 'double coincidence of demand' required in a barter system. To illustrate, our capitalist shoe producer by realising his sales of shoes in money acquired generalised purchasing power and, in so far as he is concerned, the fact of transaction is *complete* once he is able to sell his shoes for money. However, within any specified period, he may or may not use that money to buy other commodities so that, the 'final exchange' of one good against another envisaged by the 'double coincidence of demand' need not occur within that given period. Since purchases out of money can be postponed to a later date, it makes money not only a medium of exchange but also at least a temporary abode of purchasing power, separating purchases from sales. This attributes to *monetary transactions a sequential character in time*.

Marx was perhaps the first economist to exhibit the sequential nature of transactions in a monetary economy in terms of his 'circuits' of money and commodities. In such a production circuit, money (M) is spent for buying commodities (C) as raw materials which are used in the production process to make new commodities (C'). The new commodities are then sold in the market to be realised into more money ($M + \Delta M$), i.e., $M-C-C'-(M + \Delta M)$) as a sequence over time. Since this monetary circuit has to be viewed as an *intertemporal sequence* of purchases and sales always mediated by money, it is necessary for money to have generalised purchasing power not only at a point of time, but also over time. Consequently, money must act as a medium of not only temporal but also of intertemporal exchange. In this role of conducting intertemporal exchanges, money acquires its further attribute as a *store of value*, i.e., something which may be simply 'stored' or held for the present for purchasing some commodity at a future date. Since, in money, the *purchasing power is generalised in two different directions, across commodities and over time*, the latter attribute of money as a store of value makes the problem of effective demand appear in sharper focus in a monetary economy. Given a stretch of time defined as 'short-period', there is no reason to expect why monetary purchases of commodities should be exactly matched by their *intended* sales within that given period. For, it may easily happen that some individual transactors may decide to 'store', i.e., hoard money, instead of buying commodities during any given period of time. This would result in a mismatch, i.e. lack of synchronisation between purchases and sales within a given period in a monetary economy. Therefore, total *monetary* sales would have to be separated from total *monetary* purchases. Instead of the barter rule of double coincidence of demand, *intended* monetary sales may fail to materialise as corresponding monetary purchases, because some buyers may prefer to postpone their purchase by holding on to money as a store of value. Money value of supply is then separated from monetary demand precisely through the role of money as a store of value and, there is no way, in which supply can automatically create its own demand. Consequently, *Say's law fails in a monetary economy.*

Such discrepancy between sales and purchases in money during any period shows itself as changes in the *net* financial asset position of an individual household or firm. For example, with money as the only store of value or financial asset, the excess of income (sales) over expenditure (purchases) leads to increase in the *net* money balance (i.e., money balance minus outstanding debt) held by an individual. However, the decision to sell today a particular commodity and hold the proceeds of that sale as a store of value in money balance, links up the *present* act of selling with *future* plans of purchase. This makes current economic decisions involving money invariably *open-ended*, extending into the future. The very decision to sell goods for money as well as to buy goods with money then involves influences of future expectations and plans because, the device of money always provides the choice of spending it immediately on a particular commodity or holding it as generalised purchasing power for the future. This was emphasised by Keynes: 'Money, in its significant attributes is, above all, a subtle device for linking the present to the future; and we cannot even begin to discuss the effect of changing expectation on current activities except in monetary terms'.[1]

Given the influence that expectations about the future exert on the present level of activities in a monetary economy, *any notion of 'equilibrium' in the monetary economy must be conjectural in nature.* It is shaped by conjectures and expectations about an uncertain future and the state of equilibrium can be changed by a mere change in the state of expectations. It is here that the Keynesian short period in a monetary economy has altogether new attributes compared with its Marshallian predecessor: the short-period is *not* a self-contained unit of time. The Keynesian short period is necessarily open-ended. Whatever happens within a short-period involves expectations and conjectures regarding a future that lies beyond that short period. *This recognition that the short period is necessarily open-ended and any notion of 'equilibrium' is, at best, conjectural is of fundamental importance in characterising a monetary economy.*

The fact that the future is always uncertain and expectations are liable to revision, makes it almost imperative for individual participants to maintain some flexibility in their respective economic positions. Holding money as generalised purchasing power instead of specific commodities makes the economic position of an individual more flexible in so far as it allows him to revise plans more easily when his expectations change. Therefore, the greater *flexibility of economic position* that results *from a more liquid position* is a highly desirable attribute in an uncertain world. Herein lies the reason for an almost universal preference for being more 'liquid' in an uncertain world through holding money, a phenomenon which Keynes emphasised as *liquidity preference*. It stems simply from the desire for greater flexibility in revising plans in an uncertain world. At the same time, this very flexibility of economic plans of individuals permitted by the social device of money, also makes a monetary economy fundamentally volatile. A change in the mere state of expectations can have serious repercussions on current economic activities precisely because of the conjectural nature of the economic positions where quick revision is permitted by the device of money. Therefore the same device of money which permits an individual to cope better with uncertainty by keeping his economic position more flexible and liquid, may at times also make the monetary economy as a whole more volatile and susceptible to the influences of uncertainty. Paradoxically, holding money as an *individual's option* to cope better with uncertainty may fail as a *social device*, by magnifying the influences of uncertainty on current economic activities.

A consequence of the open-ended nature of conjectural monetary equilibrium in the short period may be illustrated by considering the so-called wealth or *real balance effect* (originally introduced by Pigou). Money as legal tender is held by the general public as its financial asset and is equivalent to a corresponding liability of the monetary authority (see Table 4.1 p. 106 of this chapter for elaboration). It can be argued that a cut in money wages during depression, resulting also in a fall in the cost-determined prices (see Chapter 3, Section A) would increase the *real* purchasing power of the money balance held as wealth by the public. This enhanced purchasing power of wealth held as money balance by the public, could in turn, raise their aggregate level of consumption to stimulate effective demand. In terms of our preceding discussion, it can be seen that this argument is open to doubt precisely because of the conjectural nature of monetary equilibrium. If the fall in prices resulting from a cut in money wages generate expectations of a *further* fall in prices, then the public may postpone expenditure to some future date. Such postponement will only aggravate rather than alleviate the immediate problem of effective demand. This line of reasoning, indicating that the real balance effect induced by a fall in prices may actually reduce rather than increase the level of expenditure within the short period, runs contrary to conventional wisdom. However, it becomes perfectly plausible, once it is realised that the monetary economy is necessarily open-ended where the present is unavoidably linked to an uncertain future through the social device of money.

B The Demand for Money

The demand for money originates in the multiplicity of functions that money performs in a capitalist economy. In its role as *the* medium of exchange for *temporal* as well as for *intertemporal* transactions, money would be demanded by individual households and firms both for *present* (i.e. temporal) and for *future* (i.e. intertemporal) transactions. An essential complexity in the demand for money arises because transactions planned in the future are usually far more uncertain than present transactions.

If we could imagine a world of absolute certainty where both present and future transactions would be exactly known, the distinctions between the two types of transactions would be trivial. Naturally, under absolute certainty each individual would not only know exactly his demand for money for current transactions as a medium of exchange but also his demand for money for future transactions as 'a store of wealth'. However, if other types of financial assets like government securities carrying interest rates (e.g., long-term bonds or short-term bills) are also available, then rational individuals cannot be expected to hold any money as 'store of wealth' under absolute certainty, because those alternative financial assets would earn him interest income during the interim period while their dates of maturity can be so chosen as to coincide exactly with the known dates of purchases over the certain future. Thus, if the future were known for certain, it would be blatantly irrational for anybody to hold non-interest-bearing money as a store of wealth. As Keynes put it: '. . . it is a recognized characteristic of money as a store of wealth that it is barren; whereas practically every other form of storing wealth yields some interest or profit. Why should anyone outside a lunatic asylum wish to use money as a store of wealth?'[2] Clearly, the answer to this puzzle must lie in the uncertainty that surrounds future transactions.

It must also be remembered that some money is demanded as a medium of exchange for current transactions which are more or less known. Just as firms need to hold inventories of raw materials to carry on production on a regular basis, so do individual households and firms require to hold money for current transactions conducted on a regular basis. This is called the *transaction motive* for holding money. And to the extent even present transactions are not known with absolute certainty, a further allowance must be made. Some money may also be held by individual household and firms as a precaution against sudden shortage of cash in conducting their regular transactions. This desire to hold some margin of cash over the regular requirements of transactions, largely as a precaution against a sudden shortfall in cash is appropriately described as the *precautionary motive* for holding money.

The analogy between inventories of raw materials held by firms and money held by individuals could be further exploited to analyse the consequences of transactions and the precautionary motive for holding money. The higher is the regular level of production of the firm, the higher usually is the level of raw material inventories that a firm needs to hold. Presumably, even the amount of inventories held as a precaution against sudden shortage would tend to be higher, the higher is the absolute level of inventories needed for production purposes. In a similar manner, both on transaction and on precautionary motive, individuals will tend to hold a higher amount of money, the higher is their level of transactions.

This idea that money is demanded basically for transactions fits in well with traditional versions of the so-called *quantity theory of money*, interpreted as a theory of demand for money. Using its most familiar form, the quantity theory can be written as:

$$M_d V = PT$$

or,

$$M_d = \frac{1}{V} \cdot PT \tag{4.1}$$

where M_d is the demand for money, V is the velocity of circulation of money, namely the number of times that money changes hands on an average during a period in conducting transactions, P is the general level of prices and T is the number of economic transactions during a period.

It should be noted that in relation (4.1), the quantity of money demanded (M_d) is a *stock magnitude measured at a point of time*, while both the volume of transactions T and the velocity of circulation V are *flow magnitudes measured during a period.* Consequently, if the length of the unit period is varied, say shortened from a year to six months, the measures of the resulting flow magnitudes are expected to vary accordingly, say, both T and V reduced to half their annual values to leave the demand for money (M_d) in (4.1) *independent of the length of the time unit* arbitrarily chosen.

Purely as a matter of definition, the quantity 'theory' described by (4.1) can always be assumed to be true. Given M, P and T at statistically observed values, there will always be a corresponding statistical value of the velocity of circulation V which must satisfy (4.1). *In that sense, it will not be a 'theory', but a statistical truism, when the value of V is always computed and allowed to vary* in such a manner as to satisfy (4.1). The quantity theory could become a 'theory' only when something more specific is read into a relation like (4.1).

In so far as the number of transactions conducted during a period T is concerned, it must in principle take into account all transactions including the purely *financial* ones. Thus, buying bonds in exchange for money is as much a part of the volume of transactions, as buying, say automobiles for money. But this raises some awkwardness for the quantity theory on two counts. First, the price index P must correspondingly take into account financial asset prices also on par with physical goods. Secondly, what about strictly financial transactions like conversion of short-term bills into long-term bonds? If *direct* conversion from one type of financial asset into another becomes possible without the direct mediation of money, that transaction presumably has to be ignored by the quantity theory. Nevertheless, this may affect the price level of the concerned financial asset, which as we have just seen, is supposed to enter the general price level P, since T involves all transactions including the purely financial ones. It would appear the quantity theory formulation has never been at ease with the existence of a vast and complex financial system, which not only makes the 'quantity' of money a problematic concept (see Section C, Chapter 4) but also may even cause other types of problems in interpreting the relation.

Largely ignoring difficulties resulting from transactions in financial markets, the traditional versions of the quantity theory concentrated primarily on 'real' transactions between money and *physical* goods. It was further postulated that the volume of such physical transactions T can be assumed to be proportional to the level of real output (X) in the economy. By suitable choice of units, this proportionality constant between the number of transactions (T) and the level of output (X) can be treated as unity, so that (4.1) reduces to another version, known as the 'Cambridge equation',

$$M_d = \frac{1}{V} \cdot PX = k.P.X, \qquad \text{where } \frac{1}{V} = k \qquad (4.2)$$

So long as the velocity of circulation (V), or its inverse (k), can be postulated to be an institutional constant, (4.2) describes a proportional relation between the stock of money demanded (M_d) and the money value of output $(Y \equiv PX)$. If the level of output (X) is exogenously given, say at full employment level, then the demand for money (M_d) would simply be proportional to the general price level (P) so long as the velocity of circulation of money (V) is constant in (4.2).

The assumption of rough *constancy of the velocity of circulation of money* (V), implying a regularity in the relation between the *flow* of money income (PX) and the *stock* of money demanded (M_d), is a *central postulate* in *all* versions of the quantity theory of money. In so far as money is demanded only for transaction and precautionary purposes, such regularity again suggests the analogy with the stock of raw material inventories held by a firm to carry on its regular flow of production. Given a range of technological data such as, raw material needed per unit of output, length of the production period, etc., inventories of raw materials can be expected to bear some steady relation with the flow of production. Similarly, given a range of 'institutional' factors, the demand for money may bear some steady relation with the level of economic activity. Although a whole range of institutional factors underlie the magnitude of the velocity of circulation of money, the important point is not its quantitative magnitude but its rough *constancy* so long as the underlying institutional factors do not change.

However, even in this view of demand for money as inventory, some allowance has to be made for the fact that the level of inventory holding is partly an *economy* decision. For instance, increase in the cost of raw material holding would induce firms to economise on their level of inventories. In the case of money, the rate of interest may be viewed as the indicator of the opportunity cost of holding money instead of interest-bearing financial assets. Thus, higher interest rate implies greater opportunity cost of holding money in terms of foregone interest income. As a consequence, the public may be expected to economise on their holding of money as inventory at higher interest rates. In other words, a lower stock of money (M_d) would be demanded for a *given* level of nominal income (PX) at a higher interest rate.[3] However, this would mean that the velocity of circulation (V) instead of being constant, increases and its inverse $(k = 1/V)$ decreases at higher interest rates. It enables us to rewrite (4.2) explicitly in terms of the opportunity cost of holding money through the interest rate as,

$$M_d = k(i).P.X, \quad \frac{1}{V(i)} = k(i), k'(i) \equiv \frac{\mathrm{d}k}{\mathrm{d}i} < 0 \tag{4.3}$$

where i is the rate of interest.

Nevertheless, just as some inventories have to be held to carry on production on a regular basis, similarly some money will have to be held for purposes of *regular* transactions. And unless the fluctuations in the interest rate are very violent, we can reasonably assume that the influence of interest rate changes on the transactions and precautionary demand for money will not nullify the higher demand for money as income increases. This would permit us to maintain that *the transactions demand for money* (M_d^T) is normally (i.e. when interest fluctuations are not large) an increasing function of the money value of output (Y), i.e.,

$$M_d^T = L^T(PX) = L^T(Y), \quad \frac{\mathrm{d}M_d^T}{\mathrm{d}Y} > 0, \qquad Y \equiv PX \tag{4.4}$$

where the superscript 'T' emphasises the transactions (and precautionary) demand for money as a medium of *temporal* exchange.

In so far as the demand for money exclusively as medium of *temporal* exchange is concerned, both Keynes and earlier monetary theorists were in broad agreement. But real differences begin to emerge, once the other attribute of money as a 'store of wealth' needed for *intertemporal* exchange is brought into the analysis. Because, as we have already argued in the previous Section A, expectations regarding the future in an open-ended short period begin to play a critically important role ignored by earlier theories of demand for money.

The Keynesian analysis of money as an asset, i.e., a store of wealth, is based upon two crucial assumptions. First, the whole question of future expectations was largely captured in terms of *expectations regarding the rate of interest*. Thus, as a first approximation, we may imagine that the 'long-term state of expectations' (i.e., expectations lying beyond the open-ended short period) is captured by the assumption of a 'normally' expected rate of interest i_b^* on bonds. But the reason why the interest rate and not some other variable is so important in characterising the state of expectations, follows from a second crucial assumption. Throughout Keynes' analysis, the implied assumption is that accumulated savings or wealth are held in alternative *financial* forms, e.g., choice is made between money and bonds, but not between money and other *physical* assets like capital equipment. The households' speculative demand for money then essentially becomes a decision regarding whether to hold money or to hold some other alternative form of financial asset like bonds. And, in this limited context of choice between bond and money, the rate of interest on bonds becomes the critical variable for characterising the state of expectations.

Since the annual yield of a government bond is given at say 'a', the annual bond-rate of interest i_b can be defined (in perpetuity) as,

$$\frac{a}{P_b} = i_b \tag{4.5}$$

where a is the constant annual yield (a *given* sum of money annually paid to the holder of the bond), P_b is the price of the bond in the market and i_b is the annual bond-rate of interest.

Thus, 'a' being a constant, (4.5) shows an *inverse* relation, in the form of a rectangular hyperbola, between the bond-rate i_b and the market price of bonds P_b.

Suppose, now, that the *expected* 'normal' rate of interest on bonds is i_b^*. If the ruling bond-rate i_b lies below it, i.e., $i_b < i_b^*$, then households are likely to find holding bonds unattractive on *two different types of considerations*. First, a lower than the normally expected rate of interest means that the interest income they can get by parting with their money is not attractive enough. Secondly, a relatively low bond rate i_b compared with the normally expected i_b^*) also implies that the ruling market price of bonds $P_b (= a/i_b)$ is above its *expected* 'normal' price, $P_b^* (= a/i_b^*)$, i.e., from (4.5) $P_b > P_b^*$ when $i_b < i_b^*$. This would result in *fear of capital loss*, since households will generally expect the bond price to come *down* towards its 'normal' level P_b^* from its current level P_b instead of going up further. Thus, a lower than the 'normally' expected bond rate of interest crates an overall sentiment in the market against holding bonds: on *income consideration*, it is not attractive due to a relatively low ruling rate of interest compared to what is normally expected; nor is it attractive on *capital consideration* due to fear of impending capital loss. Such market sentiments, if widely held, result in *bearishness* in the stock exchange market, i.e., a predominant sentiment towards *selling* instead of buying bonds. For opposite reasons, when the ruling rate i_b is above the normally expected i_b^*, there would generally be market sentiments in favour of holding bonds instead of money, both on income consideration of a relatively high rate of interest (i.e., $i_b > i_b^*$) as well as on capital consideration of expected capital gains. Thus, with $i_b > i_b^*$, the market is likely to turn *bullish*, i.e., a predominant sentiment towards *buying* instead of selling bonds.

From the above reasoning can be derived the notion of a *liquidity preference schedule*, showing the households'desired rate of substitution between speculative holding of money and bonds at alternative bond rates of interest *in relation to a given normally expected rate* (i_b^*). The higher is the ruling bond rate i_b in the market in relation to the normally expected rate i_b^*, the more bullish will be the market, i.e., the higher will be the attractiveness of switching from money to bonds on both income and capital consideration. It should be stressed that it is not the *absolute* level of the current interest rate, but the degree of its *divergence* from what is widely expected to be the 'fairly safe' or 'normal' rate, that matters in determining the extent of substitution between bonds and money. Therefore, the resulting liquidity preference schedule of the demand for money for speculative purposes (i.e., as a 'store of wealth') is an *inverse* function of the extent of *divergence* of the ruling rate from the normally expected rate. As $(i - i_b^*)$ increases, less money M_d is demanded for speculative purposes because, more people become 'bullish', switching from money to bonds. Formally,

$$M_d^S = L^S(i_b - i_b^*), \quad \frac{\mathrm{d}M_d^S}{\mathrm{d}(i_b - i_b^*)} < 0 \qquad (4.6)$$

where M^S is the speculative demand for money 'a store of value' (denoted by superscript 'S') and, i_b and i_b^* are the ruling and the normally expected bond-rate of interest respectively.

It is useful to present the above algebraic relation (4.6) in terms of Figure 4.1. (Note the figure clearly shows the critical influence of the state of expectations captured by i_b^*, on the *position* of the speculative demand schedule for money.)

An important point about Figure 4.1 is the different positions of the

Figure 4.1 *The influence of the state of expectations on the speculative demand for money. Two positions of the speculative demand schedule for money correspond to two different states of expectations; they are captured by the normally expected bond rate i_b^* at its two different values $i_{b_1}^*$ and $i_{b_2}^*$. In the figure $i_{b_2}^* > i_{b_1}^*$.*

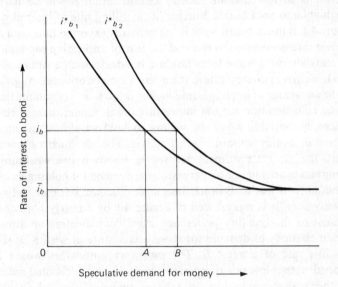

Speculative demand for money ⟶

liquidity preference schedule under alternative states of expectations, captured by the 'normally expected' rate of interest $i_{b_1}^*$ or $i_{b_2}^*$. Given any ruling rate of interest i_b, if the normally expected rate is relatively low at $i_{b_1}^*$, then households would tend to favour holding more bonds and less money at OA, both on grounds of income and capital consideration discussed above. However, if the normally expected rate were somewhat higher at $i_{b_2}^*$, both on income and on capital consideration, households would be less favourably inclined towards holding bonds and the speculative demand for holding money will be at the higher level of OB in Figure 4.1. Shifts in the *position* of the liquidity preference schedule could be caused simply by changes in the state of expectations regarding the normally expected level of the rate of interest. *Movements* along a given liquidity preference schedule are for a *given* state of expectations. This brings into sharp focus the open-endedness in the conjectural short period position of a monetary economy discussed in Section A. Because, any change in expectations regarding the 'normal' level of the rate of interest influences *current* decisions regarding the holding of money.

It is also possible to imagine situations where the ruling rate of interest is so low that on income consideration it will be hardly worthwhile to hold bonds. Further, if the ruling rate of interest $\bar{i}_b$ in Figure 4.1, is much below what is the normally expected rate, then the interest rate is expected to rise and the fear of impending capital loss prevents almost anyone from holding bonds. In such a situation of very low current interest rate $\bar{i}_b$, the interest income obtained by giving up the advantage of holding liquid money is too low. At the same time, capital consideration suggest impending losses. Under these circumstances, households would be willing to hold an almost indefinite amount of money without converting it into bonds. Such a situation where the market sentiment for selling bonds is overwhelmingly strong and bearishness is all pervasive, the demand for holding money as the 'store of wealth' is nearly insatiable. This can be described as a *liquidity trap*. It is represented in Figure 4.1 by a nearly horizontal segment of the liquidity preference schedule, indicating an almost infinite elasticity of demand for money as a 'store of wealth' at that very low rate of interest $\bar{i}_b$. The monetary authorities would be 'trapped' at that low rate of interest $\bar{i}_b$ because, any additional money that they may decide to inject into the system would simply be held as cash instead of being converted into bonds by the public. So bond prices would tend to remain constant, and so would the bond rate of interest at $\bar{i}_b$ by virtue of (4.5). Monetary policies trying to reduce the rate of interest through persuading the public to hold more bonds are then doomed to failure in situations characterised by such a liquidity trap.

Despite its simplicity in terms of working with only one type of interest-bearing financial asset namely 'bonds', this theory of liquidity preference has two outstanding features deserving emphasis. First, the theory shows how the speculative demand for money is governed by choice among the alternative *forms* in which people hold their wealth. In its simplified form, bond is the *only* alternative to holding money, for speculative purposes. Hence, the equilibrium bond rate of interest is one where, nobody at the margin wishes to exchange money for bonds given his expectations about the future. In this sense, liquidity preference theory also provides an explanation for the demand for 'barren', i.e., non-interest bearing money as an asset *coexisting* with other types of interest-bearing assets like bonds.

Second, the theory provides a powerful illustration of how expectation about the future exerts its influence on the conjectural short period equilibrium in a monetary economy. It should be recalled that it is *not* the current market rate on bonds *in isolation, but its relation to the normally expected future rate* that determines how the holding of financial wealth by the public would be distributed between money and bonds. Consequently, expectations regarding the normal rate are an essential ingredient in determining the current demand for money.

To the extent that each individual j (household or firm) has some *definite* expectation regarding the long-run 'normal' rate of interest (i_b^*), it will choose to hold *only* bonds if the current rate i_b exceeds the 'normal' expected rate (i.e., $i_b > i_b^*$). Because the interest rate is then expected to fall in the future resulting in expectations of capital gains (i.e., capital consideration); in addition, a higher than normal current rate (i.e. $i_b > i_{b_j}^*$) also yields relatively high return (i.e., income consideration). Conversely, $i_b < i_{b_j}^*$, both capital and income consideration would dictate an individual j to hold *only* money. The *liquidity preference theory at the micro-level* of an individual decision-maker therefore, suggests an 'either-or' choice of 'corner solution'; an individual j holds his money either *entirely* in bonds (if $i_b > i_{b_j}^*$) or *entirely* in money (if $i_b < i_{b_j}^*$). However, *at the macro-level*, expectations about the 'normal' rate (i_b^*) are different for different individuals. If some believe the current rate to be above while others believe it to be below their expected 'normal' rate, then the former group will hold bonds while the latter group will hold money at the same point of time. This *macroeconomic diversification of portfolios*—bonds and money being held simultaneously in the economy—is then the outcome of the coexistence of different expectations about the normal rate by different individuals.

Although there can be little doubt that such expectations about the future vary among individuals, the *microeconomic foundation* of the Keynesian liquidity preference theory can be questioned for posing so sharply an 'either-or' choice between money and bonds. Because, it is not valid to assume that there is only *macroeconomic* diversification of portfolios where some individuals *only* hold bonds while others *only* hold money in the manner described above due to their different expectations about the level of the 'normal' rate. Usually portfolios are also diversified at the *micro-level* of a single investor; the same individual may hold his wealth *partly* in bonds and *partly* in money. Perhaps an obvious explanation lies in the fact that most individuals are not confident about their own expectations of the 'normal' future rate of interest so that, rather than being rational they hedge against their own expectations about the future by holding partly money and partly bonds. However, if one insists on conventional economic rationality even under uncertainty, then an alternative explanation of individual portfolio diversification can be offered on the basis of actuarial calculations of risks.[4] Since individual investors would consider bonds to be a more risky asset than money due to possible capital loss on the former, holding a higher proportion of their wealth in bonds increases *both* expected return as well as risk for individual investors. At every given rate of interest on bonds, balance is then struck by individual investors at the margin between the conflicting motives of higher expected return and risk-aversion by holding part of the portfolio of wealth in (risky) bonds and the other part in (riskless) money. However, such an explanation of individual portfolio diversification does *not* provide the needed microeconomic foundation of the macro-theory of liquidity preference. Without any *a priori* knowledge of individual preferences and attitudes towards risk, nothing can be said about the *aggregate* demand for money and for bonds from the above analysis. Thus, the Keynesian proposition that the speculative demand for money in an economy tends to be inversely related to the rate of interest for a given state of expectations (see Figure 4.1) cannot be derived from such micro-behaviour. Instead, it must still be based on an analysis of the relation between current bond rate and its expected 'normal' rate varying among individuals. In other words, economic rationality based on actuarial calculation of risk versus expected yield by individual investors in diversifying their financial portfolios has not yet been shown to be a particularly useful framework for understanding the aggregate demand for money as an asset.

C   The Supply of Money and the Overall Liquidity Position

The central functions that money performs—as a medium of exchange and as a store of wealth – are reasonably well defined. However, there is no single commodity or debt device in a modern capitalist economy which can be said to be *uniquely* capable of performing those functions. And anything which serves as a medium of exchange or as a store of wealth must at least *partially* qualify as 'money'.

This essential problem of defining 'money' is easy to illustrate. Whenever two or more participants in the market agree on the basis of mutual trust to use either party's debt obligation as the medium for conducting temporal exchange or as a store of wealth for future exchanges, that debt obligation serves as 'money' at least in that limited context. In all such cases, mutual trust, not necessarily reinforced by the legal authority of the State, can create its own 'special money' as medium of exchange or, as a store of wealth. Thus, many types of debt obligations, like personal promissory notes of 'I-owe-you' (IOU) issued by a 'creditworthy' borrower or the modern device of credit cards where personal debt is underwritten by some large financial institution, perform the role of 'money'. As a result, what is to be treated as 'money' necessarily becomes somewhat problematic and arbitrary.

To escape such arbitrariness, it is usual to fall back upon *legalistic* rather than *functional* definitions of 'money'. For instance, in an extreme sense only the debt obligation of a Central Bank or the monetary authority in the form of 'cash' or currency notes, fully backed by the legal authority of the State, can be treated as 'money'. In a country with an underdeveloped system of commercial banking, this could have been a reasonable definition. However, such a definition is obviously too narrow in a modern industrial economy with an elaborate system of commercial banking. Consequently, a somewhat wider definition of 'money' would include debt obligation of the Central Bank in the form of 'cash' (i.e., its liabilities to the public) *plus* the *formal* debt obligations of the commercial banking system. Even this definition would be inadequate in any economy where non-bank financial institutions or intermediaries also operate on a significant scale. There is no clear justification to rule out their credit obligations from the definition of 'money'. Consider the example of an individual who draws on his account with the bank to buy a life insurance policy or to acquire savings and load shares or to deposit funds in a mutual savings bank. In such a case, he obtains a claim against some financial institution which can be readily converted into cash. The institution, in turn, acquires ownership over a part of his deposit with the bank and therefore has additional money to lend to others. This illustrates how the loans of financial intermediaries can for a time grow quite rapidly without expansion in the direct debt obligation of the commercial banks. Consequently, a wider definition of the 'stock of money' would include 'cash' *plus* formal debt obligations of the commercial banking system *plus* the debt obligations of a range of selected non-bank financial institutions. As can now be seen, the definition of the stock of 'money' is necessarily ambiguous. It can be widened or narrowed without any underlying *theoretical* principle as to which financial institution or what types of debt obligations are to be included or excluded from such a definition.

This definitional problem arises as much in theory as in practice. Therefore, major industrial capitalist economies now a days publish several indicators of 'money supply'. For instance, the *Federal Reserve Bulletin* in the United States regularly prints at least five different measures of the money stock. The narrowest measure (M_1) consists of

(a) demand deposits of commercial banks (other than domestic interbank and US Government) less cash items in process of collection and Federal Reserve Float; (b) the foreign demand balances at Federal Reserve Banks and, (c) currency outside the Treasury, Federal Reserve Banks and vaults of commercial banks.

Then, there is an intermediate measure M_1^+ 'which equals M_1 (defined above) *plus* savings deposits at commercial banks and checkable deposits at non-bank thrift institutions'. The next measure M_2 is 'M_1 plus savings deposits, time deposits open account and time certificates of deposit other than negotiable certificates of deposit of \$100 000 of large weekly reporting banks'. Then M_3, which is, 'M_2 plus deposits of mutual savings banks, savings and loan shares and credit union shares (non-bank thrift)'. On the other hand, M_4 is M_2 plus the large negotiable certificates of deposits. Finally, the widest measure of money stock is M_5 which is M_3 plus the large negotiable certificates of credit.

In comparison, the measures of money stock published in the monthly *Financial Statistics* of the Central Statistical Office in the UK, are somewhat less elaborate, although measures M_1 to M_3 correspond more or less to their American counterparts. Thus M_1 in Britain is currency in circulation plus sterling sight deposits minus adjustment items on account of interbank deposits and transit items. A larger and commonly used measure is M_3 consisting of M_1 plus 'UK private residents' deposit accounts with banks, their current and deposit accounts in non-sterling currencies, their deposits with the discount houses, and the public sector's deposits with the banks'.[5]

It should be recognised that these various legalistic conventions for measuring the 'stock of money' (e.g., M_1 to M_5) can be misleading for a fundamental reason. Broadly speaking, the narrower measure of money (e.g. M_1) is based on the idea that money is a medium of (temporal) exchange in the hands of the public; whereas the wider measures of money (e.g., M_5) clearly tries to capture the role of money both as a medium of exchange *and* as a store of wealth. A serious theoretical problem arises in so far as these two major complementary roles of money cannot always be distinguished on the basis of either the nature of debt obligations or the types of financial institutions that incur debts. As a matter of fact, the distinction between any legal, *quantifiable* definition of money and a *qualitative* assessment of the overall liquidity position of an economy stems largely from such a recognition. This latter concept of the overall liquidity directs attention to the circumstances determining the credit-worthiness of all (bank and non-bank) financial institutions and therefore, their ability to create generally acceptable debt obligations as 'money'. Needless to add, this idea of the overall liquidity position is necessarily vague and largely conditioned by the specific set of financial institutions existing in a country. Nevertheless, the fact that so many alternative measures of the stock of money can be devised and actually do coexist in monetary statistics, inescapably points to the fact that none of these measures can adequately capture the notion of the overall liquidity position.

However, overall liquidity is essentially money as credit in some form. Such credit money in a modern industrial society is invariably the outstanding debt obligation of one type of financial agent against some other in the economy. It is, therefore, useful to set out the analysis of liquidity or the quantity of money as debt obligation in terms of a simplified three-tier *balance sheet of asset and liability positions* of the major economic agents in a capitalist economy[6] (Table 4.1).

It will be noticed in Table 4.1 that if all sectors are consolidated together everything cancels on two sides of the balance sheet except the real assets (RA). Although the accountant would have to enter a notional liability against the real assets to make the balance sheets balance, it may be excluded from being shown in Table 4.1 as the pure residual item.

From Table 4.1, the overall liquidity position representing the quantity of 'money' (M) in a modern industrial economy can be

Table 4.1

	Liabilities (Outstanding credit obligations)	Assets
1. The *core* of the financial system (e.g. central bank or monetary authority)	Cash or currency money ($CM + cm$) + Any deposit of bank and non-bank financial institutions with the 'core' (d')	Financial securities (FS)
2. The periphery of the financial system (commercial banks and non-bank financial institutions)	Financial Securities ($FS + fs$)	Industrial securities (IS) + Reserve in currency (cm) + deposits with the core (d')
3. *Rest of the economy* (households and industries including public sector industries)	Industrial Securities (IS)	Real assets (RA) + Financial securities (fs) + Currency money 'in circulation' (CM)

defined as the total of financial assets held by industries and households, i.e., liquidity position represented by stock of 'money' (M) = currency money in circulation (CM) + financial securities (fs), i.e., liabilities of commercial banks and financial institutions to the public or,

$$M = CM + fs \qquad (4.7)$$

However, it would be clear from our preceding discussion of this section that the definition given in (4.7) cannot be *operationally* useful. To define 'money' or liquidity in an operational sense, one must indicate precisely what types of financial securities held by the public (*fs*), i.e., which types of liabilities (to the public) of the commercial banks *and* financial institutions, are to be treated as a part of the definition of money stock.

In oversimplified, formal discussions of the mechanics of money supply, this problem of operationally defining the stock of money is usually rendered manageable by concentrating on the credit obligation of the Central Bank or Monetary Authority, i.e., its liabilities to the public as the amount of currency held by the public (*CM*) *plus* the formal credit obligation of *only* the commercial banking system in the form of deposits held by the public in those banks. But, even here, the definition of the stock of money can have a narrower (as in M_1) or a wider (as in M_2) scope depending on which particular types of bank deposits are taken into account. In this context, particularly important is the distinction between *demand deposits* that are more or less instantly withdrawable and *time deposits* (also called savings deposits) which are not so easily withdrawable, because they usually have various restrictions on the amount or timing of withdrawal.

In a somewhat narrow, operational definition of the stock of 'money' (which roughly corresponds to M_1 or M_2), the *general* financial securities held by the public (*fs*) in definition (4.7) would be replaced by *only* the *formal* credit obligations, i.e., liabilities of the commercial banking system to the public in the form of deposits held in banks (demand deposit and/or time deposit as the case may be, in measuring M_1 of M_2). In symbols, such a narrow definition of financial securities (*fs*) held by the public can be written as,

$$fs = (d - d') \tag{4.8}$$

where d are the total deposits (assuming no inter-commercial bank deposits for simplicity) and d' are the deposits of commercial banks held with the Central Bank or Monetary Authority (i.e., the 'Core' of the Financial System in Table 4.1).

In what is known as the *fractional reserve system* of commercial banking, a commercial bank is required or expected by the Central Bank to hold only some fraction 'n' ($1 > n > 0$) of the total deposit $(d - d')$ as 'cash reserve', consisting of notes and coins *plus* deposits (d') with the Central Bank. Thus, by definition the reserve level (R_b) of the commercial bank will be,

$$R_b = d' + cm \qquad (4.9)$$

where $R_b =$ is the level of 'cash reserve' of the commercial banks, and cm is the currency (notes and coins) held by the commercial banks (see Table 4.1).

The fractional reserve system of commercial banking operates on the principle that, not all depositors will come to withdraw their entire deposits at the same point of time. Therefore, holding some reasonable fraction 'n' in cash (i.e., currency plus deposits with the Central Bank) will typically be sufficient to meet normal requirements in the form of claims for daily withdrawal by depositors. If, at any particular point of time, such claims for withdrawal by the depositors in a particular commercial bank exceeds its cash reserve, that bank can always borrow from other banks or from the Central Bank itself on a *temporary* basis to meet the claims of its depositors. But this is only a temporary device, where the *Central Bank may have to act as a lender of the last resort* to the commercial banking system. Normally, however, the conventionally stipulated ratio of reserve to deposits, namely 'n', will be enough to meet usual requirements and claims of withdrawals from banks by the depositors.

Such a fractional reserve system of commercial banking then puts a *ceiling* on the *potential* amount of credit obligation or liabilities to the public that can be incurred by the commercial banking system as a whole. Algebraically, using (4.8) and (4.9), this *potential* credit obligation can be represented as,

$$\frac{(d-d')}{R_b} = \frac{(d-d')}{(d'+cm)} = \frac{1}{n}, \qquad 1 > n > 0 \qquad (4.10)$$

where the inverse of the fractional 'cash reserve ratio', $1/n$ is the (potential) credit multiplier.

With a legally required 'cash reserve ratio' lower than unity, it follows from (4.10) that the *commercial banks can create multifold credit obligation in the form of deposits* on the basis of their reserve holding. Thus, if, n is 10 per cent, then one additional unit of cash reserve will permit the commercial banks to create $1/n = 1/0.10 = 10$ times the deposits, in accordance with relation (4.10). More formally speaking,

The credit multiplier

$$= \frac{\text{increase in deposits with commercial banks}}{\text{increase in 'cash reserve' or commercial banks}}$$

$$= \frac{1}{n}$$

In order to see how the credit multiplier works, we may imagine a unit increase in cash with the public which is kept in the form of 'primary deposit' with a commercial bank. The bank now keeps a fraction 'n' as reserve and lends out $(1-n)$ to some borrowers, who are not necessarily depositors with the same bank. This $(1-n)$ advanced as bank credit is used for purchase of goods and services by the borrower, so that it becomes someone else's income, which is again deposited with the same or some other commercial bank at the next round. Out of this again, the commercial bank concerned keeps $n.(1-n)$ as reserves and lends out $(1-n).(1-n) = (1-n)^2$ at the next round, which again returns as deposit to the commercial banking system. Thus, the total deposits with the commercial banking system as a whole takes the form of a convergent geometric series,

$$\underbrace{1}_{\substack{\text{primary deposit} \\ \text{with commercial} \\ \text{bank}}} + \underbrace{(1-n)}_{\substack{\text{first round deposits} \\ \text{with commercial} \\ \text{bank}}} + \underbrace{(1-n)^2}_{\substack{\text{second round de-} \\ \text{posits with com-} \\ \text{mercial bank}}} + \ldots$$

that sums to,

$$\frac{1}{1-(1-n)} = \frac{1}{n}$$

in conformity with the credit multiplier in (4.10).

Under normal circumstances, the credit multiplier represented by formula (4.10) *over-estimates* the credit-creating potentialities of the commercial banking system. This is because, there is usually an *internal cash leakage* in the form of the public's desire to hold a part of the credit advanced by banks in cash with themselves, primarily for regular transaction purposes. To simplify the formal argument, we may assume that the public holds a constant fraction 'a' of their bank deposits in cash. Hence, as a behavioural postulate we write,

$$\frac{CM}{(d-d')} = a, \qquad 1 > a > 0 \qquad (4.11)$$

where CM = currency held by the public.

According to (4.11), whenever bank credit is advanced to the public, it holds some steady fraction 'a', which does not return to the commercial banks as deposits and leaks away from the commercial banking system. According to this assumption, one additional unit of cash with the public (i.e., CM) can maintain the same steady ratio of cash to deposits given by (4.11), only if public holds some (unknown) quantity x as cash and deposits the rest $(1-x)$ with commercial banks. In accordance with (4.11), we can then solve for x as,

$$\frac{x}{1-x} = a \qquad \text{or} \qquad x = \frac{a}{1+a} \qquad (4.12)$$

This means that an additional unit of cash with the public leads to $a/(1+a)$ held in cash by the public and the rest, $(1-(a/1+a))$ i.e., $1/(1+a)$, deposited with commercial banks in order to satisfy relation (4.11). Consequently, out of each additional unit of cash going to the public, the banks get a 'primary' deposit $1/(1+a)$ as shown by (4.12), of which they retain only $(n/1+a)$ under the fractional reserve requirement of 'n' and advance as credit the rest, $(1-n)/(1+a)$. Out of that advance of credit from banks, the public again holds a part in cash, which is given from (4.12) as, $(a/1+a)\cdot(1-n)/(1+a)$ and deposits the rest with the commercial banks, also given from (4.12) as,

$$\left(\frac{1}{1+a}\right)\cdot\frac{(1-n)}{(1+a)} = \frac{(1-n)}{(1+a)^2}$$

So, at the next round, commercial banks advance,

$$(1-n)\cdot\frac{(1-n)}{(1+a)^2} = \frac{(1-n)^2}{(1+a)^2}$$

to the public, to receive

$$\frac{1}{(1+a)}\cdot\frac{(1-n)^2}{(1+a)^2} = \frac{(1-n)^2}{(1+a)^3}$$

as their next round of deposits.

Thus, the series of increases in *deposits* with commercial banks takes the form of a convergent geometric series,

$$\frac{1}{(1+a)} + \frac{(1-n)}{(1+a)^2} + \frac{(1-n)^2}{(1+a)^3} + \dots, \qquad 1 > a > 0; 1 > n > 0$$

$$= \frac{1}{(1+a)}\left[1 + \frac{(1-n)}{(1+a)} + \frac{(1-n)^2}{(1+a)^2} + \dots\right]$$

which sums to,

$$\frac{1}{(1+a)} \; \frac{1}{1 - \dfrac{(1-n)}{(1+a)}} = \frac{1}{(n+a)} \tag{4.13}$$

Contrasting (4.13) with (4.10) it can immediately be seen that the larger is the leakage in the form of cash from banks to the public, given by the fraction 'a', the smaller is the credit multiplier. Only in the extreme case where the public holds no cash and conducts *all* transactions in cheques of commercial banks (making $a = 0$), the credit multiplier (4.13) coincides with that in (4.10).

It is worth recalling that the credit multiplier, either in (4.10) or in (4.13), is a *potential* rather than an *actual* measure; it measures the potential of the commercial banking system in expanding its credit obligation under the fractional cash reserve system. The actual amount of credit advanced may fall short of that potential amount, in case there are not a sufficient number of eligible borrowers from the banks. To pursue further this concept of *credit potential of the commercial banking system as a whole*, it is necessary to note that there is no reason in principle to distinguish between currency held by commercial banks in their vaults as a part of their 'cash reserve' (i.e., cm in Table 4.1) and the currency in circulation (i.e., CM in Table 4.1), outside the banking system. Because, in principle, the *entire* currency money ($CM + cm$ in Table 4.1) is capable of entering the reserve base (R_b) of banks, if transactions are exclusively conducted in cheques. This has led to the notion of *high-powered money; it measures the maximum possible reserve base* of the commercial banking system.

From Table 4.1, it is evident that the entire liability of the Core (i.e., of the Central Bank) to the rest of the financial system can become high-powered money in this sense, providing reserve base for credit expansion by the commercial banks. In our simplified exposition, high-powered money (H) would then be (see Table 4.1),

H = total reserve of commercial banks (R_b)
    + currency with the public (CM)

or, using (4.9),

$$H = d' + cm + CM \tag{4.14}$$

The relation between *increment* in the stock of high-powered money (ΔH) and increment in the total 'money' stock (ΔM) defined in the narrow sense of currency in circulation plus the formal credit obligation of the commercial banking system, can be derived from the preceding analysis. Using (4.7) and (4.8), this narrow definition of 'money' can be written as,

$$M = CM + (d - d') \tag{4.15}$$

or using (4.11), $M = (1 + a)(d - d')$.

Hence, increment in the stock of this narrow definition of money is,

$$\Delta M = (1 + a) \cdot \Delta(d - d'); \tag{4.16}$$

Since the increment in the stock of high-powered money is given from (4.14) as,

$$\Delta H = \Delta(CM) + \Delta(d' + cm) \tag{4.17}$$

dividing (4.17) by (4.16), we obtain

$$\frac{\Delta H}{\Delta M} = \frac{1}{(1 + a)} \frac{\Delta(CM)}{\Delta(d - d')} + \frac{\Delta(d' + cm)}{\Delta(d - d')}$$

Substituting from (4.10) and (4.11), the above expression reduces to

$$\frac{\Delta H}{\Delta M} = \frac{(a + n)}{(1 + a)}$$

i.e.,

$$\Delta M = \left(\frac{1}{n + a}\right)\Delta H + \left(\frac{a}{n + a}\right)\Delta H \tag{4.18}$$

It will be recognised that the first and the second bracketed term on the right-hand side of (4.18) correspond respectively to the formulae for deposit expansion of commercial banks in (4.13) and increase in cash held by the public, because if bank deposit is $1/(n + a)$, then the cash held by the public is $a/(n + a)$ according to (4.11). This is really self-evident from the narrow definition of money stock in (4.15), which consists of currency held by the public (CM) and their deposits with commercial banks ($d - d'$). Since the credit multiplier operating on the reserve base of commercial banks determines both these components of the money stock as seen in (4.13), the credit multiplier together with an increment in the *potential* reserve base called 'high-powered money' also determines the *potential* increment in the overall money stock. The determinants of the credit multiplier namely, the reserve ratio 'n' of commercial banks and the internal cash or leakage ratio 'a' (see (4.13)) together with the amount of high powered money H then determine the overall *potential* for increment in money supply M. Therefore, these parameters may be called the *proximate determinants of money supply*.

It should, however, be recalled that any attempt at identifying such proximate determinants of money has to presuppose a strictly formal mechanism of credit creation (recall, for example, equation (4.8)). Nevertheless, the extent to which non-bank financial intermediaries are also in a position to create exchangeable debt obligations, such a formalistic view of the proximate determinants of money supply is likely to be misleading. The problem can be even more intricate depending on the extent to which the internal leakage from the commercial banking system flows into the non-bank financial sector (see Table 4.1). This may enhance the ability of that sector to create credit obligations outside the formal banking system. Indeed, whenever formal and informal credit obligations coexist, such possibilities of leakage from one institutional system leading to enhanced credit-creating potentiality of the other cannot be ruled out. This would make the proximate determinants of money far less easily identifiable than the above analysis suggests.

Identification of *separate* proximate determinants of money, like H, n and a, is useful in so far as these are *independent* variables not related to one another. However, existing general policy instruments for controlling money supply, like the open market operation or changing the cash reserve requirement of commercial banks under a fractional reserve system, can simultaneously affect several so-called proximate determinants of money. Thus, open market sale of government securities by the monetary authority, intended at contracting the reserve base of commercial banks by replacing their cash-holding with such securities, may set in motion portfolio adjustments by banks which, in turn, affect the cash to deposit ratio of the public that was assumed constant in (4.11). It may also affect the portfolios of non-bank financial institutions. In other words, whenever the prox-imate determinants of money tend to get interlinked, the simple view of autonomous money supply by the government linked to high-powered money and a given set of proximate determinants becomes problematic.

To sum up, the theory of *autonomous* money supply based on a set of 'proximate determinants' shown in (4.18), suffers from two fundamentally questionable assumptions. First, it has to operate on too narrow a definition of 'money' (see (4.15)), which typically excludes non-bank credit obligations. In any modern, industrial society with a complex network of financial intermediations, this may turn out to be far too simplistic a definition of the stock of money. Second, even that narrow definition of money relates to the *potential* and not the *actual* money supply. The *actual* money supply would tend to be more influenced by the *demand* for bank credits. Because, so long as the demand for bank credit falls short of its potential level of supply governed by (say) the proximate determinants of money, the commercial banking system will be *constrained by demand* to create debt obligations. In such a case, these proximate determinants of money, even if they could be identified as independent variables, would serve as poor guides to the *actual* level of credit-money created.

D The Economics and Politics of Monetarism

The older version of the 'quantity theory of money' that ruled before the Keynesian revolution can be viewed as an argument in at least three distinct steps. At the first step, it could be interpreted as a theory of demand for money for transaction purposes (see equations (4.1) to (4.3)). This also corresponds to the Keynesian idea of transactions and precautionary motive for demanding money. Assuming the volume of transactions to be related to the level of income (Y), both the traditional quantity theory and the Keynesian argument can be seen to be in broad agreement in so far as the demand for money would be an increasing, if not a strictly proportional, function of the money value of output (see equation (4.4)).

At the second step, the 'quantity theory of money' presupposes an *autonomously* given supply of money (M_s), i.e., the stock of money supplied can be assumed to be independent of the level of its demand. Historically, the 'quantity theory' originated more than two hundred years ago in the writing of the Scottish philosopher David Hume. At that time, 'money' as the debt obligation of the commercial banking system was nearly unknown. Instead, in the now antiquated case, the stock of metallic coins in circulation was related to the amount of gold (or, other precious metals like silver) in the country. Thus, 'money' in circulation, namely the supply of coins was more or less independently given by the amount of gold held by the monetary authority of a country. This system, although vastly modified through time, retained some of its essential features through the Gold Standard system, in so far as the liability or debt obligations of the monetary authority (i.e., of the 'Core' in Table 4.1, p. 106) had to be limited by the amount of gold it held in reserve to 'back' the currency.[7] Even in the present context, in so far as one concentrates only on the 'currency in circulation' *plus* the *formal* debt obligations of only the commercial banks under a fractional reserve system (see equation (4.15)), that 'narrow' definition of money still can be seen to bear some resemblance to its historical origin. Although the debt obligation or liability of the Central Bank or monetary authority is no longer governed by the gold reserve or any such extraneous factor, the debt-obligation of the monetary authority (or the 'Core' in Table 4.1) itself serves as high-powered money to limit the *potential* for credit creation by the commercial banks within a country under a fractional reserve system (see equation (4.18) in particular). However, as repeatedly emphasised this *autonomy* of the Central Bank in controlling the supply of the stock of money becomes doubtful once it is recognised that in a modern financial system there are also financial intermediaries and non-bank institutions who may be in a position to create debt obligations in response to demand. Consequently, wider definitions of 'money' – the extreme case of which is emphasised by the concept of the 'overall liquidity position' – have to include such possible credit obligations outside the commercial banking system, raising serious doubts in turn about the autonomy of the Central Bank in controlling the supply of money. The *traditional* 'quantity theory' was not required to face such complexities arising from the debt obligations of modern, non-bank financial institutions. Hence, it could comfortably be assumed that the supply of the money is autonomously decided by the gold reserve with the Central Bank.[8]

At the third or final step, the traditional 'quantity theory' often proposed a direct link between the quantity of money and the price level. As we have seen, both Keynesians and the traditional quantity theorists roughly agree that the transaction demand for money is an increasing function of the *money value* of output (see (4.4)). However, to establish the proposed link between the quantity of money demanded and the price level (P), the quantity theorists, in contrast to Keynes, tended to assume, by virtue of Say's law, that output is at the full employment level. If the level of output is fixed at full employment ($X = \bar{X}_f$), any increase in the autonomous supply of money would be matched by an increased demand for money, only though an increase in the nominal price level (P) so long as the velocity of circulation (V) is also constant. This aspect of the traditional quantity equation is already described by (4.2). It can be more explicitly written as,

$$\frac{\Delta M_s}{M_s} = \frac{\Delta M_d}{M_d} = \frac{\Delta P}{P} \tag{4.19}$$

where $X = \bar{X}_f$, constant at full employment level, and V is also postulated as constant. In other words, as (4.19) shows, any increase in money supply leads to an equivalent increase in the general price level in percentage terms because, neither output (X) nor the velocity of circulation of money (V) is presumed to adjust to the higher money supply. This stark statement of the 'quantity theory' that, the general level of prices and the supply of money increase more or less in proportion would need to be modified if it were to allow for output adjustment as well as adjustment in the velocity of circulation of money. Algebraically, instead of (4.19), we would then have,

$$\frac{\Delta M_s}{M_s} = \frac{\Delta M_d}{M_d} = \frac{\Delta P}{P} + \frac{\Delta X}{X} - \frac{\Delta V}{V} \tag{4.20}$$

i.e., the percentage change in money supply can be decomposed into percentage change in price ($\Delta P/P$), in the output level ($\Delta X/X$) as well as in velocity of circulation ($\Delta V/V$). However, such decomposition shown by (4.20) no longer has the predictive power of the preceding simpler equation (4.19). There is nothing in the 'quantity theory' to suggest how output ($\Delta X/X$) or the velocity of circulation ($\Delta V/V$) would adjust in response to changes in money supply. The appeal of the traditional quantity theory has precisely been in its utter simplicity: only by assuming negligible adjustments in the level of output and in the velocity of circulation of money, it could insist that any change in the supply of money predominantly affects the general level of prices, as seen in equation (4.19).

However, the final step of the argument by which the traditional 'quantity theory' links money supply solely to the price level runs diametrically opposite to the Keynesian view. Because once Say's law is rejected and it is shown that the level of output is determined by the level of effective demand (see especially Section C of Chapter 2), there is no reason whatsoever to assume that adjustments caused by an increase in money supply must necessarily fall on the price level (P) and *not* on the level of output (X). Further, once it is recalled (from Chapter 3) that the cost-determined prices of manufactured goods are governed by the general level of money wages, money wages rather than money supply assumes the critical role in determining the general price level.

The Keynesian view of the *speculative holding of money* as idle cash in the face of an uncertain future (see Section B of this chapter) would also suggest that the velocity of circulation of money would fall if the proportion of such idle cash balances rise. Since such speculative demand for money depends on the rate of interest, as shown by (4.6) and even recognised in some versions of the quantity theory (see (4.3)), there is no reason to treat the velocity of circulation as an institutional constant. And without the velocity of circulation constant, the simplification of equation (4.20) into (4.19) cannot obtain either.

The Keynesian macroeconomic tradition therefore clashes with traditional quantity theory on fundamental grounds. Simply stated, it does not permit the conversion of the more general decomposition shown by (4.20) into its simpler form (4.19), because neither *output adjustment* ($\Delta X/X$) nor *adjustment in the velocity of circulation* of money ($\Delta V/V$) can be assumed away. Further, it is the *money wage rate* rather than the quantity of money which exerts its decisive influence on cost-determined prices. The quantity theory of money never explained the relation between the level of the money wage rate and the quantity of money.

The *New Monetarism*, trying to reinstate the 'quantity theory' was largely in response to such challenges posed by Keynesianism. However, under the impact of Keynesian thinking in monetary matters, it had to make serious concessions by making the traditional version of the quantity theory almost stand on its head. The Keynesian view of the speculative demand for money as a store of wealth or asset, is carried to its logical extreme in the modern reformulation of the quantity theory, by suggesting that the demand function for money has to be considered *only* as an asset simultaneously with other major types of assets in the economy. In other words, *while the 'traditional' quantity theory was almost exclusively preoccupied with the transaction demand for money as the medium of exchange, its 'modern' preoccupation is exclusively with the demand for money as an asset.* In interpreting the money demand function implied by the 'quantity equation', the pendulum then swung from one extreme to the other — from money only as a medium of exchange to money only as a 'store of wealth'. In spite of this, both the old and the new version of the quantity theory, as will be seen later, insist rather surprisingly that the velocity of circulation is a rough constant so that, the demand for money as a function of nominal (or money) income remains highly stable, no matter whether money is treated exclusively either as a medium of exchange or as a store of wealth!

In this more recent reformulation of the quantity theory viewed as choice among alternative assets, there is a substantial gap between the *theoretical specification* of the demand function for money as an asset and its more manageable *'reduced form' for empirical purposes*. The theoretical specification is far too elaborate to have much practical relevance. Thus, in the 'modern' theoretical restatement of the quantity doctrine, any wealth-holder is imagined to select between money as an asset, and (four) other major types of assets in an economy, namely bonds, equities, physical goods and even 'human capital'. Money is only one of these five major forms in which wealth can be held. It is then postulated that the *expected net rates of return* on these five types of assets influence the overall pattern of wealth-holding. Consequently, in this framework, the demand for money as an asset is governed by all the factors that determine the net rates of return on the five major types of assets plus a budget constraint for total wealth.

Not surprisingly, all this adds up to a formidable list of factors in the consequent specification of the demand function for money as an asset. They can be functionally grouped under four heads:

(a) A vector or list of *interest rates*, namely i_m (on bank deposits as a form of money), i_b (on bonds) and i_e (on equities),

(b) A list of per cent *changes in interest rates* which governs the capital gains or losses on bonds and on equities, namely,

$$\frac{1}{i_b} \cdot \frac{di_b}{dt} \quad \text{and} \quad \frac{1}{i_e} \cdot \frac{di_e}{dt}$$

(c) The general *price level* P and its per cent *change*

$$\frac{1}{P} \cdot \frac{dP}{dt}$$

which govern the real yield on money and on physical goods,

(d) The overall *budget constraint* for wealth which is approximated by Friedman's notion of *permanent income Y_p* – a sort of weighted average of current and past values of income – on the assumption that the ratio of permanent income to wealth (the long-term return on wealth) is roughly constant. It is complemented by a subsidiary constraint on wealth-holding which is based on the division between 'human' and 'non-human' wealth, on the grounds that possibilities of substitution between these two types of wealth is limited. This is shown by some given ratio r_w of human to non-human wealth.

Symbolically, all this could be written in a general functional form:

$$M_d = J\left(i_m,\ i_b,\ i_e,\ \frac{di_b}{dt},\frac{di_e}{dt},P,\frac{1}{P}\cdot\frac{dP}{dt}\cdot Y_p \text{ and } r_w\right) \qquad (4.21)$$

There are serious ambiguities in the above specification of the quantity doctrine that need to be pointed out at this stage. Presumably, the demand for the stock of money (M_d) as a particular form of asset among several others in (4.21), is based upon conventional assumptions of *microeconomic* rationality of each individual maximising income from his wealth holding. However, nowhere is it explicitly indicated how such individual choices are to be *aggregated*. This problem of aggregation is especially relevant in the present context. Because, it is far from clear that individual demand functions for money can just be 'added up' without looking at corresponding changes in the debit and credit positions of individual agents in the economy when credit money itself has to be treated as some form of debt obligation (see Table 4.1). Indeed, the lack of any explicit individual-maximising model (so dear to the 'neo-classical' economic tradition!) which can then be aggregated to arrive at (4.21), makes the macroeconomic specification of (4.21) *ad hoc*.

To avoid these difficulties, it is argued that the 'test of the pudding is in eating' so that without bothering too much about the theoretical basis of the specification of (4.21), one should go ahead to test it against empirical evidence. Unfortunately, however, *the model chosen for empirical enquiry has to be considerably different.* The specification of equation (4.21) involves several variables that are empirically non-observables and therefore, cannot be dealt with directly. Thus, the list of changes in interest rates, governing capital gains or losses on bonds and equities, i.e.,

$$\frac{1}{i_b} \cdot \frac{di_b}{dt} \quad \text{and} \quad \frac{1}{i_e} \cdot \frac{di_e}{dt}$$

have to be dropped because they involve *expected* (and not actual) changes, which cannot be statistically observed.[9] Similarly, *expected* price change (dP/dt) also has to be dropped from the empirical specification of (4.21). In addition, as the parameter (r_w) representing division between human and non-human capital is empirically impossible to estimate in most instances, it is also dropped from most empirically testable versions of the modern quantity theory.

By assuming only one interest rate, *the empirically testable version* of the original specification of modern quantity theory in (4.21) is given in a highly truncated form:

$$M_d = J\left(P, Y_P, i\right) \tag{4.22}$$

It is written as the demand for *real* money balance as,

$$\frac{M_d}{P} = L\left(\frac{Y_P}{P}, i\right) \tag{4.23}$$

It deserves attention that the ultimate *empirical* specification of 'modern' quantity theory – simplified from the *generalised* demand function for money as one of the many alternative forms of assets in (4.21) to its truncated *empirical* version in (4.23) – remains hardly distinguishable from the Keynesian demand function for money. Because, it should be recalled that the Keynesian total demand for money is transaction demand as a function of current money income (see equation (4.4)) and speculative demand as a function of the rate of interest in a given state of expectations (see equation (4.6)). Consequently, at the level of *empirical* specification, the difference between the Keynesian total demand function for money and modern quantity theory appears to lie in the distinction made between *current* income (Y) in Keynesian theory (see (4.4)) and *permanent* income (Y_p), as a 'proxy' for the budget constraint for wealth in the modern quantity theory (see (4.22)). And, the extent to which most *empirical* work has to treat permanent income simply as a weighted average of incomes of various past periods with maximum weight usually being given to current income, even that distinction between current and permanent income becomes obscure. Therefore, it is fair to say that the empirical formulations put to statistical tests do *not* discriminate sufficiently between the Keynesian view of the demand for money and the modern version of the quantity theory. Indeed, the ultimate empirical determinants – income (current or permanent) and the interest rate – are so similar in both theories, that it is only in the special *equational form*, rather than in introducing new conceptual determinants of the demand for money, that the 'modern' quantity theory can be said to differ from the Keynesian view.

At the empirical level, modern quantity theory makes two inter-related claims. First, it claims to have found that the interest rate is relatively unimportant in determining the demand for money. Thus, the interest elasticity of demand for money, namely the percentage change in the demand for money resulting from percentage change in the interest rate, is claimed to be small. This in turn allows a modern quantity theorist to ignore the interest rate as one of the major determinants of the demand for money in (4.22) or (4.23).[10] This leaves him with income as the single determinant of demand for money, reducing it to a form given by (4.4). It naturally implies that the speculative demand for money which could affect the velocity of circulation as in (4.3), is rejected by the quantity theorists entirely on empirical but not on theoretical ground.

With the unstable speculative demand for money rejected on empirical grounds, the second empirical proposition of 'modern' quantity theory is hardly unexpected. It claims that the demand for money is empirically a stable function of the level of income *in the long run*. Such a stable and usually, linear relation between demand for the stock of money (M_d) and money income (Y) entails a stable velocity of circulation in conformity with the more traditional versions of the theory (see (4.2)). The 'modern' quantity theory, therefore, finds the older version as *empirically* justified, although it started out from the different premise of considering the demand for money *only* as one asset among many others (see (4.21)).

It should be noted that the demand for money as one of the many forms of assets in which wealth can be stored as postulated in (4.21), is based upon the notion of *adjustments in stocks*. However, stock items like 'human capital' or even certain types of physical capital goods take a long time to adjust. The modern quantity theorist, unlike his predecessor, therefore, likes to believe that the *demand function for money as an asset* stated in relationship (4.21) or its empirical version (4.23) is a relationship which holds only in the long-run. However, it is not clear how long should this 'long-run' be on theoretical grounds.

It must be pointed out that the empirical findings of the 'modern' quantity theorists – the insensitivity of money demand to the interest rate and a stable velocity of circulation – have not found universal support. In particular, a substantial body of empirical research has cast serious doubt on such empirical finding of a *stable* velocity of circulation.

If the empirical basis of modern quantity theory is insecure, its theoretical foundation must be seen to be still less secure. As has been already pointed out, the truncated empirical specification of the theory in (4.22) or (4.23) is very similar to the Keynesian view. Therefore, even if (4.22) and (4.23) perform well econometrically, it can in no way be treated as decisive evidence in favour of either theory. The crucial theoretical basis of the quantity theory must therefore lie in explaining the equational form, i.e., *why* the demand function for money and the velocity of circulation should be *stable* on theoretical considerations. The quantity theory – old or new – has never been able to provide a theoretical scheme to explain this. And without a clear *theoretical* scheme advanced in support of its central hypothesis of constant velocity of circulation of money, the 'modern' quantity theory often assumes the character of a 'black-box' magic; empirical tests are performed to support a hypothesis which has no theoretical basis!

In the final analysis, this mindless empiricism of the 'modern' quantity theory can be seen to be based on *three assumptions*, better described as 'articles of faith' for its disciples, none of which has adequate theoretical or empirical basis. They are:

(a) *The supply of money is (or can be) exogenously determined.* This is an article of faith, because 'money' can be so narrowly defined, as to make it exogenous, e.g., it includes bank credit based upon 'proximate determinants' but not credit obligations of other important non-bank financial institutions. Thus, even if one were to find that in actual monetary history, the supply of money has in fact strongly responded to its demand through new forms of credit obligations of non-bank institutions, the quantity theorist can continue to believe that this is unimportant. Because, 'in principle' money supply can be made autonomous by defining 'money' in a manner to suit that belief.

(b) *The functional relation between the quantity of money demanded and the nominal (or money) income is highly stable, i.e. the velocity of circulation of money is highly stable.* This is defended as an article of faith, because whenever statistical evidence contradicts it (as it often does, particularly in the case of recent British monetary history), it is claimed that slow stock-adjustments, which make the relationship valid only 'in the long-run', are not yet completed. On the other hand, why the velocity of circulation of money should be a *constant* in the long-run is never explained on theoretical grounds.

(c) Finally, even assuming the velocity of circulation (V) to be an *empirical* constant (without theoretical explanation), the quantity theory only defines the long-term *demand* for money in relation to the level of nominal income (see (4.2)). Its other aspect is *autonomous money supply* governed by a series of 'proximate determinants' see (4.18)). However, since demand (M_d) and supply (M_s) are assumed to be *independently* specified, one needs a *transmission mechanism* linking change in money supply to change in demand for money. But the quantity theory – old or new – entirely fails to specify any such mechanism of transmission. Instead, it relies on an article of faith to suggest that the level of nominal income ($Y \equiv PX$) must adjust to bridge any gap between supply and demand for money.

On this last point regarding the specification of the transmission mechanism, the Keynesian theory stands in sharp contrast. The *transmission mechanism in Keynes' theory* is clear: an increase in potential money supply, interpreted as higher debt obligation of the commercial banks, is brought about by a higher cash reserve of the banks (see (4.9)). If the Central Bank purchases securities in the open market to increase the cash reserve of the banks, then the price of securities increases and the corresponding interest rate decreases (see (4.5)). Given the state of expectation about the 'normal' rate of interest, at the lower current interest rate, the demand for money by the public (M_d) also increases (see (4.6)). Thus, higher potential for money supply by the banks can be realised at higher demand for money by the public. Consequently, an equilibrium between higher (actual) supply of money and its higher demand by the public can be reached at a lower interest rate. A lower interest rate, in turn, reduces the cost of borrowing finance from commercial banks by investors in physical capital goods. Given the state of expectations regarding the prospect for profitable investment opportunities ('the marginal efficiency of capital' as Keynes called it), the lower cost of borrowing helps in stimulating private investment. Interpreted in this way, the Keynesian transmission mechanism is *sequential in time*. The very method of augmenting money supply leads to adjustments in the market for financial securities, lowering the rate of interest and the lower interest cost of borrowing is *then* transmitted to stimulate investment in physical capital goods. The Keynesian view of the transmission mechanism therefore implies an *ordering of markets in terms of their relative speeds of adjustment*. The market for *financial* assets (i.e., the Stock Exchange) is postulated to adjust faster than the market for *physical* assets, i.e., capital goods, which adjusts only *after* the substitution between bonds and money has adjusted to change the interest rate on bonds. (See Section B of this chapter.) It is precisely such an ordering of markets by their relative speeds of adjustment that attributes to the Keynesian transmission mechanism its *sequential* character in historical time where the government can intervene at any successive stage of the sequence.

In contrast to this recursive or sequential character of the Keynesian transmission mechanism, the monetarist doctrine – in so far as it has any transmission mechanism at all – relies on *simultaneous* adjustments in all the major markets for assets (see (4.21)). It seems to suggest that people choose to buy more of physical goods or financial assets or even 'human capital', as more money is supplied to them. However, this argument has an altogether *false start*, because it fails to recognise the basic aspect of creation of *credit money*. Although it is quite plausible, as the modern quantity theory suggests, that the public might *simultaneously* choose between buying more of financial or physical goods *if* they had more money, the argument starts from the false proposition that the public simply can have more money (as if money can be sprayed from helicopters!). It has to be recognised that credit money in any modern capitalist economy is *always* the debt obligation of the financial sector (see Table 4.1, p. 106). Because such increased debt obligation can come about only through financial institutions, the argument about any change in money supply must *start* in the market for financial assets, i.e., how debt obligations are created in response to demand for them by the public. Since the quantity theory insists that the demand for money (M_d) is governed entirely by the level of nominal income (Y) and it has no theory of the determination of the level of nominal income, is unable to provide an adequate theory of how the supply of credit money can respond to its demand through adjustment in the market for financial assets.

Instead, the quantity theory falls into the dogmatism of insisting that the supply of credit money is *autonomous*, i.e., independent of its demand and therefore, independent of adjustments in the financial markets. Nevertheless, under normal functioning of the commercial banking system, described in Section C of this chapter, a 'tight' (or 'easy') money policy usually means (i) either, contraction (or expansion) of the cash reserve base brought about by open market sale (or purchase) by the Central Bank (or monetary authority), *or*, (ii) a statutory raising (or lowering) of the fractional cash reserve requirement of the banks (i.e., parameter 'n' in (4.10)). It has to be recognised that such credit squeeze succeeds at the most in terms of *potential* supply of credit. The monetary authority, for instance, succeeds in selling more financial securities to banks at a lower price for securities which also make the interest rate correspondingly higher (see (4.5)). However, this decrease in the *potential* supply of bank credit to the public may *not* reduce the *actual* supply of credit, particularly, if the *demand* for bank credit by the public does not decrease simultaneously.[11] In the simplest case, even a reduced *potential supply* of bank credit (determined by an equation like (4.18)) may still *exceed the demand* for bank credit; as a result, the *actual* credit obligations created by the commercial banks continue to be demand-determined, and the squeeze on the *potential* supply of credit does *not* affect its *actual* supply. Indeed, if the *demand* for bank credit by the public does not decrease simultaneously, commercial banks may even become unwilling to purchase enough securities from the monetary authority so that, even their *potential* for supplying credit does not decrease adequately. In a more complex situation, any decreased *potential* of the commercial banks in creating credit may simply lead to *other types* of debt obligations created by non-bank financial institutions to satisfy the higher demand for credit money by the public. In this case, as is often observed in practice, money supply may go *down* according to some narrow definition of money (e.g. something like M_1 which takes into account only currency in circulation and bank credit, as in (4.15)), but it goes *up* in terms of some other wider measure of money that also takes into account some other types of debt obligations.

The general point underlying the different cases considered above needs emphasis. The *actual* supply of money in the form of various credit obligations is strongly influenced as a rule by what the public demands as credit and *not* entirely by what commercial banks can *potentially* supply. In short, *actual* money supply tends to be demand-determined. Even in a situation where the commercial banks are supply constrained from meeting the level of demand for credit by the public, some other types of debt obligations created by non-bank financial institutions may serve as 'money' to fill that vacuum of excess demand for credit by the public.

This demand-determined nature of the level of credit money in circulation points to a fundamental defect in the monetarist perception. It fails to recognise the *commodity character of credit money under modern capitalism*. An analogy with Say's law may be helpful at this point. It will be recalled (from Section C, Chapter 2) that Say's law made the mistake of asserting that 'supply creates its own demand'. By overemphasising the supply-side, it forgot the role of effective demand in commodity production. And yet, by definition, commodities are produced only for the market, so that the size of the market, i.e., the level of effective demand must as a rule govern the level of supply of commodities. Similarly, credit money is a commodity 'produced' by banks and other financial institutions only in response to market demand. Whatever the level of demand for 'money' by the public would usually be satisfied through the creation of various types of debt obligations by the financial sector. This view of the adjustment of the supply of money to its level of demand is also strengthened by the sheer fact that there are no genuine *physical* constraints (e.g., limited capacity or raw material availability) on the supply of money, but only regulations or persuasions by the monetary authority for controlling supply. The financial institutions can normally circumvent such regulations by creating different types of debt obligations so that, the different measures of money supply often move in opposite directions. As a result the supply of credit money in one form or another tends to adjust to the level of its demand. Therefore, without controlling the *demand* for money, there is in general no way of effectively regulating its supply.

And yet, the illusion that the supply of money can be regulated independently of its level of demand by denying the commodity character of credit money remains the corner-stone of the monetarist view of economic management. However, since the control of money supply can hardly be effective in practice without controlling its demand, *monetarism in practice* relies crucially in regulating the demand for money, while *in theory* it pretends to control only the supply of money! The point may be illustrated by several typical monetarist prescriptions: it tries to reduce money supply by reducing government expenditure in general and the public sector borrowing (budget deficit) in particular. However, since such reduction in government expenditure leads to reduced effective demand and therefore, to a lower level of nominal income, it would also lead to a reduced demand for money (see (4.4)). Consequently, reduction in government expenditure or deficit can in no way be exclusively identified as an instrument for controlling the *supply* of money.

Similarly, the monetarist view that high public expenditure (investment) tends to *crowd out* private expenditure (investment) is based ultimately on the assumption of an *autonomously given* supply of money of which a higher public share must imply a lower private share. Such an argument is fallacious because higher public expenditure creates higher effective demand and, therefore, higher nominal income which in turn raises the demand for money (see (4.4)). Since money supply would tend to adjust to this higher level of demand, the crowding out argument based on a *given* supply of money also loses its force. Indeed, the crowding out argument tends to repeat an old mistake of the 'Treasury view' discussed earlier (p. 58, Chapter 2). To counter the Keynesian argument of managing effective demand through increased public investment, the 'Treasury view' contested that any increase in *home* investment would lead to an equivalent reduction in *foreign* investment, because the total amount of savings to be invested is *given*. As we now recognise, that argument was false because the total amount of savings is *not* given. It is *governed* by the level of investment (see Chapter 2, Section C). Just as the older 'Treasury view' failed to recognise the commodity-producing character of capitalism which makes the level of *supply* of commodities adjust to its level of demand, so does the crowding out postulate of modern monetarism fail to recognise the commodity character of credit money whose demand typically governs its supply.

The refusal to accept the commodity character of credit money is not merely a *theoretical* failure of monetarism. It has to be understood as a deliberate political posture. Only by insisting that money supply is autonomous, i.e., not responsive to its demand, monetarism could take a view of economic management, where the central monetary authority and its commercial banking system have the paramount role to play. By attributing to the control of money supply and to the banking system such a central regulatory role, monetarism proposes to displace Keynesian policies which argued in favour of direct demand management through active State intervention.

By concentrating on the *supply* of money as the central regulatory variable, attention is also diverted from the fundamental question of how the level of economic activity or income is determined which, in turn, governs the *demand* for money according to the quantity theory (see (4.2) and (4.4)). Instead, it is simply assumed that any discrepancy between the supply and demand for money would be eliminated through adjustment in the level of nominal income. This, however, hides the political reality of a credit squeeze through which nominal as well as real income adjusts. To the extent that a credit squeeze can be actually enforced, a major part of it takes the form of rationing the *quantity* of credit, rather than *uniformly* tightening the terms on which credit is made available (e.g., the rate of interest).[12] In effect, it leads to *highly discriminatory quantity adjustment*, as the more creditworthy from the banks' point of view still continue to have access to bank loans perhaps at a higher interest rate while the less creditworthy borrowers are simply denied credit. In such a situation of rationing the quantity of credit, the unsatisfied borrowers to be denied credit would be determined by 'creditworthiness' which, by and large, depends on the extent of ownership of property. Consequently, large firms owning more property will typically continue to have access to credit in most instances compared to smaller firms with little property that makes them less creditworthy. For example, consider a long recession, where many firms – small and large – face a serious 'cash-flow' problem, as their unrealised profits in the form of unsold inventories (see Chapter 2, Section A) do not permit them to meet their commitments of regular cash expenditure without outside borrowing. Uncreditworthy smaller firms with little property then face bankruptcy as they are unable to tide over their cash-flow problems. However, creditworthy larger firms have a better chance to tide over the same cash-flow problem as they are less likely to be rationed in terms of credits by the banks. It is this sort of a transmission process which is usually associated with general monetary restriction, recommended by the quantity theorists. Thus, reliance on generalised monetary control has usually implied strengthening the 'rule of property' by invoking discrimination against those (including marginal firms, workers and trade unions) who have little or no property and hence, are less qualified as creditworthy borrowers. Its inevitable result is a kind of quantity adjustment which relies on making the less creditworthy, smaller enterprises bankrupt by denying them credit and by increasing the rate of unemployment. Further, in so far as higher unemployment slows down the rate of money wage increase, it also slows down the rate of increase in the cost-determined prices. In short, the demand for money is reduced through a reduction in the level of economic activity brought about in the first place through unemployment caused by the bankruptcy of a large number of smaller enterprises and reducing price increases in the second place.

The nature of economic adjustment envisaged by monetarism then achieves several political objectives simultaneously. By placing the banking system at the commanding role of economic policy, it wins over the support of powerful financial circles. In the name of 'monetary discipline' it argues on the one hand against active State intervention (e.g., reduced government expenditure, the crowding out assumption, etc. discussed earlier) while on the other, the nature of monetary discipline systematically discriminates in favour of property. In short, it becomes a policy of intervention in favour of property under the paradoxical posture of non-intervention by the State. And, since such 'rule of property' has always been the guiding principle behind free enterprise capitalism, it is not surprising that the narrow academic doctrine of monetarism has been so enthusiastically turned into a potent political ideology.

Notes to Chapter 4

1. *The General Theory* (Keynes, 1936), p. 294.
2. J. M. Keynes (1937), 'The General Theory: fundamental concepts and ideas', p. 218.
3. See, W. Baumol, (1952), 'The transaction demand for cash – an inventory theoretic approach', or J. Tobin (1956), 'The interest-elasticity of transactions demand for cash', as examples trying to exploit this analogy between money and inventory-holding.
4. As in J. Tobin (1958), 'Liquidity preference as behaviour towards risk'.
5. See A. C. Bain (1976), *The Control of Money Supply* pp. 16–20 for a convenient summary of the various monetary aggregates in the United Kingdom.
6. The following tabular classification follows J. R. Hicks (1977), 'Monetary experience and the theory of money', in *Economic Perspective: Further Essays on Money and Growth*, pp. 75–7.
7. As we shall see later (in Section B, Chapter 5), the actual operation of the Gold Standard was more complex particularly because, the Bank of England could influence its gold stock through variations in the bank rate.
8. In retrospect, Keynes' argument in the *General Theory* was oversimplified

on this point in so far as it also assumed that the stock of money supply is given *independently* of demand.

9. Here again, the argument of the modern quantity theory is influenced by Keynes in so far as the *expected* normal rate (i^*) in relation to the current rate (i) determines the speculative demand for money. See equation (4.6) and Figure 4.1 in particular.

10. See, however, S. M. Goldfeld (1973), 'The demand for money revisited' which finds the long-term interest elasticity of demand for money (M_1) to be quite high (-0.7), contradicting the evidence offered by the quantity theorists. Evidence, in line with Goldfeld's is also found in the British context in several studies. See, for example, the survey by C. A. E. Goodhart and A. D. Crockett (1970), 'The importance of money'.

11. In the Keynesian transmission mechanism, the *demand* for credit money also decreases simultaneously at the higher rate of interest. This route would not be available to the quantity theory in so far as it insists on its 'empirical' claim that demand for money is insensitive to variations in the rate of interest.

12. The relevant theoretical distinction here is between quantity-rationing and price-rationing of credit. Price-rationing, e.g., raising the interest rate for borrowing funds, tends to affect almost all borrowers *uniformly*. However, rationing of the quantity typically affects the *marginal* borrowers, i.e. not every borrower has less credit by a uniform x per cent but some potential borrowers are simply denied credit altogether.

Further Reading

On the characteristics of a monetary economy, perhaps the best reading still is Keynes' article, 'The General Theory: fundamental concepts and ideas' (Keynes 1937) which should be supplemented by a reading of Chapters 12, 13, 15 and 17 or the *General Theory* (Keynes, 1936). Bain's *The Control of Money Supply* (Bain, 1976) covers material of Sections B and C in an accurate, but introductory manner. Kahn's article 'Notes on Liquidity' reprinted in his *Selected Essays in Employment and Growth* (Kahn, 1972), although difficult reading, is an excellent analysis of how to develop the Keynesian view of the demand for money.

Two articles by Tobin, 'The interest-elasticity of transactions demand for cash' (Tobin, 1956) and 'Liquidity preference as behaviour towards risk' (Tobin, 1958) apply microeconomic rationality of inventory control and portfolio choice respectively to the demand for money.

The book by Gurley and Shaw (1959), *Money in a Theory of Finance* provides a good introduction to the nature of financial intermediation in a modern capitalist economy, while the Report of the (Radcliffe) *Committee on the Working of the Monetary System* (1959) shows the importance of working with the concept of 'overall liquidity' under complex systems of financial intermediation.

Fisher's (1911) *The Purchasing Power of Money* is a classic on the traditional formulation of the quantity theory of money. It also provides the background to Friedman's reformulation in 'The quantity theory of money – a restatement' in the volume, *Studies in the Quantity Theory of Money* (Friedman, 1956). Friedman's view of monetary policy is well summarised in his 'The role of monetary policy' (Friedman, 1968) and the interested reader may also look at Friedman and Schwartz (1982), *Monetary Trends in the United States and the United Kingdom,* especially Chapters 1 and 2, for a recent statement of their position. Kaldor's two essays 'The new monetarism' (Kaldor, 1970) and 'Monetarism and UK monetary policy' (Kaldor, 1980) articulate the basic Keynesian position against monetarism. Tobin's (1981) 'The monetarist counter-revolution today: an appraisal' presents a somewhat more diluted Keynesian position.

The link between the 'real' and the 'monetary' aspect of Keynes' theory was neatly formalised in Hicks' influential article, 'Mr. Keynes and the classics' (Hicks, 1937). The resulting IS–LM technique covers pages of modern textbooks; it has been rejected in our exposition because it relies on a simultaneous ('general equilibrium') rather than a sequential transmission mechanism. On this point, see Pasinetti's 'The principle of effective demand' in his *Growth and Income Distribution* (Pasinetti, 1974) and also, Leijonhofvud, (1968) *On Keynesian Economics and the Economics of Keynes,* Chapter 2.

5
Trade and Financial Relations Among Nations

A International Aspects of Effective Demand

Production of commodities by means of commodities is anonymous by its very nature. This means that no individual capitalist needs to be concerned either about the source from which he buys his raw materials or about the market in which he sells his product. In his continuous search for higher profit, each individual capitalist is simply concerned to find raw materials from the cheapest source and in realising his potential profit by selling it at the highest price in whichever market he can. Under these circumstances, the very logic of commodity production has a tendency to expand beyond given geographical or national boundaries. Any question of the nationality of either the buyer or of the seller becomes subsidiary to the search for higher profit.

Although in their search for higher profit, individual capitalists may refuse to distinguish between the domestic and the foreign market, such a distinction is usually imposed upon them by the political reality of the modern nation-state. The distinction between the domestic or *home market* over which the jurisdiction of the nation-state prevails in terms of tariff, labour migration or foreign investment policy and the foreign or the *external market* that normally lies outside such jurisdiction of the nation-state, becomes the essential economic aspect of this political reality. Consequently, while the inherent logic of commodity production drives it towards assuming an anonymous character, the political reality of the nation-state compels it to distinguish between the home and the external market.

The economic consequence of such a distinction is perhaps most clearly visible in the old but continuing debate on *free trade versus protection.* Capitalist nations, that are economically strong enough to compete out their weaker trade rivals, typically side with the doctrine of free trade to press for the internationalisation of markets. This entails eroding the autonomy of the nation-state in regulating the home market. In contrast, economically weaker capitalist nations have to argue in favour of protectionism in economic self-defence. When the captains of domestic industry are too weak to face international competition, it is only natural for them to seek a protected home market where the nation-state can shelter them from international competition.

Protecting the size of the home market essentially means maintaining the level of effective demand for domestically produced commodities. In a *closed* economy without foreign trade, that level of effective demand is governed by the level of investment through the multiplier mechanism, as was examined at length in Chapter 2. However, in an *open* economy with significant foreign trade, exports and imports of commodities also enter into the determination of that level of effective demand. Expenditure on foreign goods by domestic consumers, i.e., imports would mean a deduction from the level of effective demand in the home market. Conversely, expenditure on domestic goods by foreign consumers, i.e. exports, would mean an addition to the level of effective demand at home. Indeed, this is the essential logic underlying the measurement of gross domestic product (i.e. total expenditure on domestically produced goods) by the *expenditure method* of national accounting for an open economy, as exhibited by equation (1.15) of Chapter 1. It may be rewritten for ready reference as,

$$\begin{aligned} \text{GDP} &= Y \\ &= \text{Final consumption expenditure } (C) + \text{final invest-} \\ &\quad \text{ment expenditure including inventory charges } (I) \\ &\quad + \text{exports } (E) - \text{imports } (M) \end{aligned} \qquad (5.1)$$

The crucial point about (5.1) is that it is only exports *net* of imports $(E - M)$, i.e., the *export surplus*, but *not* total exports, that contributes to the total final expenditure on domestically produced goods. Consequently, an expansion in the level of effective demand for domestically produced goods, i.e., an expansion in the size of the home market would require a *trade surplus* of exports over imports. Conversely, a trade deficit would reduce the size of the home market through foreign trade.

This *link between the trade surplus or deficit and the size of the home market* is simply an elaboration of the principle of effective demand examined at length in Chapter 2. Since exports are by definition *not* available for *domestic* consumption, any *autonomous* increase in exports that creates additional employment and wage bill in the export sector would also create additional demand for surplus consumption goods (in a manner described for the investment sector in Figure 2.2 of Chapter 2). If that additional demand for surplus is met *entirely* through expansion in the *domestic* production of consumption goods (as presumed in the case of a *closed* economy in Chapter 2), the resulting *foreign trade multiplier* caused by an autonomous increase in exports would be *identical* with the quantity-adjustment multiplier for a closed economy. In that case, the import bill remains constant despite the increased domestic production of exports and consumption goods. At the other extreme, if the additional demand for surplus consumption goods caused by an increase in exports is met *entirely* through the import of consumption goods, there would simply be no foreign trade multiplier. Because in that case, the *domestic* production of consumption goods is not required to respond to the additional demand created through an autonomous increase in exports.

In the more typical case of an open economy only *a part* of the additional demand for surplus consumption goods caused by an increase in exports would be met through imports, while the remaining part will be met through additional domestic production of consumption goods. As a result, the required expansion of the domestic consumption sector would be somewhat *less* in an *open* economy because part of the additional demand leaks out of the domestic market to be met through higher imports. Naturally, the more the leakage is due to higher *marginal propensity to import*, the lower will be the magnitude of the corresponding foreign trade multiplier.

Therefore, it follows that the foreign trade multiplier depends on the behaviour of imports in different sectors of the economy in response to an increase in the level of home demand brought about by higher export. This can be algebraically worked out by disaggregating total imports into its various sectoral components. Using earlier national accounting relations (1.13) to (1.15) of Chapter 1 in (5.1), we obtain,

$$Y = C + I + E - (M_c + M_i + M_{zc} + M_{zi} + M_{ze})$$

or, by collecting terms,

$$Y = [C - (M_c + M_{zc})] + [I - (M_i + M_{zi})] + [E - M_{ze}] \quad (5.2)$$

where M_j is the import of *final* (finished) goods by sector j and M_{zj} is the import of raw material (z) for production in sector j ($j = c, i$ or e).

It is important to note that each square-bracketed term on the right-hand side of (5.2) represents value added by the corresponding sector. Thus, from the total final expenditure on consumption (C) are deducted the import expenditure on finished consumption goods (M_c) as well as import expenditure on imported raw materials (M_{zc}) used in the production of domestic consumption goods to obtain the final expenditure on domestically produced consumption goods.[1] This, by definition, is the value added by the consumption sector (VA_c), i.e.,

$$VA_c \equiv (C - M_c - M_{cz}).$$

Since it is reasonable to assume (though it is not always the case in practice) that the same commodity is not exported and imported in its finished form, no *final* import is shown for the export sector. Equation (5.2) is then definitional as it corresponds to the definition of GDP by the *product method* which is obtained as the sum of the value added by all the sectors in the economy (see (1.4) of Chapter 1).

To derive the foreign trade multiplier, we assume that import as a proportion of value added, i.e., marginal and average import propensity remains constant for each sector. This assumption of constant sectoral import propensities would be more reasonable if raw material import is the quantitatively dominant component of total import by a sector. Because, the amount of raw material needed per unit of domestic value added may be treated as a rough technological constant. Otherwise, import of *finished* goods, i.e., M_c and M_i need bear no systematic relation to the value added by the corresponding sectors.

Algebraically, the constant sectoral import propensities are written as,

For the consumption sector, $\dfrac{(M_c + M_{zc})}{(C - M_c - M_{zc})} = m_c$

or,

$$(M_c + M_{zc}) = \frac{m_c}{(1 + m_c)} \cdot C;$$

For the investment sector,

$$\frac{(M_i + M_{zi})}{(I - M_i - M_{zi})} = m_i \quad \text{or} \quad (M_i + M_{zi}) = \frac{m_i}{(1 + m_i)} \cdot I;$$

and, for the export sector,

$$\frac{M_{ze}}{(E - M_{ze})} = m_e \quad \text{or} \quad M_{ze} = \frac{m_e}{(1 + m_e)} \cdot E$$

Inserting the above expressions on the extreme right in expression (5.2), we obtain GDP as,

$$Y = \frac{C}{(1 + m_c)} + \frac{I}{(1 + m_i)} + \frac{E}{(1 + m_e)} \tag{5.3}$$

where as in (5.2), each component on the right-hand side represents the final expenditure on *domestically* produced goods, i.e., the value added by the corresponding sector.

If we continue to assume that all wages are consumed (as in Chapter 2) and a constant fraction $s_p (1 \geqslant s_p > 0)$ of profit is saved, then with h_j as the share of profit in the value added by sector j ($j = c, i$ or e) the rate of savings in the economy is given as,

$$S = s_p \left(\frac{h_c}{(1 + m_c)} \cdot C + \frac{h_i}{(1 + m_i)} \cdot I + \frac{h_e}{(1 + m_e)} \cdot E \right) \tag{5.4}$$

Similarly, the total import of the economy is given as,

$$M = (M_c + M_{zc}) + (M_i + M_{zi}) + M_{ze}$$

$$= \frac{m_c}{(1 + m_c)} \cdot C + \frac{m_i}{(1 + m_i)} \cdot I + \frac{m_e}{1 + m_e) \cdot E} \tag{5.5}$$

The basic *condition for macroeconomic balance in an open economy*, corresponding to the investment–saving equality in (2.10) of Chapter 2, can be derived from the expenditure side definition of GDP in (5.1). That condition can be rewritten as,

$$I + E = (Y - C) + M$$

or,

$$I + E = S + M \tag{5.6}$$

because, $(Y - C) = S$, by definition.

By substituting (5.4) and (5.5) in the balancing condition (5.6) and simplifying, we obtain,

$$\frac{(1 - s_p h_i)}{(1 + m_i)} \cdot I + \frac{(1 - s_p h_e)}{(1 + m_e)} \cdot E = \frac{(s_p h_c + m_c)}{(1 + m_c)} \cdot C \qquad (5.7)$$

Note that equation (5.7) has a similar interpretation to our earlier equation (2.17) of Chapter 2: terms $(1 - s_p h_i)$ and $(1 - s_p h_e)$ on the left-hand side of (5.7) show the *demand* for consumption goods generated *per unit of value added* by the investment and the export sector respectively; whereas the division by corresponding expressions $(1 + m_i)$ and $(1 + m_e)$ is required to convert total final expenditures I and E to the corresponding value added figures by those sectors. (See the derivation of (5.3) from (5.2).) Therefore, the left-hand side of (5.7) shows the demand for consumption goods originating *outside* the consumption sector, namely in the investment and in the export sectors (in conformity with (2.17) p. 40 for a closed economy). Similarly, the right-hand side of (5.7) shows the surplus of consumption goods generated from domestic production as well as through imports. Thus, the interpretation of the condition for macroeconomic balance in an open economy, i.e., (5.5) is fundamentally the same as that in a closed economy in (2.10), namely the demand for consumption goods generated in sectors producing domestic non-consumables (i.e. the investment and the export sector) has to be met either through domestic surplus of consumption goods or through import. Consequently, the same principle of effective demand elaborated in Chapter 2 continues to apply resulting in quantity- or price-adjustment multiplier if, either investment or export is *autonomously* increased.

To derive the foreign trade multiplier based on quantity adjustment, we assume that investment expenditure is given in (5.7) at some constant level, $I = \bar{I}$. If there is no change in investment in the short period by assumption, $\Delta I = 0$, the required expansion in consumption (ΔC) to meet an increased demand for consumption goods generated by an autonomous increase in exports (ΔE) is given from (5.7) as,

$$\Delta C = \frac{(1 + m_c)}{(1 + m_e)} \cdot \frac{(1 - s_p h_e)}{(s_p h_c + m_c)} \cdot \Delta E, \qquad \Delta I = 0 \text{ by assumption} \quad (5.8)$$

Alternatively, with exports frozen in the short period, $E = \bar{E}$ implying $\Delta E = 0$, from the same equation (5.7), the required increase in the consumption sector (ΔC) due to an autonomous increase in investment (ΔI) can be calculated as,

$$C = \frac{(1+m_c)}{(1+m_i)} \cdot \frac{(1-s_p h_i)}{(s_p h_c + m_c)} \Delta I, \qquad \Delta E = 0 \text{ by assumption} \qquad (5.9)$$

Conditions (5.8) or (5.9) may be compared with the similar condition (2.18) in Chapter 2 for a closed economy to see how (constant) sectoral import propensities make a difference to the argument. In particular, it will be noted that a higher import propensity by any of the non-consumption sector, m_e or m_i, lowers the multiplier through a greater leakage of *demand* for consumption goods from the home market. Import of non-consumption goods reduces both the wage bill and the capitalists' profit (and their consumption) in the domestic non-consumption sectors. Consequently it also reduces the size of the home market for the realisation of surplus consumption goods into profits (see (2.7) of Chapter 2 for elaboration). A higher import propensity of the consumption sector (m_c), on the other hand, weakens the multiplier because the expansion in the *supply* of surplus consumption goods required to satisfy a given level of additional demand is less, as a higher proportion of that additional demand is met through imports. Thus, although higher import propensity of *any* sector reduces the multiplier, the reduction comes about through different economic routes. A higher import propensity by any non-consumption (i.e., investment or export) sector lowers the multiplier from the *demand* side, while a higher import propensity by the consumption sector lowers it, so to say, from the *supply*-side.[2]

The effect of the foreign trade multiplier on GDP can now be derived. From the expression for GDP in (5.3) we obtain,

$$\Delta Y = \frac{\Delta C}{(1+m_c)} + \frac{\Delta E}{(1+m_e)}, \qquad \text{if} \quad \Delta I = 0 \text{ by assumption}$$

Or, substituting the value of C from (5.8) and simplifying, we obtain the algebraic expression for the *foreign trade multiplier* as,

$$\frac{\Delta Y}{\Delta E} = \frac{(1+m_c) + s_p(h_c - h_e)}{(1+m_e)(s_p h_c + m_c)}, \qquad \Delta I = 0 \text{ by assumption} \qquad (5.10)$$

Similarly, by using (5.3) and (5.9) the *investment multiplier for an open economy* can be obtained as,

$$\frac{\Delta Y}{\Delta I} = \frac{(1+m_c) + s_p(h_c - h_e)}{(1+m_i)(s_p h_c + m_c)} \qquad (5.11)$$

If we consider the simpler case (in analogy with a one-sector model) where all sectors have the same import propensity (m) as well as the same share of profit in value added (h), i.e.,

$$m_c = m_i = m_e = m \quad \text{and} \quad h_c = h_i = h_e = h,$$

then the trade multiplier in (5.10) becomes equivalent to the investment multiplier in (5.11). In either case, the open-economy multiplier becomes,[3]

$$\frac{\Delta Y}{\Delta E} = \frac{\Delta Y}{\Delta I} = \frac{1}{(s_p h + m)} = \frac{1}{\text{m.p.s} + \text{m.p.i}} \tag{5.12}$$

where the marginal propensity to save (m.p.s) $= s_p h$ and the marginal propensity to import (m.p.i) $= m$. As is to be expected, comparison of (5.12) with (2.20) of Chapter 2 shows that the multiplier mechanism becomes necessarily weaker in an open economy, because part of the domestic demand leaks out through a positive marginal propensity to import ($1 > m > 0$).

It is important to realise that the foreign trade multiplier operates only through an *autonomous* increase in exports in exact analogy with the domestic multiplier (of Chapter 2) which also operates through an *autonomous* increase in investment. Starting from an initial position of balanced trade (i.e. export equals import initially), any such autonomous increase in export implies an equivalent *trade surplus* for the country concerned. Nevertheless, since for the world economy as a whole, total exports must identically equal total imports, such trade surplus for any one country must also imply an *equivalent trade deficit* for the 'rest of the world'. As a result, the country (or group of countries) that enjoys trade surplus is able to expand its level of effective demand or the size of the home market through the foreign trade multiplier in a manner described by (5.12). Conversely, countries with trade deficit experience contraction in their levels of effective demand through the same multiplier mechanism. This points to *conflicting national economic interests* in trade relations in so far as each country may try to attain a trade *surplus* to expand the size of its domestic market. And, a clash of national interests becomes inevitable, because *all* countries cannot enjoy trade surplus at the same time.

Such conflict in national interests, however, arises in a setting of *economic interdependence* among the trading nations. In a way, this interdependence is obvious, because exports of a country are nothing but imports by other countries. Thus, even if some countries expand their effective demand and income (GDP) through trade surplus, in so far as they also increase their imports as an increasing function of their income, the export of the deficit countries also increases in this process. This shows a degree of mutualism or *complementarity in national economic interests* because the economic prosperity of the trading partners tends to spill over through mutual expansion of exports.

Viewed in terms of the principle of effective demand, the trading nations would then appear to be locked in contradictory relations. They are *rivals* in trade with conflicting national interests in so far as each tries to obtain a trade surplus at the cost of others. They are also *partners* in trade in so far as the economic prosperity of each spills over to the others in the form of higher exports for all.

These contradictory aspects of the trade relationships can be easily formalised by assuming that there are only two groups of countries – a group with trade surplus denoted as 'country' 1 and a group with trade deficit denoted as 'country' 2. Complementarity in trade arises because the export of country 1 (E_1) is nothing but the import of country 2 (M_2) and similarly, $E_2 = M_1$. Assuming the *marginal* (which is *not* the average in the following algebra) propensity to import to be constant for either country, we write,

$$E_1 = M_2 = m_2 Y_2 + K_2, \qquad 1 > m_2 > 0 \tag{5.13}$$

and

$$E_2 = M_1 = m_1 Y_1 + K_1, \qquad 1 > m_1 > 0 \tag{5.14}$$

where K_1 and K_2 are arbitrary constants to be treated as *shift parameters*. Thus, an increase in the magnitude of say K_2 would mean an *autonomous* increase in the level of import of country 2 (i.e., M_2) over and above the increase in import *induced* by an increase in the level of its income (Y_2). Consequently, from (5.13) it also means an *autonomous* increase in the export level (E_1) of country 1.

Assuming further that the marginal (and average) propensity to save to be constant for both countries, we have,

$$S_1 = s_1 Y_1 \tag{5.15}$$

where $s_1 = s_{p1} h_1$ for notational simplicity,
and similarly,

$$S_2 = s_2 Y_2, \qquad s_2 = s_{p2} h_2 \tag{5.16}$$

Recall h_1 and h_2 are the constant shares of profit in income and s_{p1} and s_{p2} are the respective constant propensities to save out of profit in the two countries.

The condition for macroeconomic balance for country 1, is given from (5.6) as,

$$I_1 + E_1 = S_1 + M_1$$

It can be rewritten, in view of the above-mentioned complementarity in trade, i.e., $E_1 = M_2$ as,

$$I_1 + M_2 = S_1 + M_1$$

By substituting for M_2 and M_1 from (5.13) and (5.14) respectively and using (5.15), we obtain on simplification the income level of country 1 as,

$$Y_1 = \frac{I_1 + (K_2 - K_1)}{(s_1 + m_1)} + \frac{m_2}{(s_1 + m_1)} Y_2 \qquad (5.17)$$

Similarly, the macroeconomic balance condition (5.6) for country 2 in conjunction with (5.13), (5.14) and (5.16) yield the income level of country 2 as,

$$Y_2 = \frac{I_2 - (K_2 - K_1)}{(s_2 + m_2)} + \frac{m_1}{(s_2 + m_2)} Y_1 \qquad (5.18)$$

Suppose *initially* both countries had balanced trade, i.e., $E_1 = M_1$ and $E_2 = M_2$. An *autonomous* increase in the export level of country 1 from its initial trade balance raises the value of the shift parameter K_2 by $\Delta K_2 > 0$. This implies from (5.13) that the import of country 2 also shifts upwards by ΔK_2. Thus, country 1 would now have an *export surplus* by ΔK_2 and country 2 will have an equivalent *import surplus* (by $-\Delta K_2$), if the other shift parameter K_1 remains unchanged in the process. Assuming the investment levels I_1 and I_2 to be constant in the two countries, the changes in the income levels of the two countries resulting from an autonomous shift in the export level of country 1 by $\Delta K_2 > 0$, can be computed from (5.17) and (5.18) respectively as,

$$\Delta Y_1 = \frac{\Delta K_2}{(s_1 + m_1)} + \frac{m_2}{(s_1 + m_1)} \cdot \Delta Y_2 \qquad (5.19)$$

where I_1 and K_1 are constant

and,

$$\Delta Y_2 = \frac{-\Delta K_2}{(s_2 + m_2)} + \frac{m_1}{(s_2 + m_2)} \cdot \Delta Y_1 \qquad (5.20)$$

where I_2 and K_1 are constant.

Equations (5.19) and (5.20) are of considerable economic interest because they exhibit *both the conflicting and the complementary aspect* of international trade for each country. For example, in the case of country 1 shown by equation (5.19), an autonomous increase in its trade surplus by $\Delta K_2 > 0$, contributes *positively* to its change in income (ΔY_1) through its foreign trade multiplier, $1/(s_1 + m_1)$, given from (5.12). On the other hand, country 2 experiencing an equivalent trade deficit $(-\Delta K_2)$, undergoes a *negative* change in its income through its foreign trade multiplier $1/(s_2 + m_2)$, as shown by the first term on the right-hand side of (5.20). Thus, the *first term* on the right-hand side of equation (5.19) and of equation (5.20) algebraically displays the *conflictive aspect* of international trade.

In contrast, the *second term* on the right-hand side of the same equations (5.19) and (5.20) depicts the *complementary aspect* of trade. For example, this second term on the right-hand side of (5.19) shows that any increase in the income of the trading partner, country 2 by $\Delta Y_2 > 0$, will also increase the income by country 1 through a higher induced level of export ($=$ import of country 2) for country 1. And, through a similar second term on the right-hand side of (5.20), country 2 will gain in its level of income, Y_2 if its trade partner's income also increases (i.e., if $\Delta Y_1 > 0$).

However, to examine the *interplay* of the co-operative and the conflictive aspect of international trade, we must treat equations (5.19) and (5.20) *simultaneously*. This is done by inserting the value of ΔY_2 from (5.20) in (5.19) to obtain on simplification,

$$\Delta Y_1 = \frac{s_2 \Delta K_2}{(s_1 + m_1)(s_2 + m_2) - m_1 m_2} > 0, \quad \Delta K_2 > 0 \qquad (5.21)$$

where $(s_1 + m_1)(s_2 + m_2) - m_1 m_2 = (s_1 s_2 + s_2 m_1 + s_1 m_2) > 0$.

Similarly, inserting the value of ΔY_1 from (5.19) in (5.20) and simplifying,

$$\Delta Y_2 = \frac{-s_1 \cdot \Delta K_2}{(s_1 + m_1)(s_2 + m_2) - m_1 m_2} < 0, \quad \Delta K_2 > 0 \qquad (5.22)$$

As condition (5.21) shows, if country 1 can achieve an autonomous export surplus by $\Delta K_2 > 0$, its income level Y_1 will ultimately increase despite its higher *induced* import from country 2 (see (5.14)). In contrast, condition (5.22) shows that country 2 with an equivalent autonomous import surplus (ΔK_2) is an ultimate loser as its income level Y_2 decreases despite the higher *induced* import from country 1 resulting in an equivalent higher *induced* export of country 2 (see (5.13)). Since the surplus country 1 ultimately gains (see (5.21)) while the deficit country 2 ultimately loses (see 5.22)), the conflictive aspect of international trade quantitatively dominates. Thus, *rivalry rather than co-operative partnership becomes the dominant undercurrent of trade relations among capitalist nations.*

The dominant tendency towards trade rivalry can express itself in many forms depending on the particular historical and institutional circumstances. In order to achieve a trade surplus or to reduce its trade deficit a country may *devalue*, i.e., deliberately *depreciate* the value of its currency in terms of the currency of its rivals in trade. The cheapening of the home currency (say, British sterling) in terms of the foreign currency (say, American dollar) makes domestic (i.e. British) goods also cheaper for the foreigners (i.e., Americans) to buy. For instance, if the price of a commodity is say, £100 in the British home market and if sterling is devalued by 50 per cent in terms of the dollar, say from £1 = \$2 to £1 = \$1, then American buyers who had to pay (£100 × 2) = \$200 before devaluation, now pay only (£100 × 1) = \$100, i.e., 50 per cent less for the same commodity after devaluation. Thus, by making domestic commodities cheaper to the foreigners, devaluation aims at stimulating exports. On the reverse side, home (i.e. British) consumers have to pay a higher price in terms of their home currency (i.e., sterling) to buy foreign goods. For instance, a commodity which costs \$50 in the American market requires British consumers to pay (\$50 ÷ 1) = £50 after devaluation, while they paid only (\$50 ÷ 2) = £25 for the same commodity before devaluation. Thus, by making the foreign currency more expensive in terms of the domestic currency, devaluation also aims at reducing imports.

A policy of devaluation, by *simultaneously* lowering the price of exported goods to foreigners and by raising the price of imports to domestic buyers, relies on *price inducement* to attain an improvement in the balance of trade position of the devaluing country. However, such a policy can succeed only if exports and imports respond 'sufficiently strongly' to such price inducements. More formally, the percentage increase in exports due to a percentage fall in export price, i.e., the *price elasticity of exports* and the percentage decrease in imports due to a percentage rise in the import price, i.e., the *price elasticity of imports* have to be sufficiently large. Otherwise, with *inelastic* demand for exports, any decrease in export price will *not* be compensated by the *volume* of exports so that total export *revenue* falls even though devaluation lowers the price of exports. Similarly, inelastic demand for imports would actually increase the total import bill as devaluation increases the price of imports. Since devaluation is intended to stimulate exports and depress imports *simultaneously*, the *combined price elasticities of demand for exports and for imports in absolute value* (i.e., ignoring negative sign) *must at least exceed unity* for a successful policy of devaluation. Because only in that case devaluation not only increases the *physical volume* of exports and depresses the *physical volume* of imports, but it also improves the overall international *financial* position of the devaluing country by increasing its *net* earning of foreign currency.[4]

Algebraically, this condition can be obtained by defining the relevant elasticities carefully. Suppose, the exchange rate, r is the price of a unit of foreign currency in terms of domestic currency. If P_d is the price of exports in *domestic* currency, then, P_d/r = price of exports in *foreign* currency.

Consequently, the *price elasticity of the foreigners' demand for exports*, denoted by n_e ($n_e > 0$), is given as,

$$\frac{\Delta \log (X_e)}{\Delta \log (P_d/r)} = \frac{\Delta X_e/X_e}{(\Delta P_d/P_d - \Delta r/r)} = -n_e \tag{5.23}$$

where X_e is the physical volume of exports.

Similarly, if P_f is the price of imports in *foreign* currency then, $P_f r$ is the price of imports in *domestic* currency. Consequently, the *domestic buyers' price elasticity of import*, denoted by n_m ($n_m > 0$) is,

$$\frac{\Delta \log X_m}{\Delta \log (P_f \cdot r)} = \frac{\Delta X_m/X_m}{(\Delta P_f/P_f + \Delta r/r)} = -n_m \tag{5.24}$$

We assume that all supplies are infinitely elastic so that neither the domestic price of exports (P_d) nor the foreign price of imports (P_f) change when their respective supplies X_e and X_m change, i.e., $\Delta P_d = 0$ and $\Delta P_f = 0$ in (5.23) and (5.24) respectively.

In this case, the percentage increase in the volume of exports as a result of devaluation by $\Delta r / r$ per cent is given from (5.23) as,

$$\frac{\Delta X_e}{X_e} = + n_e \cdot \frac{\Delta r}{r} \qquad \text{if } \Delta P_d = 0 \tag{5.23a}$$

Similarly, the percentage decrease in the volume of import is given from (5.24) as,

$$\frac{\Delta X_m}{X_m} = - n_m \cdot \frac{\Delta r}{r} \qquad \text{if } \Delta P_f = 0 \tag{5.24a}$$

Equation (5.23a) shows the increase in the physical *volume* of exports and equation (5.24a) shows the decrease in the physical *volume* of imports brought about by devaluation which cheapens domestic currency by $\Delta r / r > 0$ per cent in terms of the foreign currency. However, a higher physical volume of exports and a lower physical volume of imports would improve the *financial balance B* of the country only if export earning in foreign currency, $E = (P_d \cdot X_e)/r$ *minus* import expenditure in foreign currency, $M = P_f \cdot X_m$ also increases as a result of devaluation. From the definition of export revenue in foreign currency, i.e.,

$$E = \frac{P_d}{r} \cdot X_e$$

the percentage change in export revenue at constant domestic price (implying $\Delta P_d = 0$) is obtained as,

$$\frac{\Delta E}{E} = \frac{\Delta X_e}{X_e} - \frac{\Delta r}{r}, \qquad \Delta P_d = 0$$

or, using (5.23a),

$$\Delta E = (n_e - 1) \frac{\Delta r}{r} \cdot E \tag{5.25}$$

Similarly, from the definition of the import bill in foreign currency, i.e., $M = P_f \cdot X_m$, the percentage change in the import bill is given as,

$$\frac{\Delta M}{M} = \frac{\Delta X_m}{X_m}, \qquad \text{if } \Delta P_f = 0;$$

or using (5.24a),

$$\Delta M = - n_m \cdot \frac{\Delta r}{r} \cdot k_0 E, \qquad \text{where } k_0 = \frac{M}{E} \tag{5.26}$$

It is to be noticed that k_0 is the *initial* ratio of the import bill to export revenue *prior to* devaluation.

The net *change* in financial balance due to devaluation can be calculated from (5.25) and (5.26) as,

$$\Delta B = \Delta E - \Delta M = (n_e + k_0 n_m - 1)\frac{\Delta r}{r} \cdot E \qquad (5.27)$$

Because, $\Delta r/r > 0$ (i.e., domestic currency cheapened by $\Delta r/r$ per cent) and initial export $E > 0$, devaluation improves trade balance, i.e., $\Delta B > 0$, if from (5.27),

$$n_e + k_0 n_m > 1 \qquad (5.28)$$

In the *special case* of an *initial* trade balance implying $k_0 = 1$, (5.28) reduces to,

$$n_e + n_m > 1, \qquad k_0 = 1 \qquad (5.29)$$

This special condition (5.29), known as the *Marshall–Lerner condition*, needs to be satisfied if devaluation is to yield a trade surplus ($\Delta B > 0$), starting from an initial position of balance in trade (i.e., $k_0 = 1$, implying $E = M$ initially).

When exports and imports are sufficiently price-elastic satisfying a condition like (5.29), devaluation may be successfully used as a weapon of trade rivalry to induce an export surplus, which in turn expands the home market through the foreign trade multiplier for the devaluing country. Nevertheless, such price advantage of devaluation would be largely lost if the foreign trade multiplier operates primarily through price rather than quantity-adjustment (see Chapter 2, pp. 45–51, Figure 2.3 in particular). In such a case, devaluation would lead to a higher domestic price level (P_d), either because the *money* wage rate rises as effective demand expands in a tight labour market, or because *imported* raw materials become more expensive. In either case, unit prime cost could rise (see Chapter 3, pp. 76–8) to such an extent as to completely outweigh the advantage of a lower export price obtained through devaluation. This can be seen from (5.23) where, if $\Delta P_d/P_d$ exceeds $\Delta r/r$, devaluation, on balance has a *negative* effect on the volume exported. Conversely, a decrease in the volume of imports may cause $\Delta P_f/P_f$ to fall so much that the volume of imports increase despite devaluation (see (5.24)). Although any such fall in import price is far less likely in practice due to the *downward* stickiness of cost-determined prices, the general analytical point should now be clear. In so far as devaluation sets in motion a multiplier mechanism based on price-adjustment, the *comparative rate of inflation* (i.e., $\Delta P_d / P_d - \Delta P_f / P_f$) among trade rivals has to be taken into account in ascertaining the *net* price advantage of devaluation. For example, a 10 per cent *higher* rate of inflation in the devaluing country is tantamount roughly to a 10 per cent *appreciation* of its currency which must be set against the percentage by which its currency is devalued.

Currency devaluation is one of the *many* possible ways in which a country may seek to obtain some price advantage over its trade rivals. Similar advantage may also be sought through *subsidising exports* or by offering *export credit* on easier terms to potential buyers. Such policies have the same broad effect of cheapening the price of exported goods. On the import side, a *tariff* on imported commodities or simply a *quota* on imports may be imposed in an attempt to restrict the volume of imports.

However, like devaluation, most of these policies are symptoms of an undercurrent of tension arising from trade rivalry. Occasionally, such rivalry may even break the surface in the form of an open *trade war*, as countries retaliate against one another through such measures as competitive devaluation or increasing tariff barriers. This results in a vicious spiral of retaliatory trade restrictions until almost every concerned trade rival finds its *absolute* volume of trade shrunk in the process.[5] Trade rivalry that originates in the motive of each country striving for a higher *relative* share of the international market may end up with countries finding the *absolute* size of their external markets reduced, as the total volume of world trade decreases through retaliatory restrictions triggered off by a trade war.

Such a vicious spiral cannot come to an end until some standstill agreement is reached. It is followed, very often, by manoeuvres towards freer trade. But freer trade, even when it leads to a larger volume of world trade does not by any means ensure that each country's *relative* share or even its *absolute* volume of trade would not decrease in the process. Indeed, the opposite is often the case, where the economically stronger country with a powerful industrial base gains disproportionately from freer trade by penetrating deeper into the markets of other countries.

Freer trade, as opposed to protection of the home market by the weaker country, is therefore *not* an indication of reduced trade rivalry. Freer trade merely sets the rules for the economically stronger nations to capture a larger share of the international market. Therefore, economically stronger nations have typically championed the cause of free trade. But a nation that could once champion the cause of free trade as the premier industrial power has also been repeatedly forced in history to argue for protectionism once its fortune changed and its international competitive power declined. This was historically most clearly visible in the *changing economic character of imperialism* in the course of the last half of the nineteenth and the first half of the twentieth century.

England, as the very first modern industrial power in the world, did not have serious capitalist trade rivals in the decades immediately succeeding the Industrial Revolution (i.e. roughly around 1840). The doctrine of free trade in commodities could then be combined with the basic rationale of capturing external markets in the absence of serious threat from other capitalist trade rivals. In this early phase, economic imperialism could assume an 'informal' character under the guise of free trade. *Militarism* and the brute force of subjugation were used for colonising territories outside Europe. But since there were enough territories to capture, England could, by and large, widen its empire without coming into direct conflict with other emerging industrial capitalist nations in Europe at least for the time being. Military conquests gave rise to the *formal Empire, which was supplemented by an informal empire or 'sphere of trade influence'*, under the guise of free trade.

It is in the later phase (from around 1880) that *enforced trade on a bilateral basis between the imperialist metropolis and the colonial periphery* begins to appear in more blatant forms. As more capitalist countries in Europe emerged as rival industrial powers, the doctrine of free trade became an increasingly unviable proposition for England. As a result, each imperialist country of Europe tried to get its share of the captive colonial market, which would be more or less its exclusive area of economic influence. Militarism, which in the earlier phase of imperialism was primarily directed to capture external markets, came home to roost. The industrialised countries of capitalist Europe fought wars among themselves to curve out and protect their respective shares of the external markets. Lenin characterised this as *imperialist war*, when militarism of one capitalist nation turns against its capitalist trade rivals in an attempt at redividing the external markets. Thus,

from the 1880s 'imperialism' – the division of the world into formal colonies and 'spheres of influence' of the great powers, generally combined with an attempt to establish deliberately the sort of economic satellite system which Britain had evolved spontaneously – became universally popular among the large powers. For Britain this was a step back. She exchanged the *informal empire* (based on free trade) over most of the under-developed world for the *formal empire* of a quarter of it, plus the older satellite economies.[6]

As the doctrine of free trade began to run out of its use as an aid to maintaining an *informal* trade empire, the economic imperative of dividing the underdeveloped world into formal colonies and de-pendencies of important capitalist powers became increasingly com-pelling. The doctrine of protectionism thus took a peculiar historical turn when each imperialist country sheltered not so much its own domestic market, but forcibly isolated the captive markets of its conquered colonies from its trade rivals. The result was a high degree of *enforced bilateralism in trade* between the metropolitan country and its colonial periphery. Such a pattern of trade persists to some degree even today. For instance, the share of exports and imports of economic dependencies (including direct political colonies) going to or originating from their respective metropolitan country compared as a ratio of the overall share of exports to and import from the underdeveloped world to that particular metropolitan country in-dicates such enforced bilateralism. This has been a marked feature of the trade of the capitalist countries with the underdeveloped world in general. On a rough statistical reckoning for the years 1960–62, the United Kingdom traded three times higher with her dependencies compared with the underdeveloped countries as a whole. For France, the same ratio was nearly eight times, while lesser imperialist powers fell back even more markedly on their dependencies for external trade. For Italy, that ratio was between 15 and 12, for Belgium between 19 and 15 and for Portugal it was a phenomenally high ratio between 64 and 73.[7]

Although it may appear paradoxical that *both* free trade and protectionism historically served the cause of economic expansion-ism, such a paradox is quite superficial. As already pointed out, individual imperialist countries took recourse to either free trade or protectionism depending on their *relative* strength *vis-à-vis* their trade rivals. Thus, trade rivalry in the guise of free trade at one time and protectionism at another time has continued as the dominant theme underlying capitalistic commodity production. In this sense, free trade or protectionism only set different rules, with the same objective of expanding commodity production. And, quite naturally, these rules are mostly set in the interest of the hegemonic capitalist power of the time. As that hegemonic role shifts from one capitalist power to another, the rules may also need to be altered. And, it is usually during this period of transition, when no capitalist country has the un-disputed authority to set the rules that all-out trade wars can more easily break out. It is therefore the nature of this hegemonic power which in the final analysis, shapes the ways in which trade rivalry among capitalist nations is conducted. Although the hegemonic power defines the trade relations among capitalist nations, its hegemony is nowhere more clearly visible than in the area of international finance. Therefore, international finance as a mirror to the power relations among trading capitalist nations deserves our special attention.

B   Lessons of International Financial History

Foreign trade influences the size of the domestic market through a *surplus* or *deficit* in trade. The influence gets magnified several times the size of the original surplus or deficit, as the surplus country expands and the deficit country contracts its domestic market through the foreign trade multiplier (see (5.12)). Since under capitalis-tic commodity production, the output and employment in a capitalist country are primarily governed by the size of its market (see Chapter 2, Section C), such imbalances in trade invariably heightens a sense of trade rivalry. With the total trade of the world *always* in balance (i.e. world export *identically* equals world import), the surplus enjoyed by some countries must have its mirror image in the deficit of others. Thus, trade rivalry typically centres on the question of surplus and deficit in trade.

Nevertheless, no country can enjoy a persistent surplus in or can another country suffer persistent deficit without some device of *international credits and liabilities*. If international trade were or-ganised on a bilateral barter principle, each country would pay for its imported goods directly in terms of its exported goods and trade would necessarily be balanced.[8] Instead, when a country enjoys a trade surplus, it spends through imports less than what it earns through exports; consequently, it must *accumulate* the balance of its income from export over its expenditure on imports as *net addition to financial assets*, showing financial claims over the future goods and services of the deficit country. Conversely, a country running a trade deficit can spend more on imports than what it earns through exports only by decumulating its stock of financial assets, i.e., by increasing its *net financial liability* position. Again, in the aggregate assets and liabilities must balance, i.e., the total increase in financial claims by *all* the surplus countries must be exactly matched by the increase in financial liabilities of *all* the deficit countries. Nevertheless, in this process of matching assets with liabilities, various debt obligations must be created on an international scale. Thus, surpluses and deficits in trade become inextricably linked with devices by which debt obligations are created on an international scale. This, in short, is the problem of creating *international liquidity* or money for conducting trade among nations.

International liquidity differs from national liquidity or money in the fundamental sense that, not every participating country in international trade has the power to create its own debt obligations. Although the right to issue currency as debt obligation has long been the monetary prerogative of the sovereign nation-state, such debt obligations created by one sovereign nation as its currency need not be accepted by another sovereign nation in settlement of international payments. In that case, that national currency or more generally, national 'money' (i.e. debt obligation of the central monetary authority plus the debt obligation of its commercial banking system, see Chapter 4, p. 106, definition (4.15) of money) of a country remains restricted only to national use. It cannot serve as an international medium of exchange or as an international store of value in settlement of payments among the trading nations.

Historically, this problem was overcome by the Gold Standard System. It facilitated trade among nations by requiring each trading country to define the value of its national currency in terms of a certain weight of pure gold. Further, by guaranteeing the *convertibility* of each national currency to an equivalent amount of gold, a major advantage of the Gold Standard System in its time was to liberate international trade from the shackles of *direct* transactions in gold (and other precious metals). Thus, the debt obligation of each trading nation denominated in gold could *indirectly* serve the purpose of gold in international transactions. Not surprisingly, it was particularly in the interest of the leading trading nation of the time, namely Britain to have such a system in order to facilitate trade.

As early as 1821, Britain guaranteed the full convertibility of its national currency into gold. By a special decree, the Bank of England was legally required to redeem its notes into gold bars and coins. At the same time, all prohibitions on melting of coins into gold and export of gold were repealed. Thus Britain, half-way through its Industrial Revolution, initiated the formal era of the Gold Standard. Other nations followed suit sooner or later. With the newly discovered gold-mines of California and Australia around 1850, the world price of gold fell drastically in relation to silver. Gresham's law of bad money driving out good money began to operate and silver coins which had considerably risen in value gradually disappeared from the market. America and France which had so long been maintaining a bimetallic standard of gold and silver, gradually drifted into a *de facto* gold standard in the process. Belgium, Italy and Switzerland whose currencies were linked to the French one, also now moved to the Gold Standard. Germany too abandoned the bimetallic standard in favour of gold, but only after she was fortified by receipts of sufficient gold from France as war repatriation following the Franco-Prussian War (1870). Thus, by 1880 most of the heartland of capitalist Europe and America, and by 1895 most other trading nations in the world had moved on to a Gold Standard.

In theory, the Gold Standard rested on an automatic adjustment mechanism: a country running into trade surplus was supposed to experience net inflow of gold, which in turn would lead to a corresponding expansion in the domestic money supply linked to the gold stock. Under the influence of the Quantity Theory of Money, this was expected to result in higher prices, including a higher price level for goods exported by that surplus country. This in turn reduced its price competitiveness in the world market leading to declining exports until the original export surplus got more or less wiped out.

In practice, such an automatic adjustment mechanism under the Gold Standard was seriously flawed. Not only was the Quantity Theory an unreliable guide in so far as increased money supply could lead to adjustment in *outputs* rather than in prices to negate such tendencies towards equilibrium, but even the basic premise that a trade surplus (deficit) would be associated with net inflow (outflow) of gold did not hold in important instances. Britain, as the most powerful industrial and financial nation of the time, was seldom required to satisfy that basic premise. The debt-obligations created (or underwritten) by the British government enjoyed unquestioned confidence of the rest of the trading world. Therefore, Britain was seldom *actually* required to liquidate her debt obligations by paying in gold to foreign governments. Instead, British debt-obligation itself was considered 'as good as gold' by other creditor nations. This climate of supreme confidence in the British government's promise to liquidate in gold its overseas liabilities allowed her *in practice* to follow an altogether different policy. Over nearly a forty-year period up to the First World War, Britain could adhere to or even manipulate the Gold Standard in a somewhat indirect way.

> "The Bank of England kept very little gold (in relation to money supply) – some say because gold yielded no interest while others are more charitable. Whatever the reason, the consequence was that the Bank was forced to react to slight losses of gold, changing the Bank Rate an incredible number of times per year".[9]

Needless to add, this mechanism of regulating the flow of gold in and out of the London money market through deliberate variations in the interest rate lay outside the theoretical equilibrating mechanism supposed under the Gold Standard. Nevertheless, it could become an eminently practical way for the Bank of England to escape the discipline of the Gold Standard only because of the complete *international confidence* in the convertibility of the British currency (and other official debt obligations) into gold.

Even this brief historical sketch of the Gold Standard emphasises the crucial distinction between the *formal and the informal aspect of convertibility* of the national currency. Formally, every currency under the Gold Standard was convertible into gold at the stipulated rate. However, *informally* the British sterling was seldom required to be converted into gold because of the complete international confidence in the immediate convertibility into gold of any official British debt obligation. This permitted the British sterling to increasingly act as a *substitute* for gold in international transactions. Thus, for several decades before the First World War (1914–18), the British sterling played the role of a *proto-reserve currency* on par with gold, i.e. like gold, it served as an *'international store of wealth'*. Therefore, notwithstanding the formal discipline of the Gold Standard, a national currency, namely the British sterling informally played the role of an international reserve, due to the total confidence it commanded of all the trading nations.

With the outbreak of the First World War (1914), all major countries were forced to suspend the convertibility of their national currencies into gold in order to finance their war expenditures. At least the temporary delinking of national currencies from their respective gold reserve base created new compulsions. Central banks of the major trading nations were now compelled as a matter of expediency to hold in reserve other national currencies instead of gold to settle international payments. Although even at the height of the Gold Standard during the pre-1914 period, several countries had invested part of their gold reserves in London to obtain in exchange interest-bearing British financial assets denominated in sterling, the system now extended to some other national currencies. This system in which *several* national currencies (along with the British sterling) served at least partly as international *reserve* in exchange of gold is known as the Gold Exchange Standard. The Gold Exchange Standard differed from the earlier Gold Standard not so much in economic content as in the changed balance of financial powers among nations. The privilege so far informally enjoyed *only* by the British sterling now came to be extended to *several* other national currencies, as many central banks openly held various national currencies as part of their international reserve. Thus, the Gold Exchange Standard saw the emergence of more than one national currency in the role of international reserve currency. This threatened the earlier undisputed supremacy of the British sterling. Thus, by the early 1920s, central banks of several countries reported significant holdings of British sterling, American dollar as well as French franc (roughly in that order of quantitative importance) along with gold as their reserve.

In an attempt to regain the pre-war supremacy of her currency, Britain prematurely returned to the Gold Standard in 1925, pegging the pound at the *old* pre-war rate of gold parity. However, this attempt to reassure other nations of the convertibility of the sterling into gold at the old rate soon turned out to be unviable. The competitive position of Britain in world trade had considerably declined in the mean time. Thus, between 1926 and 1930 both the United States and France ran large trade surpluses. And, the Bank of France also began to steadily convert the payments surplus into sterling claims for a final show-down with Britain over the British attempt to reinstate the sterling. The impending 'run' on the small gold reserve of Britain finally began in early 1931. Britain was largely defenceless; with international confidence in her currency shaken, she could no longer effectively resort to drawing in other countries' gold reserves to London by just raising her bank rate. At this critical moment, France also began to convert her accumulated sterling claim into gold and Britain was forced to abandon the Gold Standard in the summer of 1931.

With the collapse of the convertibility into gold of the most important reserve currency of the time, namely the British sterling, a major financial crisis developed on two fronts. On the one hand, several countries holding a substantial sterling reserve in place of gold had no option but to leave the Gold Standard as well. This in turn caused wide fluctuations in the exchange rates of their currencies. On the other hand innumerable bankruptcies and financial failures resulted, signalled first by the collapse of Credit Anstalt Rothschild Bank in Vienna.

In this chaotic financial climate surrounded by the deep depression of the early 1930s, the United States too temporarily left the Gold Standard to devalue the dollar in 1933 and returned again to the Gold Standard in 1934 at a lower rate of gold parity. However, except for a brief period of non-convertibility into gold, France along with Italy stuck to a sort of Gold Standard between 1931 and 1936. But these 'gold bloc countries' had to take increasing recourse to tariff and other forms of trade barrier to protect themselves against the depreciating currencies of their trade rivals who had quit the Gold Standard. This triggered off large-scale *trade war* and 'beggar-my-neighbour' policies in trade where each country was trying to protect or even increase its exports and cut down on its imports. The mutually annihilating trade war resulting in a shrinking international market could be called to a halt only after a 'Stand Still Agreement' was reached in 1936 between the 'gold bloc countries' led by France on the one hand and Britain and the United States on the other.[10]

Such an all-out trade war against the background of the collapse of the Gold Exchange Standard demonstrates the *inherent instability of trade rivalry among capitalist nations without the hegemonic role of any single capitalist power*. Although that hegemony originates in *trade* superiority, it is gradually consolidated through the *financial* supremacy of a national currency serving as international reserve. With *several* national currencies simultaneously serving as international reserve, the Gold Exchange Standard clearly marked the end of the undisputed financial supremacy of Britain. And, when Britain was unable to regain her hegemony by being forced to abandon the Gold Standard in 1931, no other country could assume that role of hegemony to set its own rules of international finance. Without such established rules, the stage was set for the unrelenting trade war of 1931–6.

In a way, the experience of the Gold Exchange Standard also had a positive aspect. It demonstrated the possibility of creating *any required level of international liquidity through national debt obligations* (i.e., national currency) without the constraint of gold. However, this could be achieved only if international confidence in national currencies could be maintained. On the other hand, an individual nation can create any amount of such debt obligations in its national self-interest. And, such national self-interest is almost certain to clash with international interest in the longer run because, the *use of any national currency as international reserve bestows on the country the right to 'borrow' internationally* without restraint. Thus, the country can 'purchase' any amount of real goods and services from other countries simply by accumulating monetary liabilities abroad. However, as financial liabilities accumulate abroad, international confidence in that national currency gradually gets shaken (as happened in the case of the British sterling in 1931) and acute financial instability returns to the international scene. As experience showed (1931–6), this could even degenerate into fierce trade wars.

Such instability in international trade and finance could largely be overcome if *two conditions* could be satisfied through mutual agreement among the trading nations. First, it requires the enforcement of *stable exchange rates* so that no nation would use devaluation as a means to creating trade surplus (see pp. 143–6, Chapter 5). The second and politically more difficult condition is to create a genuinely *international mechanism for settling international payments which depends neither on gold nor on any national currency.* These, in effect, were the main objectives of the Keynes Plan (1942).

As Keynes argued, it had to be a payment mechanism based on an internationally agreed form of debt obligation created by an International Clearing Union. It was called the 'bancor' and a vital provision of the Plan required commitment of all member states to accept, in lieu of gold payment and without limit, such units of 'bancor' transferred to their credit in the accounting books of the

Clearing Union in settlement of any balances due to them from any other member. The practical soundness of the argument lay in its obvious analogy with credit creation by the national banking system: just as 'no depositor in a local bank suffers because of balances, which he leaves idle, are employed to finance the business of someone else',[11] so would no surplus country suffer by accepting such 'bancor' to its credit. It would only leave its command over the resources of the countries in the *general* pool of the Clearing Union rather than in the vault of its own central bank. But the surplus country always remains entitled to use its credit accumulated in 'bancors' to finance its international payment at any time, just as it could have used the reserve held in its own central bank. In short, it was a proposal to create an internationally agreed credit mechanism, instead of hoarding in gold or in other national currencies by the individual central banks of the surplus countries.

In the Agreements at Bretton Woods (1945) that followed, the Keynes Plan was modified to the point of being virtually defeated, not on grounds of logic but on grounds of the immediate post-war balance of economic power among nations. The ultimate failure to create a genuine international credit mechanism at Bretton Woods, delinked from national currencies or gold, must be traced back to the dominant national self-interest of the United States. The area of agreement was politically limited because the United States which by the end of the Second World War had acquired an unassailable position of economic and political hegemony over the rest of the capitalist world, was in no mood to accept any international monetary system that could possibly restrict her hegemonic role. Refusing to learn from the earlier British experience, the United States insisted on the American dollar serving as the *'reserve currency'*. With a war-devastated Europe desperately requiring American help and America already controlling around 80 per cent of the monetary gold reserve of the (non-socialist) world and over 20 per cent of world trade, there could possibly be no serious challenge to this scheme. The dollar was accepted at its pre-war (1934) convertibility rate at 35 dollars to an ounce of pure gold, while all other currencies were required to maintain their fixed par value *vis-à-vis* the dollar. Thus, *in appearance it was a system of indirect convertibility of all currencies into gold through their dollar parity; in practice it soon turned out to be a system of their convertibility only into dollar.*

The *dollar standard* created at Bretton Woods formally bestowed on the national currency of the United States the privilege of being the international reserve currency. Nevertheless, this privilege could not be enjoyed during the period of reconstruction of war-devastated Europe under the Marshall Plan. The Marshall Plan, between the years 1948 to 1952, provided Western Europe with massive *bilateral* aid (of the order of US 17 billion dollars). And yet, until about the mid-1950s, the world saw a period of acute *dollar shortage* because all such US grants and aids for reconstruction were almost immediately spent back on American goods and services, resulting in large and systematic trade surplus for the United States during this period. The systematic trade surplus of the United States created the shortage of dollars in Europe. International liquidity in the form of the dollar was available to Europe only through *net capital account lending* and transfer (e.g. as grant or aid) by the United States.

The dollar shortage illustrated with particular force the *logistical problem inherrent in the use of any national currency as international reserve.* So long as the United States ran a persistent trade surplus and was spending less on imports than what she earned through exports, foreign countries could not earn adquate dollars for their international reserve. It required either the United States to run a large trade deficit or to lend massively on its capital account to create adequate international liquidity in the form of dollars. Paradoxically, however, such persistent trade deficit or capital account lending, say, through foreign investment, could only undermine international confidence in the dollar as foreign countries kept accumulating the monetary liabilities of the United States.

The course of events that followed over the next two decades or so (roughly, 1953–73) largely bore out this paradoxical pattern. With the restoration of their war devastated economies, countries of Western Europe and Japan began to improve their trade position *vis-à-vis* the United States. In December 1958, thirteen major European capitalist nations introduced the *convertibility* of their currencies into dollars in accordance with the agreement at Bretton Woods. The system of convertibility envisaged at Bretton Woods now came into operation involving, (i) *official*, i.e. central bank to central bank, convertibility of the dollar into gold and, (ii) *free market* convertibility of major west European currencies into dollars.

The free convertibility of the major European currencies into dollars marked the end of the period of acute dollar shortage. It also indicated that the central banks of those European countries were holding enough dollars in reserve to support the free market convertibility of their currencies. However, it is of crucial importance to realise that such adequate *dollar reserve* of the European countries was made possible *not through their trade surplus vis-à-vis* the United States, *but mostly through direct foreign investment by the United States* since the mid-1950s. Although the United States sustained on an average a trade *surplus vis-à-vis* the rest of the world till the late 1960s, this did *not* result in a dollar shortage, because through this period she was massively *lending on capital account* in the form of direct foreign investment (and military and other transfers). Thus, the cumulative total of American direct foreign investment rose from $7.2 billion at the time of the agreement at Bretton Woods (1945–6) to $34.7 billion in 1961 and $86.0 billion in 1971, i.e., the annual rate of American direct foreign investment was over $3 billion during this entire period (1946–71). The major part of this investment, about 60 per cent on an average, went to Europe. As a result, major European countries acquired enough dollars in reserve to make their currencies freely convertible into dollars from 1958 onwards.

The broad mechanism of financing of American investment in Europe was *initially* (i.e., till about the mid-1960s) through the central banks in Europe. The European central banks advanced equivalent national currencies against the dollar liabilities of the United States which they held in reserve. The national currencies thus obtained were used mostly by American multinational corporations to invest aggressively in Europe, often taking over earlier European-owned firms. Thus, while American direct foreign investment extended control over productive assets in Europe, European central banks had to be largely content with the holding of the monetary liabilities of the United States.

Although the Bretton Woods Agreement presumed that all such international financial transactions would be conducted mostly through the central banks, the situation began to change rapidly from around the mid-1960s. Commercial banks of American and European origin, located *outside* the United States began holding dollar deposits against which they also advanced credit in dollars. Thus began the phenomenal growth of the *Euro-dollar market*, where commercial banks although located outside the United States, created debt obligations denominated in dollars. Such dollar denominated loans originating outside the United States grew at the phenomenal compound rate of over 26 per cent per annum between 1965 and 1982.

And, by 1973, such dollar-denominated transactions by the commercial banks outside the United States *exceeded* the total volume of dollar transactions by the European central banks.

The transition from a situation of acute *dollar shortage* to its abundance or *dollar glut* therefore came in two distinct phases. In the first phase, European central banks acquired adequate dollar reserves through large direct foreign investment (and military aid) by the United States in Europe. In the second phase, this mechanism was overtaken by dollar denominated loans created in the Euro-dollar market. Analytically, however, the same dollar performed two rather distinct functions of money in this process. During the period of the dollar shortage, the dollar primarily served *as a medium of* (temporal) *exchange*, e.g., dollars made available to Europe through Marshall aid were more or less directly and immediately spent back on American goods and services. In this sense, the dollar transfers meant equivalent transfers of *real goods and services from the United States to Europe*. However, the dollar served quite a different function *as a store of international wealth* through its reserve currency status, as a dollar glut began to develop, because American multinational firms now purchased real goods and services in Europe against their overseas dollar liabilities. Consequently, a transfer of *real goods and services from Europe to the United States* took place under the reserve currency status of the dollar.

This privilege of 'shopping around the world' by simply accumulating monetary liabilities abroad could be (and was) exercised by the United States in the name of providing the world with enough international liquidity (i.e. dollars) under the Bretton Woods arrangements.

However, such accumulation of overseas dollar liabilities mirroring the privilege of the reserve currency status of the dollar, was an unviable proposition in the longer run. It gradually reduced international confidence in the convertibility of the dollar into gold and other currencies. As a result, most countries began diversifying their currency portfolios by converting dollars into other currencies or into gold. This meant a steady erosion of the reserve position of the United States. In 1950, the ratio of total international reserve (gold plus foreign currencies) to dollar liabilities held abroad stood as high as 2.7 times. This ratio of the *reserve backing* of the dollar came down to 1.6 by 1956, it was less than 0.5 by 1967 and even less than 0.3 by 1970.

By this time, the United States was in no position to maintain the convertibility of the dollar in terms of the international reserves that she held. Heavy speculation against the dollar was already underway since at least November 1967, when the British sterling was devalued. There were several piecemeal attempts made to save the dollar. For instance, in a Washington meeting in March 1968, major central bankers agreed to a two-tier price system for gold – *official* conversion rate only among central banks at the same old Bretton Wood parity of $35 to an ounce of gold and a free market price for *non-official* conversion. A little later in 1968, the then President of the United States announced a programme for eliminating US payments deficits through such measures as restriction on direct foreign investment by American firms, reduction in American military spending abroad (especially on the Vietnam war) and finally, through attracting foreign finance into the United States by means of interest rate differential and forward market intervention. This was followed by the United States persuading West Germany to appreciate her currency in 1969 in an attempt to improve the balance of trade position of the United States.

Nevertheless, such manoeuvres proved ineffective. The inherent instability of using a national currency as the international reserve had, by now, surfaced as an irreversible process because of the enormous overhang of accumulated dollar liabilities abroad. Massive conversion of those dollar liabilities into gold and other currencies, especially into West German Mark and Japanese Yen, emerged as the unmistakable sentiments in all major foreign exchange markets. Between the first quarter of 1970 and the second quarter of 1971, foreign exchange (mostly dollar) holdings of West Germany doubled from 6 to 12 billion dollars while that of Japan went up more than five times from 2.4 to 12.7 billion dollars. These two close allies of the United States were intervening in the market to buy dollars against the rising tide of selling dollars in order to maintain the exchange rate of the dollar in terms of their own currencies. Both West Germany and Japan also had their national self-interest in not letting the dollar depreciate so that, their competitive trade position did not deteriorate *vis-à-vis* the United States as their major trade partner. However, the situation was already beyond control; in May 1971 several European countries felt compelled to allow a *joint float* of their currencies. It meant letting the forces of demand and supply in the foreign exchange markets settle the exchange rate between the dollar and their currency basket. Major cracks in the foundations of the Bretton Woods System were now apparent and the United States confirmed it by taking the *unilateral* decision to indefinitely suspend the official Bretton Wood convertibility of dollar into gold in August 1971. *Gold became demonetised* and for all practical purposes, the Bretton Woods System collapsed from that date.

Attempts at restoration followed. The Smithsonian Agreement (December 1972) tried to appreciate all major currencies simultaneously in relation to a make-believe 'central value' of the dollar at $38 to an ounce of gold, while the United States continued with her policy of non-convertibility of dollars into gold. However, such *de facto* depreciation of the dollar failed to improve US balance of payments and there was hardly any reason for restoration of confidence in that make-believe Smithsonian 'central value' of the dollar. By March 1973, there was yet another round of massive selling of dollars, which forced major currencies to finally delink from the dollar. Some European countries (e.g., France, Germany, Benelux, Denmark, Norway and Sweden) agreed to a *joint float* as an extension of their earlier 'snake-in-the-tunnel' agreement (April 1972). This agreement had already created a mechanism of narrow variation in the exchange rates among these currencies through co-ordinated intervention in the foreign exchange market. It subsequently evolved into European Currency Unit (ECU) agreement. Some other countries like Japan, Canada and Switzerland decided on an *independent float* of their respective national currencies. The Bretton Woods system had no longer any relevance, except perhaps for some financially less important countries which continued to peg on the dollar either directly (54 countries in 1975) or indirectly through their continued peg on the French franc (13 in 1975) and the British sterling (10 in 1975). The par value system originally erected at Bretton Woods was thus replaced by a non-system – some countries on joint float, some on independent float, and some less important currencies pegged to the dollar, franc or sterling as the case may be. It only remained for the IMF to formally accept this non-system, which its Interim Committee obligingly did, in its Jamaica meeting of January 1976. Since then the capitalist world has been operating on such a confused system comprising different types of 'floats' between major national currencies or groups of currencies, where both the nature of the 'floats' and the currency groupings keep changing from time to time. International monetary arrangements have been largely left to the blind forces of 'demand and supply' in all the major foreign exchange markets, strongly influenced by speculation on currencies.

Despite differences in details, there is an obvious *historical parallel* between Britain's abandonment of the Gold Standard in 1931 and the collapse of the Bretton Wood official convertibility of the dollar into gold in 1971. The analogy is based on the fact that both Britain and the United States lost the international status of their currencies as proto-reserve and reserve currency respectively under the increasing weight of the overseas monetary liabilities they had gradually built up. And yet, the building up of such foreign liabilities is an inevitable aspect of the use of any national currency as international reserve, because it bestows on that national currency the privilege to 'shop around the world' against its mere paper liabilities at least in the short run. Consequently, that privilege becomes an essential weapon in an attempt to maintain trade supremacy. The reserve currency country undertakes a massive programme of direct foreign investment (and military adventures) to extend its control over world resources. It finances such a programme by accumulating monetary liabilities abroad. A national currency in its role as international reserve thus helps to *shift the focus of trade rivalry from simply achieving a trade surplus to controlling external resources through foreign investment* (or 'export of capital' as Lenin called it). At least in the short run, the reserve currency country has a decisive advantage in so far as it finances such foreign investment through creating monetary liabilities abroad. Its trade rivals have to finance their foreign investments only through achieving surplus in trade. Nevertheless, such a strategy is self-defeating in the longer run because the fundamental strength of a national currency depends on the strength of its national *industries* to out-perform trade rivals and sustain a steady trade surplus over time. Indeed, both the British sterling at its time and the American dollar later were internationally accepted as reserve currencies precisely because Britain and America had been the leading industrial powers of the time. In the longer run, such financial supremacy cannot be maintained without industrial supremacy.

And yet, the historical compulsions of financial supremacy pulls the country in a different direction. The extensive use of any national currency as international reserve brings with it a steady development and consolidation of financial interests in the form of international banking, insurance and financial intermediation in general. Such interests of 'high finance', which we may describe as the interests of *finance capital* (as opposed to industrial capital), gradually acquire a *supranational* dimension through its role as the financier of the world. Thus, 'the City' emerged as the dominant international financial centre at the height of the Gold Standard and so did 'Wall Street' at a later date. In both cases, their importance as centres of international finance gradually outstepped the industrial or trading importance of the country. Consequently, an *asymmetry developed between the 'real' and financial weight* of the country in the world economy. For instance, on a rough estimate (relating to 1983), the United States contributed about 25 per cent of the gross product of the world and about 38 per cent of the OECD total, while its trading weight was only 13 per cent of world exports and about 15 per cent of world imports of primary products. In contrast to these weights in 'real' terms, 75 to 80 per cent of all international loans were denominated in dollars; some 55 per cent of world trade was invoiced in dollars (over 90 per cent of world trade in oil is denominated in dollars) and the central banks around the world hold about 75 per cent of their foreign currency reserves in dollars. Such marked *disproportionality between the 'real' and the financial weights becomes the breeding ground for conflict between supranational financial and national industrial interests.*

Historically, this happened in the case of Britain after the First World War when she hurriedly returned to the Gold Standard in 1925, pegging the pound at the old, pre-war gold parity rate. The objective of a strong national currency in the interest of the *international* role of British finance capital was counterposed against the objective of a high level of employment in domestic industries. Even Winston Churchill observed, 'the Governor [of the Bank of England] shows himself perfectly happy in the spectacle of Britain possessing the finest credit in the world simultaneously with a million and a quarter unemployed . . . . I would rather see Finance less proud and Industry more content'.[12] And yet, the City badly needed that rating of 'the finest credit in the world' through creating the image of a strong and unfaltering sterling, although it undermined the international competitiveness of British industries. Only when Britain was forced to abandon the Gold Standard (1931), the prestige of 'the City' was sufficiently discredited at least temporarily, to make arguments in favour of domestic industry and employment politically more acceptable. Keynesian theory in support of *national* economic policies, designed to defend the level of employment in domestic industries against depressive influences of an over-valued national currency could find political acceptance only under those circumstances.

Again the historical parallel with the United States is not far away. Similar experiences are being repeated now (1980–84) in the United States under the guise of monetarism and in a reversal of Keynesian policies.[13] So long as the United States was the top industrial power among the trading nations, no contradiction emerged between her *national industrial* and *international financial* interests. Indeed, the two *complemented* each other just as British industrial and financial interests could maintain a symbiotic relationship at the height of the Gold Standard. However, along with the extensive use of the dollar as the international reserve currency under the Bretton Woods System (1946–73), American finance capital also began to assume inevitably its *supranational* character. American banking expanded overseas and began lending to industries not necessarily of American origin; American shipping and insurance coverage extended to world trade in which American firms were not involved. In short, these operations of international, financial intermediation assumed *relative autonomy* from the national industrial base in the United States. Repeating a familiar historical course traced by Britain in an earlier period, this relative autonomy of US finance capital paved the way for the emergence of the contradiction between finance and industry. The contradiction grew as the relative industrial and trading position of the United States in the world economy declined. Such decline became increasingly visible in the persistent trade deficit of the United States.[14] However, the supranational interest of finance capital in the United States requires the image of a strong dollar to be maintained despite such trade deficits. At least temporarily, this is being achieved in the name of 'monetary discipline'; the tight control of monetary targets preached by monetarism allows the American rates of interest to soar high. In so far as it also creates a high *differential* in the interest rates between the United States on the one hand and most other countries on the other (including Japan and major European countries), it helps to attract speculative 'hot money' from abroad to bridge the trade deficit of the United States. It also creates the illusion of a 'strong' dollar where expectations of capital gains from an appreciating dollar feeds on itself to attract further speculative flows from abroad. Such an artificially bloated dollar, so long as it lasts, serves well the interests of American finance capital, although it makes national industries increasingly less price-competitive and creates serious unemployment at home. Thus, the ideology of monetarism finds a natural ally in the supranational interests of finance capital (and perhaps, not accidentally, both the United States and Britain embraced monetarism because they have historically the two most articulated supranational financial interest groups in the capitalist world, namely the Wall Street and the City).

The paradox inherent in the process of attaining maturity as a capitalist nation is thus reflected in the course of development of finance capital. Finance capital emerges on the strength of the national industrial base and a symbiotic relation exists between finance and industry at the initial stage. It is the industrial supremacy of a country which raises its national currency to the status of the international reserve currency. This creates the conditions necessary for finance to acquire its supranational character. However, as this international role expands, finance capital attains relative autonomy from the national industrial base at the next stage. Conditions for contradiction are thus created. In the final stage, finance capital representing relatively independent economic interests and detached from its earlier national industrial base begins to oppose the national industrial interest, as it requires a 'strong' currency despite a relative decline in the industrial and competitive position of the nation. Such a suicidal confrontation between industry and finance is capable of destroying ultimately the economic hegemony of a nation which created the supranational character of its finance in the first place.

Notes to Chapter 5

1. Recall that all required domestic raw materials are produced (as in Chapter 2) in the vertically integrated consumption, investment and export sectors respectively. Hence, final expenditure (C, I and E) on any of these sectors is *net* of expenditure on *domestic* raw materials.
2. This is again similar to the multiplier analysis for a closed economy given in (2.19) of Chapter 2 (p. 41). Because raising the value of h_i in (2.19) lowers the multiplier from the *demand* side, while raising h_c lowers the same multiplier value from the *supply* side.
3. Recall $\Delta Y/\Delta E$ is defined at $I = \bar{I}$, i.e., $\Delta I = 0$ in (5.12), similarly $\Delta Y/\Delta I$ is defined at $E = \bar{E}$, i.e., $\Delta E = 0$ in (5.12). In more exact notations,

$$\left.\frac{\Delta Y}{\Delta E}\right|_{I=\bar{I}} = \left.\frac{\Delta Y}{\Delta I}\right|_{E=\bar{E}} = \frac{1}{\text{m.p.s.} + \text{m.p.i.}}$$

4. A distinction should be made between the physical and the financial

aspect of devaluation. In so far as devaluation necessarily increases the *physical* volume of exports it creates more employment and output at home through the foreign trade multiplier. However, such increase in the physical volume of exports need not increase export *revenue* if price elasticity of export is small. A similar argument also applies to the reduction in the physical volume of imports induced by devaluation.

5. In Section B of this chapter, we briefly describe the trade war that ensued in 1931 when Britain was forced to abandon the Gold Standard. It did not come to a halt until the Stand Still Agreement was reached in 1936.

6. E. Hobsbawm (1972), *Industry and Empire*, p. 150.

7. The two ratios for each country represent calculations on the basis of export and import share respectively (For England and France these two ratios are sufficiently close.) See, E. Kleiman (1976), 'Trade and the decline of colonialism', especially Tables 1 and 2.

8. In other words, bilateral barter trade would have ensured a double coincidence of demand. As we have already pointed out (see p. 88, Chapter 4), such double coincidence of demand does not necessarily hold in a *monetary* economy in which the act of monetary sale has to be distinguished from the act of monetary purchase.

9. W. Arthur Lewis (1977), *The Evolution of the International Economic Order*, pp. 47–8.

10. Interestingly, when the exchange rates finally settled down following the Stand Still Agreement of 1936, they were not all that different from what they were in 1931. This suggests that competitive devaluation as a part of a trade war may leave the *relative* positions roughly unchanged.

11. Quoted from Article 12 of the 'Proposals by British experts for an International Clearing Union' (dated 18 April 1943), reproduced in the *Proceedings and Documents of the United Nations Monetary and Financial Conference* (United Nations Organization, 1948), pp. 1548–73.

12. Minute of 22 February 1925.

13. Except for the large projected budget deficit of the Government of the United States which is mostly explicable in terms of tax cuts to stimulate private business (the so-called 'supply-side' economics) and sharp rise in military expenditure.

14. The United States had already an average annual trade deficit of 0.6 billion dollar during the years the Bretton Woods System collapsed (1971–3). With some fluctuations, the trade deficit widened over the years. The United States ran a deficit of $42.7 billion in 1982, $64.6 billion in 1983 and is projected (at the time of writing) to cross the $100 billion mark in 1984).

Further Reading

Most standard textbooks on international economics would provide the definition of a country's balance of payments and its relation to national accounts, e.g. Kindleberger (1958), *International Economics*, Chapter 2; also Chapters 9 to 11 discuss materials covered in Section A. Robinson's 'A graphical analysis of the foreign trade multiplier' (Robinson, 1958) sets the analysis in terms of mutual repercussions between two countries, while Metzler's 'Underemployment equilibrium in international trade' (Metzler, 1942) is one of the best, but advanced, readings in this field.

A good historical background to international finance is provided by Kindleberger, *The World in Depression 1929–1939*, especially Chapters 5 to 10 (Kindleberger, 1973). Lewis' *The Evolution of the International Economic Order* (Lewis, 1977) is a highly readable, short account. Johnston's *The Economics of the Euro Market* (Johnston, 1982) provides a comprehensive treatment of some recent developments in international finance.

Lenin's influential essay *Imperialism, the Highest Stage of Capitalism* (Lenin, 1979) was partly inspired by Hobson's *Imperialism: A Study* (Hobson, 1938) which also remains a classic. Kleiman's 'Trade and the decline of colonialism' (Kleiman, 1976) is an interesting empirical essay on the link between the pattern of trade and colonialism in the early 1960s. Rowthorn's essay 'Britain in the world economy', reprinted in his *Capitalism, Conflict and Inflation* (Rowthorn, 1980) provides some data and analysis of British 'finance capital' in the 1970s while Bhaduri and Steindl in (1983), 'The rise of monetarism as a social doctrine' try to understand the politics of monetarism in relation to developments in 'finance capital'.

6
The Instability of Commodity Production

A Business Cycles: Instability in the Level of Commodity Production

A central implication of the commodity producing character of capitalism – namely, the size of the market determining the level of commodity production – is analytically captured by the Keynesian proposition that investment *governs* savings through the multiplier mechanism (see Section C, Chapter 2). Viewed as a circular flow of income, the level of expenditure or investment is the *independent* variable that determines the size of the market and therefore income as well as saving as its fraction as *dependent* variables. This theory of effective demand also captures the *conditions for realisation of profit*. Assuming all wages are consumed, the larger is the expenditure decision of the capitalists on their consumption and on investment, the larger becomes the size of the market for realising the surplus of consumption goods into monetary profits (see, in particular equations (2.7) to (2.9) of Chapter 2). Thus, when workers spend, by assumption, what they get as wages, the profit that the capitalists make depends on what they spend.

In so far as capitalists' consumption (C_p) depends on their profit (say, a constant fraction $(1 - s_p)$ of profit $R = C_p$, as in equation (2.15) of Chapter 2), their consumption expenditure (C_p) is *induced* by profit (R). Therefore, it cannot be treated as a variable independent of profit. It is the other component of capitalists' expenditure namely, *investment* (I) which becomes the *independent variable* of the system *determining the level of profit* (R). This is captured by the simple equation, analogous to the one-commodity model (given in (2.30) of

Chapter 2) as

$$\overrightarrow{I = s_p R} = s_p hY, \qquad \text{where} \quad \frac{R}{Y} = h \tag{6.1}$$

As the direction of the arrow in the above equation (6.1) shows, it is investment (I) which *determines* the level of profit (R) for a given (marginal and average) propensity to save out of profits (s_p). By the same logic, investment also determines the level of income (Y), when both the propensity to save (s_p) and the share of profit in income (h) are given.[1]

However, it can hardly be doubted that investment is not altogether autonomous. Capitalists invest with a view to making profits. The higher are the *expectations* of profit induced by a higher level of *realised* profit, the larger is the investment that capitalists are willing to undertake in general. At the same time, a higher level of *realised* profit also provides capitalist firms with more of *internal* funds to finance new investments. There is an obvious attraction of financing a higher proportion of investment through such internally generated funds because it reduces the risk of investment in illiquid capital goods. When firms borrow funds from outside sources, they have to pay interest charges on the borrowed fund, no matter whether they earn enough profit or not, to cover such interest charges. The *risk of illiquidity* of not having enough monetary profit to service outside loans is less severe, the lower is the *gearing ratio*, i.e. the ratio of borrowed to own funds, in the asset structure of firms. Naturally, a higher level of realised profit creates more favourable conditions for firms to finance their investment plans without exposing themselves to the increasing risk associated with higher gearing ratios.[2]

The level of realised profit therefore has a strong feedback on investment decisions in at least *two* different ways. First, in so far as higher *realised* profit also raises *expectations* of profit, it stimulates investment. Second, higher realised profits reduce the risk of *financing* investment through outside borrowing. Thus, in general, higher *realised* profit favourably influences investment *decisions*.

Nevertheless, such feedback from realised profit to investment decisions is not shown in equation (6.1), in so far as it treats investment as an independent or autonomous variable in the short run. To capture such feedback, it is necessary to treat *investment as a dependent variable*, influenced by considerations of profit. More generally, we would need to postulate a functional relation showing the demand for investment goods, i.e., an *investment function*, in which investment as a dependent variable is induced by other variables (e.g., realised profits) of the economic system.[3]

Although in the present state of economic theory, no generally accepted investment function exists, even the broad nature of the feedback from profit to investment (in lieu of a more precise investment function) should make us aware of an important *two-way relation between investment and profit*. Higher investment causes higher profit through the multiplier relation depicted in (6.1); but higher profit also leads to higher investment *decisions* through some not clearly specified investment function. Schematically, this two-way causation can be summarised as

$$I \xrightarrow[\text{feedback through 'investment function'}]{\text{multiplier relation, as in (6.1)}} R \qquad (6.2a)$$

So long as the share of profit in income remains constant so that the multiplier mechanism operates through quantity- rather than price-adjustment, the two-way relation in (6.2a) can be easily translated into a *similar two-way relation between investment and the level of income (output)*. As before, higher investment leads to higher income through the multiplier; but higher income also has a positive feedback on investment decisions, again through some (ill-specified) investment function. In an important special case, such feedback is often assumed to be transmitted to investment from the *rate of change* rather than the *level* of income. Since investment (net of depreciation) adds to the existing level of productive capacity, the rate of change in expected productive capacity, i.e., *expected change* in the potential level of output may be assumed to exert a strong influence on investment decisions. This special form of the investment function (which has not done too well empirically in many instances) is commonly known as the *acceleration relation*.[4] Taking into account this special form, the two-way causation between investment and income can again be schematically represented as,

$$I \xleftarrow[\substack{\text{feedback through 'investment function'} \\ \text{(with 'acceleration relation' as a special case)}}]{\text{multiplier relation}} Y \qquad (6.2b)$$

The two-sided relation between investment on the one hand and profit or income on the other, represented by (6.2a) and (6.2b) respectively, points to the nature of instability in the level of commodity production that may result. If for some reason the level of investment rises, the level of profit as well as the level of income would rise through the multiplier mechanism given in (6.1). However, higher profit and income has positive feedback on investment as emphasised by the lower arrows in (6.2a) and (6.2b) respectively. As a result investment rises further, raising in turn profit and income again in the next round in a process of *cumulative* expansion. Conversely, a lower level of investment by lowering profit and income through the multiplier (i.e., equation (6.1)) would lower investment in the next round and trigger off a process of *cumulative* contraction.

However, unless such a cumulative process converges, any small autonomous increase (or decrease) in investment would lead to an *indefinite* expansion (or contraction) in the level of profit and income. Such an highly *unstable* economic system cannot survive in reality because, any chance decrease (or increase) in investment would destabilise the system through indefinite contraction (or expansion). Consequently, realistic analysis must, in general, deal with stable systems by identifying *the condition for stability* namely, the condition under which such a cumulative process converges over time.

In order to investigate such stability properly, the time sequence in which the feedbacks occur must be specified more carefully. This may be done by means of *period analysis*. We assume that investment of the *current* period denoted by time 't', leads to generation of profit and income in the same current period 't' through the multiplier relation (6.1). Thus, introducing the time-periods explicitly, (6.1) becomes,

$$I(t) = s_p R(t) \tag{6.3a}$$

$$= s_p h Y(t), \qquad h = \frac{R(t)}{Y(t)}, \text{ a constant} \tag{6.3b}$$

However, current periods profit $R(t)$ or income $Y(t)$ influences investment *decisions* in the current period which materialises as investment expenditure $I(t+1)$ in the *next* period. Thus, the feedback from profit and income to investment assumed in (6.2a) and (6.2b) respectively can be given a more precise algebraic form,

$$I(t+1) = A + aR(t), \qquad a > 0 \tag{6.4a}$$

$$= A + ahY(t), \qquad \frac{R(t)}{Y(t)} = h, \text{ a constant} \tag{6.4b}$$

where A is an arbitrary constant, representing the autonomous part of investment; h is a constant share of profit in income and a is a parameter whose positivity ensures positive feedback from profit to investment with one-period lag.

By making investment dependent on profit or income (lagged by one period), equations (6.4a) or (6.4b) represent *special cases* of the investment function. It should be emphasised that many such more or less equally plausible forms of the investment function are possible which may differ both in terms of the *structure of time lags and the particular variables* that are supposed to influence investment. However, it is worth repeating that no generally acceptable investment function exists because *none* of them captures adequately the investment behaviour of the capitalists. Indeed, all such precisely formulated investment functions turn out in reality to be far too mechanical a description of the investment decisions by the capitalists. Expenditure on long-lived investment goods in an uncertain economic world is perhaps guided more by the gambler's instinct than by any mechanical or rational response. As Keynes had once remarked, rational investment decisions can turn out to be suicidal in an irrational world.

Despite the limited validity of any specific investment function, precise investment functions such as (6.4a) and (6.4b) are analytically useful devices for tracing through time the consequences of the feedback on investment from other economic variables. For example, the two-way relation between investment and profit, postulated in (6.2a), is now fully described by the pair of algebraic equations (6.3a) and (6.4a). Similarly, the mutual feedback between investment and income are captured by (6.3b) and (6.4b).

A graphical analysis of either of these pairs of equations – (6.3a) and (6.4a) or (6.3b) and (6.4b) – clearly demonstrates the *stability condition*, namely the condition that requires to be satisfied for mutual feedback between investment and profit (or income) to gradually *converge* over time. This is illustrated in Figure 9.1 which plots equations (6.3a) and (6.4a) as a pair of straight lines showing the two-sided relation between investment and profit.

Consider, for example an arbitrary initial investment level $I(0)$. Through the multiplier relation (6.3a), as depicted by ray OE through the origin, investment $I(0)$ causes realised profit $R(0)$ at point P_0 on OE. However, profit level $R(0)$ has its feedback on next period's investment through relation (6.4a) which is shown by line AE. Thus,

Figure 6.1   *Relation between investment and profit: the stable case. Ray OE represents the profit realisation condition through the multiplier relation (6.3a), hence* $\tan EOR^* = s_p$. *Line AE represents the feedback from profit to investment, given by (6.4a). The slope of AE corresponds to parameter 'a' and the intercept OA with the vertical axis corresponds to the arbitrary (positive) constant 'A' in equation (6.4a).*

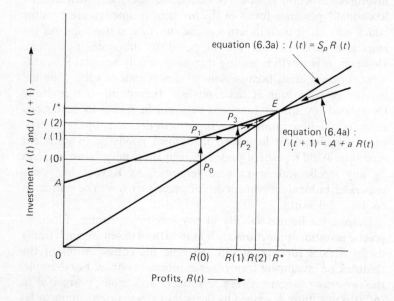

profit $R(0)$ leads to higher investment level $I(1)$ at point P_1 on line AE; that higher investment $I(1)$ causes higher profit $R(1)$ again through the multiplier relation at point P_2 on OE. Higher profit at $R(1)$ now causes higher investment $I(2)$ at point P_3 on AE and so on, until the sequences of rising investment $(I(0), I(1), I(2), \ldots)$ and of rising profit $(R(0), R(1), R(2), \ldots)$ converge at their respective equilibrium values I^* and R^*, represented by point E in Figure 9.1.

Such convergence of rising investment and profit to their equilibrium values is possible only if the *slope* of the line OE, representing the multiplier relation (6.3a) *exceeds* the *slope* of the line AE, representing investment as a function of profit in (6.4a).[5] Algebraically, this yields *the condition for stability* as,

$$s_p > a \tag{6.5}$$

In other words, the two-way relation between investment and profit, depicted by the pair of equations (6.3a) and (6.4a), is *stable* if the marginal propensity to save out of profits (s_p) *exceeds* the marginal propensity to invest out of profits (a).

Similar graphical analysis of equations (6.3b) and (6.4b) would establish an equivalent stability condition,

$$s_p h > a h, \qquad 1 > h > 0 \tag{6.6}$$

This means that the two-way relation between investment and income is stable, provided the marginal propensity to save out of income ($s_p h$) *exceeds* the marginal propensity to invest out of income (ah). Needless to add, the two stability conditions (6.5) and (6.6) are *equivalent*, as (6.6) is algebraically derivable by simply multiplying both sides of (6.5) by the positive fraction h.

The two-sided relation between investment and profit means that higher current investment $I(t)$ causes higher current profit $R(t)$ through (6.3a), which, in turn, stimulates investment of the next period $I(t+1)$ through (6.4a). Thus, a *recursive relation* is established between investment of any two successive periods, which is obtained by inserting (6.3a) in (6.4a) to yield,

$$I(t+1) = A + \left(\frac{a}{s_p}\right) . I(t) \tag{6.7}$$

Thus, investment of period 1 is related to initial investment $I(0)$ by,

$$I(1) = A + \frac{a}{s_p} I(0)$$

Similarly, $I(2) = A + (a/s_p)I(1)$.

However, we substitute for $I(1)$ in terms of $I(0)$ from above to obtain,

$$I(2) = A + \frac{a}{s_p}\left[A + \frac{a}{s_p} I(0)\right] = A\left[1 + \frac{a}{s_p}\right] + \left(\frac{a}{s_p}\right)^2 I(0)$$

Continuing in this manner and substituting for $I(2)$,

$$I(3) = A + \frac{a}{s_p} I(2) = A\left[1 + \frac{a}{s_p} + \left(\frac{a}{s_p}\right)^2\right] + \left(\frac{a}{s_p}\right)^3 . I(0)$$

Note that we can write for the general term $I(t)$,

$$I(t) = A\left[1 + \frac{a}{s_p} + \left(\frac{a}{s_p}\right)^2 + \ldots + \left(\frac{a}{s_p}\right)^{t-1}\right] + \left(\frac{a}{s_p}\right)^t \cdot I(0)$$

Summing the geometric series within the square bracket term on the right-hand side of the above expression, we obtain,

$$I(t) = A\left[\frac{1 - \left(\dfrac{a}{s_p}\right)^t}{1 - \left(\dfrac{a}{s_p}\right)}\right] + \left(\frac{a}{s_p}\right)^t \cdot I(0) \tag{6.8}$$

Thus, by repeatedly using the recursive relation (6.7), the above expression (6.8) relates investment of *any* period t uniquely to the *initial* investment level $I(0)$.[6]

Note that the satisfaction of the earlier stability condition (6.5) would make (a/s_p) a positive fraction *less* than unity. Consequently, $(a/s_p)^t$ will become negligibly small for large values of t. Thus, from expression (6.8) $I(t)$ will show gradual convergence to its equilibrium value I^*, namely

$$I(t) \to I^* = \frac{A}{\left(1 - \dfrac{a}{s_p}\right)} \quad \text{in (6.8) as } t \to \infty \text{ if } s_p > a \tag{6.9}$$

In other words, equation (6.8) depicts the time-path of investment $I(t)$ to provide an algebraic restatement of the earlier graphical analysis of Figure 9.1.[7]

The most important economic aspect of the two-way relation between investment and profit (or income) described so far by means of equations (6.3a) and (6.4a) (or equations (6.3b) and (6.4b) for income) is that it implies a *unidirectional movement* between investment and profit through mutual feedback. This is indeed obvious from the recursive relation (6.7) between investment levels of any two successive periods. Because, no matter whether such a system is stable or not (namely, condition (6.5) is satisfied or not) higher (lower) investment in the current period $I(t)$ leads to still higher (lower) investment in the next period $I(t+1)$ as the coefficient (a/s_p) is positive in (6.7). Such a sequence of rising (or falling) investment level *converges* to an equilibrium value in the stable case (see (6.9)) or it explodes through *indefinite* expansion (or contraction) in the unstable case. However, in neither case does the mutual feedback between investment and profit explain *fluctuations* in the level of investment, i.e., investment rising for some periods and then falling and vice versa. In other words, no *turning points* in the direction of investment can be explained by the mutual feedback between investment and profit discussed so far.

Nevertheless, for a theory of *endogenously generated business cycles* in a capitalist economy, it needs to be shown that there is such an endogenous or internal mechanism by which the level of investment fluctuates on its own over time. Otherwise, we must rely on *exogenous* explanations, where, random external shocks from time to time (e.g., outbreak of war, opening up of new foreign market, technological breakthroughs, etc.) create conditions for such fluctuations in the level of investment. In the course of its actual history, any economy would undoubtedly be subject to such exogenous shocks from time to time. Nevertheless, the remarkable *regularity* with which business cycles occur would seem to suggest that there may be an endogenous mechanism inherent in the capitalist economy which causes investment and therefore, the level of income, determined through the multiplier mechanism, to fluctuate ever time.

For investment to fluctuate in such an endogenous manner, it must be subject to systematic *contradictory pulls*. This can come about through a more *complex structure of time lags* among the relevant economic variables. For instance, instead of the simple one period lag assumed in the feedback from profit to investment in (6.4a), it may be equally plausible to assume that investment *decisions* of the current period depend *both* on the current *level* of profit $R(t)$ as well as on the *rate of change of actual profit*, $[R(t) - R(t-1)]$. In so far as current profit $R(t)$ makes investment less risky through *internal financing* by firms, it would have a positive influence on current investment *decisions*, materialising as next period's investment $I(t+1)$. However, the expected *rate of return on investment* $(\Delta R/I)$ depends on the incremental profit (ΔR) rather than on the total profit (R). Thus, if *expectation* of the incremental profit, $[R(t+1) - R(t)]$ from new investment is guided by the *actual* increment in profit during the current period, i.e. $[R(t) - R(t-1)]$, then we may plausibly assume that the *actual* increment in profit currently realised, i.e., $[R(t) - R(t-1)]$ has a positive feedback on investment decisions.[8] In that case, instead of (6.4a), the feedback from profit to investment could be represented by

$$I(t+1) = A + aR(t) + b[R(t) - R(t-1)]; \qquad a, b > 0$$

Slight rearrangement of terms on the right-hand side of the above investment function clearly shows the *contradictory pulls* generated by the profit levels $R(t)$ and $R(t-1)$ on the level of investment, i.e.,

$$I(t+1) = A + (a+b)R(t) - bR(t-1); \qquad a, b > 0 \tag{6.10}$$

Next period's investment $I(t+1)$ *increases* with $R(t)$, but it *decreases* with $R(t-1)$ in (6.10). Such contradictory pulls of profit levels on investment, when combined with the usual multiplier relation (6.3a) would give rise to fluctuations in the level of investment and income under particular values of the parameters.[9]

Similarly, opposing pulls of the levels of income on investment would be generated if the investment function (6.4b) is replaced by an *acceleration relation*, where the *actual* rate of change of income, $Y(t)$ $- Y(t-1)$ has a positive feedback on current investment *decisions*, realised as *next* period's investment $I(t+1)$. Such an acceleration relation depending on the *actual* change in income yields, instead of (6.4b),

$$I(t+1) = A + V \cdot [Y(t) - Y(t-1)] \tag{6.11}$$

Since $Y(t)$ has a *positive* and $Y(t-1)$ has a *negative* influence on investment $I(t+1)$, the acceleration relation (6.11) in conjunction with the usual multiplier relation (6.3b) can again lead to *fluctuations* in the level of investment and income under certain values of the parameters.[10] This is the simplest case of the *multiplier–accelerator interaction mechanism* leading to business cycles.

It should be noticed that (6.10) and (6.11) represent analytically similar investment functions, because it is the *actual rate of change* in profit or in income that generates the opposing pulls on investment. Thus, the *contradictory* influence on investment through the relevant economic variable, R or Y, provides the common theme in the analysis of the endogenous mechanisms generating business cycles. However, a major problem with such a linear acceleration relation, described by (6.11) or (6.10), arises from the fact that they generate cycles which either gain or lose steadily in amplitude over time. The cycles become larger or die out over time. Consequently, any such linear accelerator is incapable of explaining *sustained* oscillations of more or less constant amplitude that persist indefinitely through time without outside shocks.

The level of investment may oscillate persistently over time through an endogenous mechanism of *self-excitation and relaxation,* if the contradictory influences on the level of investment *vary in intensity* at different levels of investment.[11] Thus, unlike in the case of a linear accelerator described by (6.11), the intensity of those contradictory pulls change over the *phases* of the business cycle as the level of investment varies. This gives rise to various types of *non-linear accelerators,* or more generally, *non-linear feedback* mechanisms from profit (or income) to investment. Such a mechanism can come into operation when investment decisions depend not only on profit or income as in (6.4a) and (6.4b), but also on the existing level of *investment opportunities* in general. For instance, a high current level of investment $I(t)$ realises a high current level of profit $R(t)$ through the multiplier relation (6.3a). This feeds back positively on the next period's investment in the recursive manner shown by equation (6.7). However, as investment keeps rising in a *self-exciting* manner through the recursive relation (6.7), existing opportunities for investment begin to get exhausted rapidly. Thus, a phase of high and rising investment characteristic of an economic 'boom' contains its own seed of destruction through dwindling opportunities for further investment. When such opportunities dwindle sufficiently, the negative influence on investment becomes strong enough to *relax* the self-excitation mechanism of recursively rising investment shown by (6.7). This is the *upper turning point* of a typical business cycle. At that point, a positive but no longer rising level of investment may still continue to exhaust investment opportunities. Hence that negative pressure continues to depress the level of investment further, now in a self-exciting manner operating in reverse. The level of investment could then go on falling, until perhaps, the rock bottom is reached with zero *gross* investment. When *gross* investment is zero, *net* investment is negative which means that even replacement of worn-out capital equipment is not undertaken. In particular, inventories of finished goods are allowed to run down without being replaced and the economy reaches *the* lowest point of the business cycle. This also represents a *lower turning point* of the business cycle, because continued negative *net* investment over time as well as run-down stocks of inventories create opportunities for new investment through replenishing stocks and replacing worn-out capital equipment. Just as high and rising investment contains its own seed of destruction, so does a low level of investment generate its own method of revitalisation through recreation of investment opportunities. With accumulating investment opportunities exerting a positive influence on the level of investment, the level of investment begins to rise gradually. The upturn of the cycle marking the phase of economic recovery starts, only to repeat the cycle all over again.

Formally, such persistence of business cycles through dwindling and recreation of investment opportunities could be captured by treating the autonomous part of investment 'A' in (6.4a), *not* as a constant, but as a time-dependent shift parameter representing the 'state of investment opportunities' in each period. In so far as investment opportunities are diminished by *accumulated* investment from the past, this could be formally exhibited as,

$$A(t) = B - b[I(t) + I(t-1) + \ldots + I(t-n)]$$

$$= B - b \sum_{j=0}^{n} I(t-j), \qquad b > 0 \tag{6.12}$$

where B is an arbitrary (positive) constant and n is the average lifetime of machines, i.e. the average number of periods over which investment embodied in a particular machine-design (technology) survives before it requires replacement.

Using (6.12) in the self-exciting, recursive relation for investment in (6.7), *persistent* business cycles may be generated through continuous dwindling and recreation of investment opportunities in a manner described above. Because high investment over several past periods, i.e., high values of $I(t)$, $I(t-1)$, etc., makes the negative term on the right-hand side of (6.12) large to represent dwindling investment opportunities, so that $A(t)$ shifts downwards, depressing the level of investment. Conversely, low levels of investment over several past periods make the negative term on the right-hand side of (6.12) small to represent a state of high investment opportunities. Thus, high past levels of investment make the shift parameter $A(t)$ assume a low value, whereas low past levels of investment make the parameter $A(t)$ assume a high value roughly in conformity with the pattern of exhaustion and recreation of investment opportunities at the peak and trough of the business cycle assumed in our earlier discussion.

In this theory, business cycles are caused because investment has a tendency to create contradictory effects on *itself*. Higher investment, on the one hand realises higher profit to stimulate further investment as shown by (6.7); but, on the other hand, higher investment saturates the market more rapidly to curb opportunities for further investment, as indicated by (6.12). This is best summed up in Kalecki's remark: 'The tragedy of investment is that it causes crisis because it is useful. Doubtless, many people will consider this theory paradoxical; but it is not the theory which is paradoxical but its subject – the capitalist economy'.[12]

Nevertheless, such a built-in bias of high investment to destroy itself over time can be partly overcome through continuous *innovation* and introduction of *new products*. In addition, persuasive *advertising* can artificially create demand to blur the distinction between 'useful' investment opportunities and investment opportunities that are meant to satisfy artificially created needs by encouraging a culture of 'consumerism' in capitalist societies. Thus, the very logic of successful commodity production must somehow prevent the market from ever becoming saturated so that the very usefulness of investment does not pave the way to crisis through the exhaustion of investment opportunities at any point of time.

From this perspective technological development itself may assume a special role in a capitalist economy. Since the technology for new products embodied in current investment usually has a tendency to make obsolete older forms of capital goods, investment in new technologies and new products may create investment opportunities by accelerating the rate of obsolescence. This is a process of 'creative destruction' – to borrow a term from Schumpeter – which technological dynamism under capitalism almost invariably implies.[13] However, it is not always recognised that, at least part of that technological dynamism springs from the paradoxical nature of investment under capitalistic commodity production: unless current investment can continuously destroy the usefulness of past investment through such technological obsolescence to create space for further investment, the success of commodity production on an expanding scale is not ensured. This destructive role of technology carried out through new investment is at least as important as its productive role in averting regular crises in commodity production in a capitalist economy.

B   The Inflationary Process

When all wages are consumed by assumption, any *increase* in the level of investment must be matched by a corresponding *increase* in saving out of increased profits. This multiplier relation, shown as the profit realisation equations (6.1) or (6.3a) earlier, therefore yields,

$$\Delta I = s_p \Delta R \qquad (6.14)$$

In general such increase in profit (ΔR) can come about through *two* distinct routes. First, the higher effective demand induced by an increase in investment (ΔI) leads to higher output, i.e., the quantities produced adjust upwards to be realised into greater volume of sales. The resulting larger volume of sales at any *given profit margin* per unit of sale, leads to a higher level of profit. This is the quantity-adjustment multiplier described in Chapter 2 (see Figure 2.2 in particular). Alternatively, the profit margin per unit of sale itself may increase in response to higher demand so that, for any *given volume of sales* (and, no quantity-adjustment), higher profits are realised through a *redistribution* of income from wage to profit, which raises the share of profit in income (h). This is the price-adjustment multiplier also described in Chapter 2 (see Figure 2.3 in particular).

The working of *both* the quantity- and the price-adjustment multiplier is shown in Figure 2.4, p. 53, in a simple case based on the analogy with the one-commodity model. In this simple case, recall from equation (2.31) that the percentage increase in *real* investment ($\Delta L_i / L_i$) is matched by corresponding saving in terms of percentage increase in total output and employment ($\Delta L / L$) which shows the quantity-adjustment *plus* percentage increase in the share of profit ($\Delta h / h$) arising from price-adjustment, i.e.

$$\frac{\Delta L_i}{L_i} = \frac{\Delta L}{L} + \frac{\Delta h}{h} \qquad (6.15)$$

Since the share of profit (h) depends on the relationship between the price level (P), the *money* wage rate (w) and the level of labour productivity (x) through the relation given, for example, in (3.2) of Chapter 3, i.e.,

$$\frac{w}{P} = x(1-h)$$

we obtain the percentage change in the share of profit from logarithmic differentiation of the above equation. It yields on simplification,

$$\frac{\Delta h}{h} = \frac{(1-h)}{h} \cdot \left[\frac{\Delta P}{P} + \frac{\Delta x}{x} - \frac{\Delta w}{w} \right] \qquad (6.16)$$

We can now combine equations (6.15) and (6.16) to obtain on rearrangement of terms,

$$\frac{\Delta P}{P} = \frac{h}{(1-h)} \cdot \left(\frac{\Delta L_i}{L_i} - \frac{\Delta L}{L} \right) + \left(\frac{\Delta w}{w} - \frac{\Delta x}{x} \right) \tag{6.17}$$

Thus, equation (6.17) shows the percentage increase in the price level $(\Delta P/P)$ required to balance higher investment $(\Delta L_i/L_i)$ with higher saving *given* the extent of quantity-adjustment $(\Delta L/L)$ as well as percentage increases in the money wage rate $(\Delta w/w)$ and in the level of labour productivity $(\Delta x/x)$. In particular, it should be noted that w/x represents wage cost per unit of output (see (3.2), p. 67) so that, the last bracketed term on the right-hand side of (6.17), namely

$$\left(\frac{\Delta w}{w} - \frac{\Delta x}{x} \right)$$

simply shows the percentage increase in unit variable (or prime) cost which has to be compensated through a percentage increase in price.

A *special case* of equation (6.17) arises when there is no quantity adjustment at all. For instance, the economy may be at full employment or at full capacity utilisation so that, by assumption, the quantity adjustment term $\Delta L/L$ vanishes. In this case, (6.17) reduces to its simpler form,

$$\frac{\Delta P}{P} = \frac{h}{(1-h)} \left(\frac{\Delta L_i}{L_i} \right) + \left(\frac{\Delta w}{w} - \frac{\Delta x}{x} \right), \text{ because } \frac{\Delta L}{L} = 0 \tag{6.17a}$$

Equation (6.17a) shows the extent of price rise required to close an *inflationary gap*, i.e., the gap opened by investment exceeding its full employment level, namely

$$\Delta L_i = (L_i - L_i^f) \tag{6.17b}$$

where L_i^f is the number of workers in the investment sector required to maintain full employment in the economy.[14]

Consider now an arithmetical example which illustrates the extent of price rise required to close such an inflationary gap.

Suppose $L_i^f = 100$, i.e., the full employment level of investment requires 100 workers in the investment sector. An inflationary gap in terms of higher demand for consumption goods may be created by employing more than 100 workers in the investment sector, i.e. say, L_i = 114. Or, from (6.17b), $\Delta L_i = 14$. If the *initial* share of profit in income (h) at full employment (i.e., when $L_i^f = 100$) is given at 30 per cent, i.e.

$$h = 0.30$$

and the percentage rise in the *money* wage rate and in labour productivity are 5 per cent and 2 per cent respectively[15] i.e.,

$$\frac{\Delta w}{w} = 0.05 \quad \text{and} \quad \frac{\Delta x}{x} = 0.02$$

then the required percentage increase in price to close the inflationary gap can be computed from (6.17a) as,

$$\frac{\Delta P}{P} = \frac{0.3}{(1-0.3)} \cdot \left(\frac{14}{100} \right) + (0.05 - 0.02) = 0.09$$

i.e., 9 per cent. Alternatively, in terms of (6.16) this entails $\Delta h/h$ = 0.026 (approximately), so that the share of profit in income increases from an initial 30 per cent to almost 31 per cent in order to generate enough savings to match a higher level of investment at full employment (see also, Figure 2.4, p. 67).

Although the *demand* for surplus consumption goods created by additional employment in the investment sector (e.g. 14 per cent in the above example) is met through a fall in the *real* wage rate and a corresponding rise in the share of profit (h), over and above any gain in labour productivity (2 per cent in the above example), such fall in the *real* wage rate occurs despite increased *money* wages (by 5 per cent in the above example). Thus, the *nominal* (money) price level rises due to two analytically distinguishable effects:

(a) Prices rise as labour cost per unit of output (w/x) increases. This is shown in percentage terms by the last bracketed expression ($\Delta w/w - \Delta x/x$) on the right-hand side of (6.17) or (6.17a), and amounts to $(0.05 - 0.02) = 0.03$, i.e. 3 per cent in the above example. This constitutes the *cost-push* element in the price rise.

(b) If prices rise merely to cover such labour cost per unit of output, the share of profit, defined as $h = (1 - w/px)$, would remain constant, as price (p) and labour cost per unit of output (w/x) increase by the same proportion. To finance a higher level of *real* investment ($\Delta L_i/L_i = 14$ per cent in the above example), the share of profit must increase and the *real* wage rate must fall, if no quantity adjustment (except for gain in labour productivity) is permitted by assumption. This is shown by the first term, $(h/1 - h) \cdot (\Delta L_i/L_i)$ on the right-hand side of (6.17a). It constitutes the *demand-pull* element of price rise and shows the reduction in the *real* wage rate necessary to eliminate the excess demand for consumption goods generated by higher investment at full employment (see also (2.29a) and (2.29b) of Chapter 2, p. 50).

However, once prices have risen *sufficiently* either through cost-push or through the demand-pull effect or both (as shown by (6.17a)) to generate enough additional saving to match the additional investment (see (6.14)), the basic macroeconomic balance is restored. Consequently, the inflationary gap is closed at full employment with perhaps a higher share of profit (h) to neutralise the forces of demand-pull.

Such neutralisation is impossible and the share of profit cannot increase if *money* wage rate rises faster than price *plus* labour productivity in percentage terms. This is evident from (6.16), where Δh cannot be positive (i.e., $\Delta h \leqslant 0$) if,

$$\frac{\Delta w}{w} > \left(\frac{\Delta P}{P} + \frac{\Delta x}{x}\right) \tag{6.18}$$

In particular, if labour productivity remains constant ($\Delta x/x = 0$), *money* wage rate rising faster than price must imply that the *real* wage rate is inflexible downwards. Consequently, no redistribution of income from wage to profit is possible to bridge the inflationary gap of excess demand for consumption goods created by additional investment at full employment. Such downward inflexibility of the *real* wage rate creates an *inflationary barrier* at full employment. Any additional investment at that full employment level creates an inflationary gap that can no longer be closed due to the operation of the inflationary barrier. As a result, a process of inflationary price rise, propelled by persistent excess demand for consumption goods, continues *indefinitely* through time (see Figure 2.4, p. 67).

Such an inflationary barrier points to a situation where workers successfully defend their *real* wage rate at full employment. However, even if workers fail to defend their real wage rate, they might continuously *attempt* to protect it, and in the very *attempt* at restoring their real wage rate, a persistent process of inflation may be triggered off *despite the elimination* of the excess demand for consumption goods through an *initial* reduction in the real wage rate.

To analyse such a situation where inflation persists despite no excess demand, consider a case where there is no rise in *money* wage rate ($\Delta w/w = 0$) or in the level of labour productivity ($\Delta x/x = 0$) in the *initial* period. However, during that initial period, real investment increases by $\Delta L_i/L_i$. If the price level rises by k per cent in the *initial* period, where k is given from (6.17a) as,

$$k = \frac{\Delta P}{P} = \frac{h}{1-h} \cdot \left(\frac{\Delta L_i}{L_i} \right), \quad \frac{\Delta w}{w} = \frac{\Delta x}{x} = 0 \quad \text{by assumption,}$$

then the *real* wage rate is sufficiently reduced by k per cent, to close *entirely* the inflationary gap caused by higher initial investment ($\Delta L_i/L_i$). Hence on the basis of a conventional *demand-pull* explanation of the inflationary process, there should be no reason for *further* price rise. However, in an *attempt* to restore their *real* wage rate to its earlier level, if workers bargain for a k per cent increase in their *money* wage rate in the *next* period, then this may trigger off a process of *cost-push* inflation. Because in response to that k per cent rise in money wage, which raises labour cost per unit of output (w/x) by an equivalent k per cent at constant labour productivity (x), capitalists would also have to raise their prices by the same k per cent to protect their profit margin per unit of sale. And, as prices rise by k per cent, workers again demand k per cent higher *money* wage in the *next* period only to induce a further price rise by the capitalists. Thus, although a k per cent decrease in the *real* wage rate from its *initial* level wipes out the inflationary gap, the one-period-lagged adjustment of *money* wage rate to prices keeps the inflationary process going through time.

Such an inflationary process can be formally captured by noticing that for all time periods beyond the initial one, the *real* wage rate is lower by k per cent, i.e.

$$\frac{w(t)}{P(t)} = \frac{w_r(0)}{(1+k)}, \qquad \text{for all } t > 0 \tag{6.19}$$

where $w_r(0)$ is the *initial real* wage rate at $t = 0$.

This reduction in the *real* wage rate by k per cent is maintained only because the *money* wage rate rises in the same proportion as the price level, but always with one-period lag. If this lag were not there, real wage could be maintained at its initial level $w_r(0)$ i.e.,

$$\frac{w(t)}{P(t-1)} = w_r(0) \tag{6.20}$$

Dividing (6.20) by (6.19), we obtain a *recursive* relation between the price levels of any two successive periods as,

$$P(t) = (1+k)P(t-1) \tag{6.21}$$

Thus, if the initial price level is $P(0)$, then the price level in period 1 is given from (6.21) as

$$P(1) = (1+k)P(0)$$

Similarly for period $t = 2$, $P(2) = (1+k)P(1)$ or, by substitution for $P(1)$, $P(2) = (1+k)^2 P(0)$.

By such repeated substitution, the price level for any period t is obtained from (6.21) as,

$$P(t) = (1+k)^t P(0) \tag{6.22}$$

It shows an inflationary time-path, where the price level increases by a steady k per cent in every period.[16]

It would be customary to describe the above as a process of cost-push inflation, because although there is *no excess demand* in the system after the initial k per cent reduction in the *real* wage rate (see (6.19)), the price level keeps rising as the *money* wage rate rises. Therefore, the rising labour *cost* per unit of output (w/x) is seen as the causal factor underlying such an inflationary process. Nevertheless, such a view is one-sided; the money wage rate rises only because the price level rises. The *mutual* feedback between prices and money wages clearly makes it meaningless to single out either as *the* causal factor.

An increase in the price level induces an increase in the money wage rate because the workers try to protect their *real wage rate*.

Conversely, an increase in the money wage rate leads to an increase in the price level, because the capitalists attempt to protect their *profit margin* per unit of sale (recall Chapter 3, p. 68 and 78). When both sides feel powerful enough to defend their economic interests, prices as well as money wages may keep rising with or without excess demand. A persistent inflationary process then becomes a symptom of the underlying *conflict* in economic interests among the classes.

Both the economic and the political aspects are inextricably linked in such a process of inflation sustained by the conflicting interests among the classes. Economically, such an inflationary process continues because, the claims in terms of shares of national income made by the various classes cannot be reconciled. For instance, in our preceding analysis the initial level of the *real* wage rate $w_r(0)$ which the working class tries to protect cannot be reconciled with the higher profit margin that the capitalists demand to finance a higher level of investment (by $\Delta L_i / L_i$). It needs to be emphasised that such competing claims are more easily reconciled when *quantities* adjust upwards in response to a higher level of demand. However, if for some reason (e.g., full capacity utilisation or full employment) quantity adjustment is restricted, it becomes all the more difficult to reconcile such competing claims by the classes. Note that the quantity-adjustment multiplier increases *both* the *absolute* level of wage and of profit, leaving the share of wage and profit unaltered in national income. Such a *co-operative* scheme of capitalistic commodity production (which the Keynesian policies emphasised) tends to break down when the price-adjustment multiplier takes over, because it tries to *alter* the relative shares of the classes, usually in the near-full employment situation. This generates *conflict rather than co-operation* among the classes which expresses itself through the inflationary process.

Politically, the capitalist economy becomes more prone to such conflict and, therefore, to inflation as the economic power of the classes becomes more evenly balanced. The greater the organised power of the workers and the stronger their economic position in a situation of relative labour scarcity at near-full employment, the less inclined they would be to accept a lower *real* wage rate (or *real* wage rising slower than labour productivity, implying increasing share of profit over time). This pushes the capitalist economy towards inflation not only through the operation of an inflationary barrier at which the real wage rate is inflexible downwards, but it may even *accelerate the rate of inflation by shortening the time-lag* between price and money wage rise. For instance, if the initial price rise is 9 per cent (as in our earlier arithmetical example, p. 184, $k = 0.09$), then a one-year lag between price rise and money wage rise (see (6.20)) would imply that the money wage rate will rise by 9 per cent and price by another 9 per cent next near. However, if this time-lag is shortened to say 6 months, then even *before* the next year, money wage would have risen by 9 per cent and prices would have risen by $(1.09)^2 - 1$, i.e., almost 19 per cent, to keep the *real* wage rate down by 9 per cent from its initial level (see (6.19)).

A shorter time-lag between price rise and subsequent *money* wage rise accentuates the annual rate of inflation in a conflictive inflationary process only because the workers respond faster in their attempt to protect the *real* wage rate. This is sharply in *contrast to a pure demand-pull inflation*, where the inflationary gap is gradually closed by steady reduction in the *real* wage rate. For instance, with earlier numerical values in p. 184 inserted in (6.17a), the *overall* reduction in the *real* wage rate needed to match investment with savings by eliminating *excess* demand is given as,

$$\left(\frac{\Delta P}{P} - \frac{\Delta w}{w} \right) = \frac{0.3}{0.7}(0.14) - 0.02 = 0.04$$

i.e., 4 per cent, where $h = 0.3$, $\Delta L_i/L_i = 0.14$ and $\Delta x/x = 0.02$ in (6.17a).

If prices rise by 9 per cent and money wage by 5 per cent per year, then the inflationary gap is closed in one year. However, when the time-lag is shorter, so that prices rise by the same 9 per cent and wages by the same 5 per cent in six months, the inflationary gap is closed in half a year. A shorter time-lag in this case would bring the inflation to an end by closing the inflationary gap faster only because *further feedback* between prices and money wages that results from the workers' *attempt* to restore their *real* wage is ignored. Paradoxically then, any such shortening of the time-lag that closes more rapidly the inflationary gap, may end up by accelerating the *subsequent* rate of inflation generated through conflicting claims by workers to restore their *real* wage and by capitalists to protect their profit margin.

When inflationary redistribution actually succeeds in reducing the *real* wage rate, it imposes in effect one of the *most regressive tax systems* possible on the working class. It is more regressive than even a direct tax imposed *only* on wages, because left to the forces of an unregulated market, higher investment is financed by additional saving generated from higher profit (see (6.14)). But as profit increases, there is additional consumption by the capitalists which is *also* financed by the inflationary redistribution against the workers. In short, the burden of financing additional investment as well as additional consumption by the capitalists falls on the workers. The arithmetical logic is simple: as s_p $(1 > s_p > 0)$ is the marginal (and average) propensity to save out of profit, one additional unit of saving requires $1/s_p$ units to be redistributed from wage to profit. However, that additional unit of saving could be generated simply by a direct tax on wages which would have reduced wage income by only one unit to increase government savings by one unit. Thus, inflationary redistribution imposes an additional burden *per unit of saving* compared to a direct tax only on wage which is given by,

$$\left(\frac{1}{s_p} - 1 \right) = \left(\frac{1 - s_p}{s_p} \right) > 0, \qquad \text{If} \quad 1 > s_p > 0 \tag{6.23}$$

Although a direct tax on wage may impose a lighter burden on the workers compared with inflationary redistribution, there is no reason why an economically powerful working class should obligingly accept such a burden alone. Just as capitalist firms generally try to pass on the burden of an additional tax on (corporate) profit to their consumers through higher prices, the workers may claim higher *money* wages to pass on such burden of additional (income) tax to the capitalists. In general, capitalists would try to maintain their *post-tax profit margin* while workers would try to protect their *post-tax real wage* and neither side would accept an additional tax burden. In such a situation the *conventional fiscal role of the State* is engulfed by the economic conflict among the classes. For instance, a higher direct tax imposed by the State to control the level of effective demand in an inflationary situation may actually *accelerate* the rate of inflation, as the burden of the additional taxes keeps being passed on from one class to the other, in the form of rising money wages and prices. Such *shifting of the burden of additional taxes* could make conventional tax policies of the State counter-productive in controlling inflation, because the inflationary process gets *accelerated*, rather than being subdued by such additional taxes.

In a regime of *progressive* income tax, such additional tax burden may come into effect through a higher tax rate on the *marginal* compared to *average* money income. For instance, the *post-tax earning* (e) of a worker is given as,

$$e = w - d = (1 - t_a)w, \qquad t_a = \frac{d}{w} \qquad (6.24a)$$

where w is the *money* wage rate, d is the direct (income) tax paid, and t_a is the *average* tax rate.

However, *increment* in post-tax earning is given as,

$$\Delta e = \Delta w - \Delta d = (1 - t_m)\Delta w, \qquad t_m = \frac{\Delta d}{\Delta w} \qquad (6.24b)$$

where t_m is the *marginal* tax rate.

The *progressive* nature of the direct (income) tax system ensures,

$$1 > t_m > t_a > 0 \qquad (6.25)$$

Dividing (6.24b) by (6.24a), the percentage increase in *post-tax* earning ($\Delta e/e$) is obtained as,

$$\frac{\Delta e}{e} = \left(\frac{1 - t_m}{1 - t_a}\right)\left(\frac{\Delta w}{w}\right) \qquad (6.26)$$

It is immediately evident from (6.26) that the percentage increase in the post-tax earning is *less* than that in the money wage rate – i.e. $(\Delta e/e)/(\Delta w/w)$ is less than unity – because, t_m exceeds t_a in (6.25).

Nevertheless, it is the percentage increase in *post-tax* earning rate ($\Delta e/e$), rather than in the *pretax* money wage rate ($\Delta w/w$), that must keep pace with percentage rise in price ($\Delta P/P$), if the workers have to protect the purchasing power of their 'take-home' pay. From (6.26) this means that there would be *no decline in post-tax* real earning if,

$$\frac{\Delta P}{P} = \frac{\Delta e}{e} = \left(\frac{1 - t_m}{1 - t_a}\right)\left(\frac{\Delta w}{w}\right)$$

i.e.,

$$\frac{\Delta w}{w} = \left(\frac{1 - t_a}{1 - t_m}\right)\left(\frac{\Delta P}{P}\right) \qquad (6.27)$$

Thus, if the marginal and the average income tax rate are 40 and 20 per cent respectively, i.e., $t_m = 0.4$ and $t_a = 0.2$, then from (6.27), a 9 per cent increase in price (i.e., $\Delta P/P = 0.09$) requires *money* wage rate to increase 12 per cent (i.e., $\Delta w/w = 0.12$), only to protect the level of 'take-home', *post-tax real earning* from declining. But this 12 per cent increase in money wage rate, in the absence of any rise in labour productivity (x), raises variable cost per unit of output (w/x) also by 12 per cent (see equation (6.17)). Consequently, to protect their profit margin, capitalists increase prices by another 12 per cent, while that 12 per cent price rise feeds back through (6.27) to induce a 16 per cent rise in money wage in the next period (with t_a and t_m assumed constant at 20 and 40 per cent respectively). Thus, the rate of inflation *accelerates* from an initial 9 per cent to 12, 16, . . . per cent, and so on over time.

The economic content of such an accelerating inflationary process is similar to the one described earlier by equations (6.19) to (6.22). Inflation occurs because both workers and capitalists try to defend their *post-tax* real wage and profit margin respectively. However, a *progressive* system of income tax imposes an increasing burden of tax in money terms, as both wage and profit income rise in money terms during an inflationary process.[17] And, as both the classes refuse to bear that increasing tax burden, it gets continuously shifted from one class to another through spiralling rise in prices and money wages in an *accelerating* process of inflation.

If the marginal and average tax rates (i.e., t_m and t_a respectively in (6.27)) are assumed *constant* for simplicity, such *acceleration* of the inflationary process can be formally described by simply introducing a one-period lag between money wage rise and price rise (as in (6.20)) so that (6.27) becomes,

$$\frac{\Delta w(t-1)}{w(t-1)} \equiv \left[\frac{w(t) - w(t-1)}{w(t-1)} \right] = \left(\frac{1 - t_a}{1 - t_m} \right) \left[\frac{P(t-1) - P(t-2)}{P(t-2)} \right]$$

$$= \left(\frac{1 - t_a}{1 - t_m} \right) \left(\frac{\Delta p(t-2)}{p(t-2)} \right) \tag{6.27a}$$

However, prices rise *instantaneously* with money wages (as in (6.19)) implying,

$$\frac{\Delta P(t-1)}{P(t-1)} = \frac{\Delta w(t-1)}{w(t-1)} \tag{6.28}$$

Using (6.28) in (6.27a), we obtain a *recursive relation* between *percentage rise* in price (k) of any two successive periods, i.e.,

$$k(t-1) = \left(\frac{1-t_a}{1-t_m}\right)k(t-2) \tag{6.29}$$

where

$$k(t-1) = \frac{\Delta P(t-1)}{P(t-1)} \quad \text{and} \quad k(t-2) = \frac{\Delta P(t-2)}{P(t-2)}$$

Thus, given any initial percentage rise in the price level as $k(0)$ (which is 9 per cent in the preceding arithmetical example), the percentage rise in price in period 1, i.e., $k(1)$ is computed from (6.29) as,

$$k(1) = \left(\frac{1-t_a}{1-t_m}\right)k(0)$$

Similarly,

$$k(2) = \left(\frac{1-t_a}{1-t_m}\right)k(1) = \left(\frac{1-t_a}{1-t_m}\right)^2 k(0)$$

and proceeding in this manner through repeated substitution, the percentage rise in price in period t, i.e., $k(t)$ is given from (6.29) as,

$$k(t) = \left(\frac{1-t_a}{1-t_m}\right)^t k(0) \tag{6.30}$$

where the marginal and average tax rates, t_m and t_a respectively, have been assumed *constant*.[18] Equation (6.30) shows how the rate of inflation, measured by percentage rise in price $k(t)$ *accelerates* over time under a *progressive* income tax system (i.e., so long as (6.25) holds).

An inflationary process, such as the one described above, is rooted in the social conflict among the classes, which ultimately extends to the mediating role of the State in terms of its conventional fiscal policies. The capitalists resist any decrease in their (post-tax) profit margin which tends to justify the wage-unit hypothesis (see (6.28) above). On the other hand, workers' resistance to any decline in their (post-tax) *real* wage rate sets in operation an *inflationary barrier*. In this way, the wage-unit hypothesis and the inflationary barrier exhibit two sides of the same phenomenon; they suggest that *neither* class would accept any *unfavourable* change from the *status quo* of existing class distribution of income. In such a situation the capitalist economy becomes highly susceptible to inflation. Not only an additional tax burden imposed by the State, but even an accidental rise in say, the price of *imported raw materials* (e.g. oil) may trigger off an inflationary process, as neither side accepts any additional burden.

It is also in the general logic of such economic conflict, that each class not only tries to *protect* but *improve* its income share, whenever its relative economic power increases. In addition to the organised power of trade unions, the bargaining position of the workers generally improves when the *unemployment rate* (u) is low. Such a hypothesis found some empirical support in a series of findings – commonly known as the *Phillips' curve* – which reported that the percentage rise in *money* wages ($\Delta w/w$) tends to be *inversely* related to the rate of unemployment (u), i.e.

$$\frac{\Delta w}{w} = H(u), \qquad \frac{\mathrm{d}H}{\mathrm{d}u} \equiv H'(u) < 0 \qquad (6.31)$$

where w is the *money* wage rate and u is the unemployment as a proportion of total labour force.

The inverse relation postulated in (6.31) may come about either because capitalist employers themselves bid up the *money* wage rate faster in situations of labour scarcity characterised by low unemployment rate, u; alternatively, *money* wage rate may rise faster because organised workers are in a better position to negotiate for higher *money* wages when there is less unemployment in general. Generally money wages would increase faster in situations of low unemployment through both these routes. In addition, trade unions are likely to take into account the rate of price rise ($\Delta P/P$) in an attempt to protect their *real* wages. This latter consideration is more explicitly shown in the *augmented version of the Phillips' curve* which yields in place of (6.31),

$$\frac{\Delta w}{w} = H(u) + n \cdot \frac{\Delta P}{P}, \qquad H'(u) < 0, n > 0 \qquad (6.32)$$

Note that, so long as the value of the parameter 'n' is less than unity, i.e., $1 > n > 0$ in (6.32), it means that workers are only *partially* able to protect their *real* wage through such negotiated settlements. However, $n \geqslant 1$ implies that the workers *fully* or even more than fully compensate for price rise ($\Delta P/P$) through *money* wage rise ($\Delta w/w$), *irrespective* of the rate of unemployment (u). In other words, the value of the parameter 'n' in (6.32) is meant to reflect the extent of conflict over inflationary redistribution.

On the basis of the empirical relationship put forward by the original Phillips' curve (6.31), it is tempting to suggest that there would be a certain rate of unemployment u^*, at which there would be no increase in money wages, i.e., at $u = u^*$, $H(u^*) = \Delta w/w = 0$ in (6.31), and in so far as the inflationary process is *pushed* by rising wage cost, a sufficiently high rate of unemployment at $u = u^*$ can bring such inflation to an end. However, the augmented Phillips' curve (6.32) should caution us against so simplistic a view. In so far as rise in money wages is at least partly in response to rising prices, negotiated settlements for higher money wages may continue so long as prices are rising. Thus, in (6.32), even if we assume, $H(u^*) = 0$, money wages continue to rise ($\Delta w/w > 0$) if prices continue to rise ($\Delta P/P > 0$), *irrespective* of a relatively high unemployment rate at $u = u^*$.

Nevertheless, in a process of inflation generated by economic conflict among the classes, it is always attractive to produce apologetic theories that would justify curbing the economic power of the working class by inflicting a heavy rate of unemployment on them. The idea of *a 'natural' rate of unemployment* is used by economists belonging particularly to the Monetarist School to provide precisely such a justification. Although the original Phillips' curve (6.31) or its augmented version (6.32) attempted to set out an *empirical* description of the *observed* behaviour of money wages in terms of *observed* price changes ($\Delta P/P$) and unemployment rate (u), this could be turned into an *empirically non-testable* hypothesis about the nature of wage bargain in a capitalist economy by introducing *expected* rather than *actual* (observed) price change. Because, being a statistically non-observable variable, a hypothesis involving *expected* price change ($\Delta \hat{P}/P$) cannot be directly tested. Replacing *actual* by *expected* price change in (6.32), the *expectation-augmented version of the Phillips' curve* is derived as,

$$\frac{\Delta w}{w} = H(u) + n \cdot \left(\frac{\Delta \hat{P}}{P} \right), \quad H'(u) < 0, \quad n > 0 \qquad (6.33)$$

where $\Delta \hat{P}/P$ is the percentage change in price *expected* or anticipated by the workers.

Thus, (6.33) says that the *money* wage rise claimed and obtained by the workers is *in anticipation* of price rise. This reverses the lagged adjustment of money wages to prices assumed for example, in (6.20) or (6.27a). It also relies strictly on the pre-Keynesian notion that wage bargain is in *real* and not in *money* terms because workers bargain for *money* wage taking into account anticipated price rise. Indeed, if the parameter '*n*' in (6.33) takes the value of unity, we have a *special case* of the expectation-augmented version of the Phillips' curve where, wage-bargain is *entirely* in real terms, i.e.

$$\frac{\Delta w}{w} = H(u) + \left(\frac{\Delta \hat{P}}{P}\right), \qquad \text{because } n = 1 \text{ by assumption (6.33a)}$$

Since the percentage change in *real* wage $(\Delta w_r / w_r)$ is definitionally equal to percentage changes of money wage *minus* price, namely

$$\frac{\Delta w_r}{w_r} = \frac{\Delta w}{w} - \frac{\Delta P}{P}$$

we can use the above definition in (6.33a) and rearrange terms to obtain,

$$\left(\frac{\Delta P}{P} - \frac{\Delta \hat{P}}{P}\right) H(u) - \frac{\Delta w_r}{w_r} \tag{6.34}$$

The left-hand side of (6.34) shows the actual $(\Delta P/P)$ *minus* the anticipated price change $(\Delta \hat{P}/P)$ by the workers. Consequently, there would be no *unanticipated change* in price, if the right-hand side of (6.34) is zero, i.e.,

$$\frac{\Delta P}{P} = \frac{\Delta \hat{P}}{P} \qquad \text{implying } H(u) - \frac{\Delta w_r}{w_r} = 0 \tag{6.34a}$$

If the change in *real* wage $(\Delta w_r / w_r)$ is *exogenously* given by, say, the growth in labour productivity $(\Delta x/x)$, then a 'natural' rate of unemployment (u^*), where there is no *unanticipated* change in price can be defined from (6.34a) as,

$$H(u^*) = \frac{\Delta w_r}{w_r} = \frac{\Delta x}{x} \qquad \text{(exogenously given)}$$

or,

$$u^* = H^{-1}\left(\frac{\Delta x}{x}\right) \tag{6.34b}$$

If the *actual* unemployment rate is somehow (e.g., through Keynesian policies) kept *below* its 'natural' rate, i.e. $u < u^*$, then $H(u)$ *exceeds* the *exogenously* given growth rate in *real* wage ($\Delta w_r/w_r = \Delta x/x$). Consequently, the right-hand side of (6.34) is positive implying, actual price rise ($\Delta P/P$) is greater than that anticipated by the workers ($\Delta\hat{P}/P$). This results in *unanticipated* inflation which has a tendency to *accelerate* over time, because workers would further increase their money wage claims in the next period by anticipating higher inflation (see (6.33a)).

Such a theory of 'natural' unemployment is most implausible. It rests on a very special version of collective wage bargain given in (6.33a), where workers and their trade unions are supposed to have almost *unrestricted* economic power *irrespective* of the existing unemployment rate (u). Thus, it is assumed in (6.33a) that the workers can actually raise their money wage rate ($\Delta w/w$) in line with *whatever* price rise they anticipate ($\Delta\hat{P}/P$). Clearly, such an assumption would be unreal in most instances, particularly if the unemployment rate is already high. And yet, this unreal hypothesis about collective wage bargain given in (6.33a) cannot be statistically questioned, because the anticipated variable ($\Delta\hat{P}/P$) is statistically non-observable!

Again, such a theory of 'natural' unemployment rate is questionable, because it assumes an *exogenously* given growth rate in the *real* wage rate (see (6.34b)). When *money* wages rise at the same rate as labour productivity *plus* actual price rise, i.e.,

$$\frac{\Delta w}{w} = \frac{\Delta x}{x} + \frac{\Delta P}{P}$$

the *existing* share of wage in income defined as, $(1 - h) = w/xP$, remains constant (see (6.18)). Nevertheless, nothing in economic theory suggests that *existing* shares – whatever they happen to be – can serve as the basis for computing a 'natural' unemployment rate (u^*) in (6.34b). Only by assuming that the existing *status quo* of income shares is always accepted as 'natural' by the workers, the concept of 'natural' unemployment is defined in (6.34b).

Finally, the theory is far too simplistic in terms of its treatment of expectations. Even on its own terms, this theory only shows that there is no *unanticipated* inflation at the 'natural' rate of unemployment only in so far as the workers are concerned (see (6.34a)). However, if capitalists have *different* expectations about say, money wage rise ($\Delta\hat{w}/w$) in setting their prices, expectations of different economic agents will come into conflict. It is far from clear that a 'natural' rate of unemployment can even be defined under such *conflicting* expectations. Only by taking recourse to the oversimplified assumption of expectation by one type of economic agent, namely the workers, some definition of 'natural' unemployment is arrived at in (6.34a).

Despite such numerous difficulties and questionable assumptions underlying the concept of the 'natural' rate of unemployment, it has become a 'respectable' concept because of the political purpose it serves. In any inflationary process propelled by conflict among the classes, as we have already seen (equations (6.24a) to (6.30)), even the conventional fiscal role of the State may become counter-productive in controlling inflation. Under these circumstances, only through curbing the economic power of the working class by inflicting a high rate (the 'natural' rate) of unemployment on them can the capitalist State hope to succeed in controlling inflation, because the burden of higher investment or of higher tax could be borne by a working class weakened through a severely high unemployment rate. Concepts such as the 'natural' rate of unemployment intellectually justify such an economic strategy and, in the ultimate analysis, this is also what Monetarism is all about (see Chapter 4, Section D).

So long as both the classes remain powerful enough the role of the State as an economic mediator among them visualised in '*social democratic*' *ideologies*, comes to be increasingly questioned. The State apparatus may find it increasingly difficult to finance its welfare programmes without running the risk of accelerating the inflation, as the contending classes refuse to bear the additional tax burden. *Economic conservatism* as an ideology begins to find a large audience: it argues against the 'inefficient' policies of the Welfare State and wants to replace State intervention by the 'discipline of the market place' that is usually loaded against the workers (see condition (6.23)).

Within the working class itself, two opposite tendencies are likely to develop as the inflationary process persists or even accelerates. On the one hand, the *unorganised workers* find themselves increasingly unable to defend their standard of living without becoming a part of the collective bargaining process. This creates condition for greater unionisation of hitherto unorganised workers, calling for wider *uniform* wage settlement throughout the economy. On the other hand, such uniform settlement of wages tends to put greater stress on the relative structure of money wages, i.e., *money wage differentials* traditionally established among various industries and occupations.

Considerable empirical evidence now exists to suggest that higher money wage settlements may first take place in those industries which are placed in particularly favourable economic circumstances. Thus, in industries with an exceptionally high growth in labour productivity or in industries where demand conditions are exceptionally favourable like successful export industries, higher money wage settlements may take place first. Then comes into operation the 'propagation effect' of a *wage–wage spiral* which tries to restore the *relative* money wage structure. As a result, wages in most other industries also rise, led by such 'key industries' with high productivity or demand growth. This in turn creates a situation of internally generated upward pressure on the *entire* money wage structure. The link between growth in labour productivity in *particular industries* and general money wage increase in the process tends to depress further the profit margin of the 'weaker' industries with little or no productivity growth. It is a process of 'cumulative disequilibrium', rather than any automatic tendency towards restoring equilibrium, where weaker industries seek protection from the State, while weaker organised labour seek protection against inflation through increased unionisation. The economic conflict among the classes can only heighten in such a process of cumulative disequilibrium. This allows economic conservatism, through such implausible construction as the 'natural' unemployment rate and monetarist policies to provide ideological justification for breaking the power of organised labour in the name of controlling inflation.

Notes to Chapter 6

1. A higher level of investment may increase profit level, because *either* real income increases (i.e. the quantity-adjustment multiplier) *or* income is redistributed from wage to profit (i.e., the price-adjustment multiplier). By assuming, the share of profit in income (h), to be constant, we focus attention exclusively on the quantity-adjustment multiplier. See Figure 2.4, p. 53, for further elaboration.
2. Of the total realised (i.e., monetary) profit of any period, a firm operating on the principle of joint liability usually retains a part and distributes the rest of the profit to its shareholders. The retained profit, if invested in financial assets provides the firm with an interest income. However, when the firm invests its retained profit as well as borrows from outside to finance its physical investment plans, it not only loses its assured interest income (which is the opportunity cost of retained profit) but runs the additional risk of having to pay interest on borrowed funds.

3. Recall that we had avoided facing the problem of how profit of the investment sector (R_I) is realised throughout our discussion in Chapter 2. Such discussion of realisation of profit in the investment sector would have required us to specify an investment function showing the *demand* for investment goods. Instead in Chapter 2, we were forced to assume that whatever the investment sector produces (autonomously) is demanded so that, Department I (the investment sector) faces no problem of realisation of profit. This unreal assumption is needed only because there exists no generally accepted investment function.

4. See equation (6.11) later in the text showing a simple accelerator relation. Note, however, the important difference between *expected* change in income given as, $Y(t+1) - Y(t)$ and *actual* change in income given as $Y(t) - Y(t-1)$. Actual change substitutes for expected change in (6.11) only if expectations are formed by direct extrapolation of immediate past experience, known as the assumption of 'static expectation'.

5. It can be easily checked that, if line *AE* (i.e., equation (6.4a)) has a larger (positive) slope than the line *OE* (i.e. equation (6.3a)), the time path shown by arrows in Figure 6.1 *diverges* from equilibrium *E*, even if such an equilibrium exists. The existence of equilibrium implies that the two lines intersect in the positive quadrant. However, with slope of *OE* ($ = s_p$) less than the slope of *AE* ($ = a$), intersection of the two lines in the positive quadrant is possible if line *AE* has a *negative* vertical intercept, i.e., the constant '*A*' in (6.4a) is negative.

6. (6.8) is the *particular solution* (when $I = I(0)$ at $t = 0$) of the *first-order difference equation* (6.7). For such first-order difference equations with constant coefficients, this method of repeated substitution is adequate to arrive at the solution.

7. Note (6.8) can be written as,

$$I(t) = \frac{A}{\left(1 - \dfrac{a}{s_p}\right)} + \left(\frac{a}{s_p}\right)^t \left[I(0) - \frac{A}{\left(1 - \dfrac{a}{s_p}\right)} \right]$$

$$I(t) = I^* + \left(\frac{a}{s_p}\right)^t [I(0) - I^*], \qquad I^* = \frac{A}{\left(1 - \dfrac{a}{s_p}\right)}$$

Hence, the second term on the extreme right-hand side, showing initial divergence from equilibrium value $[I(0) - I^*]$, vanishes gradually for large t if $s_p > a > 0$, as in stability condition (6.5).

8. This implies *expectations* of additional profit from new investment, i.e. $[R(t+1) - R(t)]$, is formed by extrapolation of current *actual* experience of realised profit $[R(t) - R(t-1)]$. This is the case of 'static expectation' also mentioned in Note 4 of this chapter.

9. Substituting for $R(t)$ and $R(t-1)$ from (6.3a), we rewrite (6.10) as a

second-order difference equation in I as,

$$I(t+1) - \left(\frac{a+b}{s_p}\right)I(t) + \frac{b}{s_p}I(t-1) = A$$

The left-hand side of the above equation representing the homogeneous part of the equation has the characteristic equation (obtained by trying for $I(t) = Hm^t$) given by the quadratic equation,

$$m^2 - \left(\frac{a+b}{s_p}\right)m + \frac{b}{s_p} = 0$$

The roots of the quadratic equation,

$$m_1, m_2 = \frac{\left(\frac{a+b}{s_p}\right) \pm \sqrt{\left(\frac{a+b}{s_p}\right)^2 - \frac{4b}{s_p}}}{2}$$

These roots have imaginary parts (i.e., the roots are conjugate complex) if,

$$\left(\frac{a+b}{s_p}\right)^2 - \frac{4b}{s_p} < 0, \quad \text{i.e. } (a+b)^2 < 4.s_p.b$$

Such conjugate complex roots generate cycles (like a trignometric consign function) that gain or lose in amplitude over time (For details of reference, see the further reading suggested at the end of this chapter.) For example, if $a = 0.15$, $b = 0.10$, $s_p = 0.6$, then the above-mentioned inequality is satisfied, i.e., $(0.15+0.10)^2 = (0.25)^2 = 0.0625 < 4.(0.6).(0.1) = 0.24$.

The reader may satisfy himself with numerical examples (any given $I(0)$ and $I(1)$) that the level of investment *fluctuates* with these parameter values.

10. As in the preceding note, conjugate complex roots of the second-order difference equation obtained from (6.3b) and (6.11) ensure fluctuations. In this case, the required condition for fluctuation in income is, $v < 4 s_p h$.

11. These two terms 'self-excitation' and 'relaxation' are borrowed from non-linear oscillations occurring in certain electrical circuits.

12. *Essays in the Theory of Economic Fluctuations* (Kalecki, 1939) p. 149.

13. See, J. A. Schumpeter (1947), *Capitalism, Socialism and Democracy*, especially Chapters VII and X. Formally, a higher rate of obsolescence reduces the average life time 'n' of machines and may thus weaken the contribution of the negative term on the right-hand side of (6.12) despite high levels of past investment.

14. At $L_i = L_i^f$, the demand generated for consumption goods is just sufficient to employ enough workers in the consumption sector (L_c) to maintain full employment in the economy (see (2.25) of Chapter 2).

Strictly speaking, additional employment in the investment sector (ΔL_i) can take place only by *withdrawing* an equivalent number of workers from the consumption sector under full employment, i.e., $\Delta L_i = -\Delta L_c$, if $L_i + L_c = L^f$, constant full-employment labour force. Instead of making this extreme (unrealistic) assumption of strict full employment, we presume a near-full employment situation, where employment in the investment sector can be marginally increased (by ΔL_i) without withdrawing labour from the consumption sector, as L_c remains constant.

15. Increase in labour productivity (assumed away in Chapter 2) introduces *autonomous* increase in quantities to reduce the required extent of price adjustment. We take into account possible increase in labour productivity during an inflationary process to facilitate later discussion (e.g., (6.34b)).

16. (6.22) represents the particular solution to the first-order *homogeneous* difference equation (6.21). Note that (6.7) and (6.21) are solved by the same method of repeated substitution, although (6.7) represented a *non-homogeneous* first-order difference equation involving a constant term 'A'.

17. To keep the analysis simple, we abstracted from progressive rate of taxation of corporate profit. Its introduction would further accelerate the inflationary process.

18. Equation (6.29), like (6.21), is a first-order homogeneous difference equation whose particular solution at $k = k(0)$ is given in (6.30). When the tax rates are *not* assumed constant, by repeated substitution we obtain,

$$k(t) = \left[\left(\frac{1-t_a(0)}{1-t_m(0)}\right) \cdot \left(\frac{1-t_a(1)}{1-t_m(1)}\right) \cdots \left(\frac{1-t_a(t)}{1-t_m(t)}\right) \right] k(0)$$

where $t_a(j)$ or $t_m(j)$ represent average and marginal tax rates of period j ($j = 0, 1, \ldots, t$).

Further Reading

Haavelmo's *A Study in the Theory of Investment* (Haavelmo, 1960) part I on 'Survey of problems' would provide the reader with one of the best introductions to the problem of constructing an 'investment function'. Far more limited in scope is Knox's, 'The acceleration principle and the theory of investment: a survey' (Knox, 1952), which explains in detail the 'acceleration principle' used in the construction of a class of business cycle models (see equations (6.10) and (6.11) in the text), e.g., Samuelson's 'Interaction between the multiplier analysis and the principle of acceleration' (Samuelson, 1939). Perhaps the most fruitful economic application of this class of fluctuation models is in Metzler's 'Nature and stability of inventory cycles' (Metzler, 1941).

Our analysis in Section A mainly follows Kalecki's analysis, e.g., 'Outline of a theory of the business cycle' (Essay No. 1) in his *Selected Essays on the*

Dynamics of the Capitalist Economy (Kalecki, 1971) which was lucidly explained in Lange's essay, 'Michal Kalecki's model of the business cycle' in his *Papers in Economics and Sociology* (Lange, 1970). Two similar models are Kaldor's 'A model of the trade cycle' in his *Essays on Stability and Growth* (Kaldor, 1960) and Goodwin's 'The non-linear accelerator and the persistence of the business cycle' (Goodwin, 1951) which clearly identified the nature of non-linearity required for sustained fluctuations.

Despite many surveys and studies that appeared on inflation since the early 1970s, Bronfenbrenner and Holzman, 'A survey of inflation theory' (Bronfenbrenner and Holzman, 1963) remains one of the relatively early, and yet most balanced, introduction to the problem. Keynes' *How to Pay for the War* (Keynes, 1940) is still interesting reading and two interpretative essays on it, Maital's 'Inflation, taxation and equity: 'How to pay for the war' revisited' (Maital, 1972) and Trevithick's, 'Keynes, inflation and money illusion' (Trevithick, 1975) discuss some of the materials covered in Section B. Phillips' influential article, 'The relation between unemployment and money wage rates in the United Kingdom, 1861–1957' (Phillips, 1958), Dicks-Mireau and Dow, 'Determinants of wage inflation: United Kingdom, 1946–56' (Dicks-Mireau and Dow, 1959) and, Eatwell, Uewellyn and Tarling, 'Money wage inflation in industrial countries' (Eatwell *et al.*, 1974), systematise some of the essential empirical material in the modern discussion of wage-inflation. A recent statement of the notion of a 'natural' rate of unemployment is to be found in Friedman's rather obscure discussion in *Unemployment versus Inflation* (Friedman, 1975), clearly reformulated and criticised by Cripps in 'Money supply, wages and inflation' (Cripps, 1977) on which the discussion in the text relies. Class conflict as the basis of inflation also involving the State, is discussed in Rowthorn's article, 'Conflict, inflation and Money' reprinted in his *Capitalism, Conflict and Inflation* (Rowthorn, 1980), while the monograph by Jackson, Turner and Wilkinson, *Do Trade Unions Cause Inflation?* (Jackson *et al.*, 1975) is useful as background reading. McCallum's 'Inflation and social consensus in the Seventies' (McCallum, 1983) also provides interesting empirical material.

7
Capitalistic Accumulation: a Long Term View

A Conditions for Steady Accumulation

The distinction between the short and the long period in economic analysis is meant to be a device to deal with the complex process of economic change through time. Its essential rationale depends on a *classificatory* scheme which groups variables contributing to economic change separately, according to their *relative* speeds of adjustment: Variables that adjust relatively rapidly are short period variables; whereas, other variables that adjust more slowly may be assumed to change only negligibly during the short period. Consequently, this latter group of variables may be treated as provisional constants during the short period. They are variables having a significant role to play only in the context of the long period analysis.

The purpose of classifying economic variables according to their relative speeds of adjustment into short and long period variables is *analytical* rather than *historical*. In an actual historical process, all the relevant variables change *simultaneously* through time. Nevertheless, because these variables change at different speeds, the method of long period analysis tries to achieve an analytical simplification by displaying the interconnection among a group of variables that change relatively slowly over time while assuming at the same time that the faster moving variables maintain their *completely adjusted* equilibrium values. In other words, the situation is analytically reversed. In a short period analysis, the long period variables are assigned *constant* values. In contrast, in long period analysis, the short period (i.e. faster-adjusting) variables are assigned their *fully adjusted*, equilibrium values.[1]

This method has proved to be particularly useful in analysing the *dual role of investment* in capitalistic accumulation. On the one hand, additional investment (ΔI) creates *additional demand* for consumption goods (ΔC^d) through the usual multiplier mechanism described in Chapter 2. On the other hand, investment, *net* of replacement requirements, also creates additional productive capacity *to augment the supply potential* of the economy. However, the demand-creating effect of investment may be assumed to have a higher speed of adjustment, so that the *increase* in demand for consumption goods (ΔC^d) resulting from an *increase* in investment (ΔI) may be treated as a short period adjustment variable. Consequently, it is assigned its equilibrium value, given by the multiplier relation (2.18), p. 41 i.e.,

$$\Delta C^d = \frac{(1 - s_p h_i)}{s_p h_c} \cdot \Delta I \tag{7.1}$$

where ΔC^d is the *total* additional demand for consumption goods resulting from additional investment ΔI.[2]

Net investment, on the other hand, creates additional capacity as a long period variable because construction and installation of new capacities take considerably longer time. For this reason, this supply-creating aspect of (net) investment as a slower adjusting variable appears only in the long period analysis which could be abstracted from, in our short period analysis of effective demand in Chapter 2.

By defining *net* investment J as *gross* (or total) investment I *minus* replacement investment F we obtain,[3]

$$J = I - F = (1 - f)I, f = \frac{F}{I}, \quad 1 > f > 0 \tag{7.2}$$

where J is the *net* investment that creates additional capacity and f is the ratio of replacement (F) to gross investment (I).

Of the *net* investment J in any period, a certain proportion λ, $1 > \lambda > 0$ is devoted to the investment sector to expand capacity there; the remaining proportion $(1 - \lambda)$ of net investment is devoted to expand capacity in the consumption sector. Thus, the *net* investment going to the consumption sector (J_c) during any period is,

$$J_c = (1 - \lambda)(1 - f)I, \quad (1 - \lambda) = \frac{J_c}{J}. \tag{7.3a}$$

Similarly, net investment going to the investment sector during the same period is,

$$J_i = \lambda(1-f)I, \qquad \lambda = \frac{J_i}{J} \tag{7.3b}$$

If we assume that to create every *additional* unit of productive capacity in C-sector, v_c amount of (net) investment is required on average, then *investment cost per unit of potential output* flow of the consumption sector is given as,[4]

$$v_c = \frac{J_c}{\Delta C^s} \tag{7.4a}$$

where J_c is the net investment in consumption sector and ΔC^s is additional capacity, i.e., increase in the *potential* supply of consumption goods. Similarly, investment cost per unit of potential output flow in the investment sector is given by,

$$v_i = \frac{J_i}{\Delta I^s} \tag{7.4b}$$

where J_i is the net investment in the investment sector and ΔI^s is additional capacity, i.e. increase in the *potential* supply of investment goods.[5]

Using (7.3a) in (7.4a), we obtain the increase in the *potential supply* of consumption goods as,

$$\Delta C^s = \frac{(1-\lambda)(1-f)I}{v_c} \tag{7.5a}$$

And from (7.3b) and (7.4b), the increase in the *potential supply* of investment goods is obtained as,

$$\Delta I^s = \frac{\lambda(1-f)I}{v_i} \tag{7.5b}$$

Additional demand for consumption goods (ΔC^d) generated by the multiplier relation (7.1) must exactly match the *additional supply* (ΔC^s) of consumption goods given by (7.5a), if the *newly created capacity* in the consumption sector is to be *fully utilised*. Thus full utilisation of newly created capacity in the consumption sector in every period requires,

$$\Delta C^d = \Delta C^s \tag{7.6}$$

Or, from (7.1) and (7.5a),

$$\frac{(1 - s_p h_i)}{s_p h_c} \Delta I = \frac{(1 - \lambda)(1 - f)}{v_c} \cdot I$$

The above relation yields the proportional rate of growth of gross investment $(\Delta I / I)$ required to maintain *full utilisation of newly created capacities in the consumption sector* in every period as,

$$\frac{\Delta I}{I} = g_i = \frac{s_p h_c}{v_c} \cdot \frac{(1 - \lambda)(1 - f)}{(1 - s_p h_i)} \tag{7.7}$$

However, for investment to expand at the rate g_i specified by (7.7), it is also necessary that the *additional supply of investment goods* given by (7.5b) must match its *additional demand* given in (7.7), i.e.

$$\frac{\Delta I}{I} = \frac{\Delta I^s}{I} \tag{7.8}$$

Or, from (7.7) and (7.5b),

$$\frac{s_p h_c}{v_c} \cdot \frac{(1 - \lambda)(1 - f)}{(1 - s_p h_i)} = \frac{\lambda(1 - f)}{v_i} \tag{7.9}$$

Condition (7.9) ensures that *newly created capacities are fully utilised in the investment sector*. In particular, (7.9) specifies the equilibrium proportion $\lambda = \lambda^*$ in which investment is to be distributed between the two sectors (see (7.3a) and (7.3b)), so that there is no excess demand for or excess supply of investment goods in the economy. This equilibrium value is obtained by solving for λ in (7.9) to yield,

$$\lambda = \lambda^* = \frac{v_i \cdot s_p h_c}{v_c \cdot (1 - s_p h_i) + v_i \cdot s_p h_c} \tag{7.10}$$

If λ exceeds its equilibrium value λ^* in (7.10), it is clear from (7.7) that a *lower* growth rate in the demand for investment goods g_i is required to maintain full utilisation of new capacities in the consumption sector (because g_i falls as λ rises in (7.7)). However, such higher value of λ exceeding λ^* implies that the rate of growth in the supply of investment goods $\Delta I^s / I$ is increased because λ is increased in (7.5b). It follows that the equilibrium condition (7.8) which ensures full utilisation of new capacities in the investment sector is violated, as there is under-utilisation of capacities in the investment sector when $\lambda > \lambda^*$. Similarly, there would be excess demand for investment goods if $\lambda < \lambda^*$, as the rate of growth in the demand for investment goods, g_i in (7.7) will then exceed the growth in the supply of investment goods, $\Delta I^s/I$ in (7.5b).

Therefore, if conditions (7.7) and (7.10) are *simultaneously* satisfied, there would be no under- or over-utilisation of new capacities created through net investment in *either sector*. Algebraically this is ensured by inserting the equilibrium value of $\lambda = \lambda^*$ from (7.10) in (7.7). This yields, on simplification, a *rate of growth in investment* (g_i^w) *which is warranted by full utilisation of new capacity in every sector* of the economy, i.e.,

$$g_i = g_i^w = \frac{s_p h_c (1-f)}{[v_c(1 - s_p h_i) + v_i s_p h_c]} \tag{7.11}$$

In analogy with the one-commodity case, if we assume,

$$v_i = v_c = v$$

and

$$h_i = h_c = h$$

then (7.11) reduces to its simpler form

$$g_i = g_i^w = \frac{s_p h (1-f)}{v} \tag{7.11a}$$

Further, if replacement investment is ignored as a relatively minor item (which means installed capacities have long service life in both sectors), then (7.11a) reduces to,

$$g_i = g_i^w = \frac{s_p h}{v}, \qquad f = 0 \tag{7.11b}$$

Equation (7.11b) has an analogous economic interpretation. It shows the *additional demand* for commodities (ΔY^d) resulting from the multiplier mechanism due to an increase in investment, i.e.,

$$\Delta Y^d = \frac{\Delta I}{s_p h} \quad \text{(see (2.20) in Chapter 2, p. 41)}$$

has to be matched by the *additional supply* of commodities (ΔY^s) through (net) investment, i.e.,

$$\Delta Y^s = \frac{I}{v}$$

assuming $I = J$ if $f = 0$. Consequently,

$$\Delta Y^d = \Delta Y^s \quad \text{implies} \quad \frac{\Delta I}{I} = g_i^w = \frac{s_p h}{v} \quad \text{as in (7.11b).}$$

However, when we consider two separate departments producing investment and consumption goods as distinct physical commodities, we need to ensure *separately* that there is no excess demand for or excess supply of *either* consumption goods (i.e., (7.6) yielding (7.7)) *or* of investment goods (i.e., (7.8) yielding (7.10)). And, it is the *combination* of these two separate conditions which yield (7.11) in a more general case.

Equation (7.11) also exhibits in a simple way the condition for *realisation of profit along the growth-path of investment*. It will be noted that the *rate of return* on investment (ζ), i.e., additional profit generated per unit of net investment ($\Delta R / J$) is *definitionally* given from (7.4a) and (7.4b) for the two respective sectors. Thus, from (7.4a) we write, for the consumption sector,

$$\frac{h_c}{v_c} = \frac{h_c \cdot \Delta C^s}{J_c} = \frac{\Delta R_c^s}{J_c} = \zeta_c^s \tag{7.12a}$$

where $\zeta_c^s = \Delta R_c^s / J_c$ rate of return on net investment in the consumption sector with *full* utilisation of new capacities (denoted by superscript 's').

Similarly, from (7.4b), for the investment sector,

$$\frac{h_i}{v_i} = \frac{h_i \Delta I^s}{J_i} = \frac{\Delta R_i^s}{J_i} = \zeta_i^s \tag{7.12b}$$

where ζ_i^s is the rate of return on net investment in the investment sector with full utilisation of new capacities.

Unless the rate of return on investment is *uniform* in both the sectors, the sectoral pattern of investment (λ) would tend to shift in favour of the sector enjoying a higher return. Thus, for maintaining a constant value of $\lambda = \lambda^*$ from (7.10) along the steady growth path, the uniformity of the rate of return on investment must be ensured. From (7.12a) and (7.12b), *uniformity in sectoral rates of return* implies,

$$\zeta_c^s \equiv \frac{h_c}{v_c} = \zeta_i^s = \frac{h_i}{v_i} \tag{7.13}$$

Since, $v_c h_i = v_i h_c$ in (7.13), using this in (7.11) we obtain,[6]

$$g_i^w = s_p \zeta^s \qquad \text{if } f = 0 \text{ by assumption} \qquad (7.14)$$

where $\zeta_c^s = \zeta_i^s = \zeta^s$ = the uniform rate of return.

This can also be rewritten as,

$$\zeta^s = \frac{g_i^w}{s_p} \qquad (7.14a)$$

where ζ^s is the *uniform* rate of return on net investment, when all *new* capacities created through net investment of every period are *fully utilised* (superscript 's' represents such fully utilised potential supply). It follows from (7.14a) that the higher is the growth rate of investment (g_i^w), the higher is the rate of return on investment defined at full capacity (ζ^s) for any given propensity to save out of profit (s_p). Therefore, equation (7.14a) recaptures the multiplier relation that a higher level of investment leads to the realisation of a higher level of profit (see (6.1) and (6.14) of Chapter 6). But that relationship is now restated in the context of a steadily growing economy with full utilisation of new capacities, continuously created through net investment.

In a private enterprise capitalist economy any such steady rate of growth (g_i^w) is sustainable only if the capitalists always *realise* the rate of return they *expect* on their net investment. Unless, the rate of return realised on investment conforms to *their* expectation, the capitalists would be induced to change their investment plans. This will naturally disturb any steady rate of growth g_i^w in (7.11). In other words, steady growth with full utilisation of new capacities must mean that the profit expectations of the capitalists are continuously fulfilled.[7] This implies from (7.14a),

$$\zeta^e = \zeta^s = \frac{g_i^w}{s_p} \qquad (7.15)$$

where ζ^e is the *expected* rate of return on investment by the capitalists, while ζ^s is the *realised* return at full utilisation of new capacities (see (7.14a)).

It now needs to be pointed out that the characterisation of full capacity growth in (7.11) is still deficient in one crucial respect. Steady growth at the rate g_i^w specified by (7.11) fails to ensure full utilisation of *all existing capacities*. It merely guarantees that *additional* capacities (ΔI^s and ΔC^s) created through net investment of every period remain fully utilised along such a growth path. Indeed, this is evident from the balance conditions between *additional* demand and *additional* supply obtained for the consumption for the investment sector respectively in (7.6) and (7.8). In contrast, we require *total* (not additional) demand of each sector to be matched by *total* supply of that sector at full capacity production. However, during the *intitial period*, the economy inherits from the past *arbitrary* levels of capacities in each sector as its initial condition. If these initial capacities historically inherited are such that there is over- or under-utilisation of capacity in one sector or the other, such *initial imbalance* in sectoral capacity utilisation would persist through time without being corrected even if condition (7.11) is satisfied. Such initial sectoral imbalance which upsets the possibility of steady accumulation in a capitalist economy has been described by many Marxist writers as the *proportionality problem*.[8]

Since the proportionality problem is essentially the historical legacy of an arbitrary initial condition, we may consider productive capacities $X_i(0)$ and $X_c(0)$ in the investment and in the consumption sectors respectively which are arbitrarily inherited by the economy in the initial period. Given initial labour productivity $x_i(0)$ and $x_c(0)$ in the two sectors, full utilisation of existing, i.e. the inherited capacities would require employment in the two sectors to be distributed in the proportion,

$$\frac{L_c(0)}{L_i(0)} = \frac{X_c(0)/x_c(0)}{X_i(0)/x_i(0)} = \bar{\theta}(0) \qquad (7.16a)$$

Nevertheless, this proportion $\bar{\theta}(0)$, being arbitrarily given by the initial condition, need not correspond to the proportion in which employment needs to be distributed between the two sectors to realise surplus of consumption goods into monetary profits. That *profit realisation proportion* is given from equation (2.25), p. 48, of Chapter 2 as,

$$\frac{L_c}{L_i} = \frac{(1-h_c)}{(1-h_i)} \cdot \frac{(1-s_p h_i)}{s_p h_c} \cdot \left(\frac{w_i}{w_c}\right) = \theta_R \qquad (7.16b)$$

Thus, two distinct proportions $\bar{\theta}(0)$ and θ_R, are dictated simultaneously by the double need of full utilisation of *initial* capacity, i.e. $\bar{\theta}(0)$ in (7.16a) as well as of realisation of surplus into profits, i.e. θ_R in (7.16b). In other words, an equality between (7.16a) and (7.16b), i.e.,

$$\bar{\theta}(0) = \theta_R, \qquad \text{at} \qquad t = 0 \qquad (7.17)$$

has to be satisfied to guarantee that the initial condition of the economy is characterised by full utilisation of capacities in all sectors. And only with this additional condition (7.17) holding, the earlier condition (7.11) ensures full utilisation of *both* new and old or historically inherited capacites along the steady growth path g_i^w of the economy.

To appreciate more fully the *structural* problem inherent in full capacity utilisation under arbitrary initial condition, consider Figure 7.1 below. It assumes an arbitrary initial situation, historically inherited by the economy where condition (7.17) is violated.

Consider, historically given proportions along the ray OP_2 representing (7.16a). Suppose OG workers are employed in the investment sector to utilise *existing* capacities in that sector fully. Thus,

Figure 7.1   *Realisation and proportionality problem. Ray OR through the origin corresponds to the profit realisation equation (7.16b). Rays OP_1 and OP_2 shows two different proportions of historically inherited capacities corresponding to equation (7.16a). Along OP_1 the consumption sector has a relatively higher proportion of historically inherited capacities than along OP_2.*

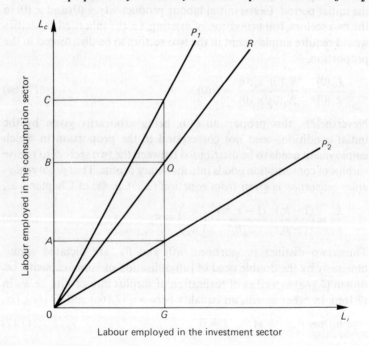

Labour employed in the consumption sector

Labour employed in the investment sector

$OG = L_i(0) = X_i(0)/x_i(0)$. However, OG workers in the investment sector create effective demand for surplus consumption goods which can be produced by OB workers in the consumption sector (see Figure 2.2, p. 37, for elaboration). In other words, with OG as the employment level in the investment sector, realisation of profit requires OB workers to be employed in the consumption sector. Consequently, the proportion OB/OG equals the profit realisation proportion θ_R in (7.16b), where the ray through the origin OR represents the profit realisation equation (7.16b).[9] However, by assumption historical proportions inherited along OP_2, permit only OA workers to be employed in the consumption sector. In consequence, *structural excess demand* for consumption goods, measured by the output producible by AB workers (i.e. AB multiplied by constant labour productivity x_c), exists in the initial situation.

Alternatively, suppose historical proportions are defined along ray OP_1 by (7.16a). The same OG number of workers in the investment sector generate demand for surplus consumption goods that can be produced by the same OB workers in the consumption sector to satisfy the profit realisation condition (7.16b) along ray OR. But, the historical proportion along ray OP_1 requires OC workers to be employed in the consumption sector for full utilisation of inherited capacity in that sector. Consequently, in this case *structural excess capacity* in the consumption sector, measured by output producible by BC workers (i.e., BC multiplied by x_c) would emerge in the economy. Thus, if OG represents the number of workers needed to be employed in the investment sector to fully utilise the inherited level of capacity of that sector, namely $OG = X_i(0)/x_i(0)$, then *structural excess demand or excess capacity* emerges in the consumption sector so long as condition (7.17) is violated.

This problem of an *arbitrary initial composition* of the capital stock resulting in structural excess demand or excess capacity in some sectors could be overcome through the flexibility of the *product* wage rates in the different sectors. This would, for instance, make the shares of profit in sectoral value added (i.e. h_c and h_i) flexible or would change the *money* wage relativities (w_i/w_c) to render the realisation proportion, θ_R more flexible in (7.16b). Nevertheless, such adjustment between prices and money wages altering the class distribution of income or the alteration of the money wage structure would be generally *incompatible* with a *steady* rate of accumulation over time in a capitalist economy.

Similarly, the share of investment between the two sectors, given by λ in (7.3a) and (7.3b), could change over time to bring the historical proportion $\overline{\theta}(0)$ in (7.16a) gradually in line with the realisation proportion θ_R in (7.16b). Nevertheless, such *changing* pattern of investment over time is not compatible with a *steady* rate of accumulation. Nor is there any compelling reason to suppose that the *autonomous* investment decisions by the capitalists would necessarily be directed the overcome over time the mismatch between realisation and proportionality shown in Figure 7.1. In short, an arbitrary initial composition of sectoral capacities can render the capitalist economy incapable of achieving steady state growth with full utilisation of capacities in all the sectors.

On the basis of the preceding analysis, we may now present a *list of conditions* that need to be satisfied for full utilisation of capacity along a steady growth path in a capitalist economy. It requires:

Condition 1. A rate of growth in investment such that there is *no over- or under-utilisation of new* (additional) *capacities* created through net investment in any sector. This is shown by conditions (7.6) and (7.8) which are ultimately combined to yield the growth rate g_i^w in investment in (7.11).

Condition 2. A *uniform rate of return* on investment in all sectors, shown by (7.13). Only with a uniform return in investment in all sectors, would the sectoral pattern of investment (λ) be stable over time at its equilibrium value λ^* given by (7.10). At that equilibrium value $\lambda = \lambda^*$, there is neither excess demand for nor excess supply of investment goods (see (7.10)). And, at that sectoral distribution of investment, $\lambda = \lambda^*$, the full capacity growth path of the consumption sector is also defined from (7.7).

Condition 3. A uniform rate of return on investment is steadily *realised* along the full capacity growth path given by (7.11). This is shown by (7.14a). However, for the growth path to remain undisturbed over time, this *realised* rate of return must also correspond to the *expected* rate of return by the capitalists, as shown by (7.15), because only then the *expectations* of capitalists regarding return on investment are exactly *fulfilled*. As a result, they would have no reason to change their investment plans over time and deviate from the steady growth path (g_i^w).

Condition 4. Finally, the *initial composition of the capital stock* arbitrarily inherited from the past must be in the 'right proportions', as shown by (7.17). Unless, this happens to be the case, discrepancy would arise between *the realisation and the proportionality problem*, as shown in Figure 7.1. Only if condition (7.17) holds, such discrepancy does not arise. Consequently, there would be no *structural* excess demand or supply in some sectors and the *initial* situation would not tend to vitiate the conditions for steady growth. Paradoxically, however, this requires the initial conditions *not* to be arbitrary, but to be moulded by the requirements of steady growth. This is a contradiction in terms. It shows the extremely unlikely, almost *accidental* nature of steady state growth in a capitalist economy, where (7.17) holds by fluke or accident.

Even if the set of analytical Conditions 1 to 4 (equations (4.11) to (4.17)) are assumed to be satisfied, such full capacity growth in a capitalist economy may not be *socially sustainable*. Because, it is satisfactory from the point of view of *only one class*, namely the capitalists. There is no reason to believe that such steady growth would necessarily be satisfactory to the working class for two major reasons. First, their *expected* real wage rate may differ from the real wage rate that is *realised* along such a steady growth path. Formally, the realised *product* wages are implied by the *given* value of h_c and h_i needed in defining the multiplier relation (7.1), restated also as the realisation proportion (7.16b). Recall that, by definition (see (3.2) of Chapter 3), the *real* wage, in terms of consumption goods is $w/P_c = x_c(1 - h_c) = w_r$, at each given level of labour productivity x_c. Unless the expected real wage rate of the workers (w_r^e) corresponds to the *realised* real wage rate (w_r), i.e., $w_r^e = w_r$, along the steady growth path – in analogy with the earlier condition (7.15) for the capitalists – the class distribution of income (given by h_c and h_i) cannot be said to have attained a *mutually* accepted pattern. Without such mutual acceptability, the conflicting economic claims by the competing classes would tend to upset the steady nature of growth, probably degenerating into an inflationary process (examined in Chapter 6, Section B).

Secondly, *full capacity growth does not mean full employment growth*. Indeed, the steady rate of accumulation (g_i^w) warranted by full utilisation of capacities may not create a sufficient number of new jobs for all the fresh entrants into the labour market in each period. In that case, the capitalists could be content with the steady rate of growth that fetches them their expected return on investment (see (7.14a) and (7.15)), but the workers face a mounting *absolute* level of unemployment ever time.

The number of jobs available in a sector during any period is *definitionally* given by the level of output of that sector divided by the level of labour productivity. Thus, $C/P_c x_c$ = the number of jobs available in the consumption sector (L_c) and $I/P_i x_i$ = the number of jobs available in the investment sector (L_i). It is important to note that, the *higher* is the level of labour productivity ($P_c x_c$ or $P_i x_i$) in either sector, the *lower* must be the number of jobs available to produce a *given* level of output (C or I), as a matter of definition.

The total number of available jobs, i.e., the employment level (L) of the economy is then definitionally given as,

$$L = L_i + L_c = \frac{I}{P_i x_i} + \frac{C}{P_c x_c}$$

or

$$L = \left[\frac{1}{P_i x_i} + \frac{1}{P_c x_c} \cdot \left(\frac{1 - s_p h_i}{s_p h_c} \right) \right] \cdot I \tag{7.18}$$

because the multiplier relation implies, $C/I = (1 - s_p h_i / s_p h_c)$, as in (2.17), p. 40, of Chapter 2.[10] In analogy with the one-commodity case, if we assume (see (2.30) of Chapter 2),

$$P_i x_i = P_c x_c = Px \text{ (uniform labour productivity)}$$

and $h_i = h_c = h$ (uniform profit share), then (7.18) reduces to its simpler form,

$$L = \left(\frac{1}{Px} \right) \cdot \frac{I}{s_p h} \tag{7.18a}$$

Equation (7.18a) shows that the level of employment (L) is simply the level of income (Y) determined by the multiplier relation, i.e., $Y = I/s_p h$ (see (2.20) of Chapter 2) divided by the uniform labour productivity (Px). With both the price level (P) and the share of profit (h) remaining *constant*, the percentage growth in employment is given from the logarithmic differentiation of (7.18a) as,

$$\frac{\Delta L}{L} = \frac{\Delta I}{I} - \frac{\Delta x}{x}, \qquad \text{if } h \text{ and } P \text{ are constants} \tag{7.18b}$$

Writing $(\Delta x/x) = q$ = growth in labour productivity in *physical* terms, the rate of growth of employment ($\Delta L/L$) along the full capacity growth path, $\Delta I/I = g_i^w$ is given from (7.18b) as,

$$\frac{\Delta L}{L} = g_i^w - q \tag{7.18c}$$

Unless this rate of growth in employment creation given by (7.18c) equals the rate of growth in the labour force ($\Delta N/N$), there would be either growing unemployment (if, $\Delta N/N > \Delta L/L$) or growing shortage of labour (if, $\Delta N/N < \Delta L/L$). This in turn may ultimately upset the steady growth rate (g_i^w) of full utilisation of capacities. Therefore, growth with full capacity *and* full employment requires from (7.18c)

$$\frac{\Delta L}{L} = g_i^w - q = \frac{\Delta N}{N} = n$$

or,

$$g_i^w = n + q \tag{7.19}$$

where q is the growth in *physical* labour productivity ($= \Delta x/x$) and $\Delta N/N = n$ is the rate of growth of labour force. Note 'n' also equals the rate of growth of population, if the demographic 'participation rate', i.e., the ratio of 'active' to total population remains constant.

However, condition (7.19) only guarantees that the growth of employment creation ($\Delta L/L$) keeps pace with the growth of new entrants in the labour market ($\Delta N/N$). Unless the economy is *initially* in a position of full employment, i.e.,

$$L(0) = N(0) \qquad \text{at } t = 0 \tag{7.19a}$$

(in analogy with full utilisation of initial capacity in (7.17)), *only new entrants* in the labour market (ΔN) would be absorbed in *new* jobs (ΔL), whereas any *initial* unemployment given by, $[N(0) - L(0)]$ would persist through time.

The growth rate of labour force (n) plus of labour productivity (q), shown on the right-hand side of (7.19), may be called the *natural rate of growth* of the economy. It specifies the *maximum* rate at which the *potential output* of the economy can grow through increase in numbers as well as in the efficiency of the labour force. Thus, when the rate of growth warranted by full utilisation of capacity (g_i^w) in (7.11b) equals the natural rate of growth ($n + q$) in (7.19), the economy is maintaining its *maximum, feasible rate of steady growth*.

In general, technological progress inducing growth in labour productivity ($\Delta x/x$) would be *incompatible* with *steady* growth. Thus, in (7.11b), unless the rate of return on investment (h/v) remains constant *despite* technical progress, the growth rate g_i^w cannot be steady over time. Only if *technological progress is neutral* in the sense of leaving the investment cost per unit of output (v) *constant* at a *constant* rate of return on investment (h/v), can steady growth proceed through time with technological progress.[11]

Such neutrality of technical progress, where both the rate of return (h/v) and the investment cost per unit of output (v) remain constant entails that the *share of* profit (i.e., $h \equiv h/v \cdot v$) is constant. Definitionally, however,

$$h = \left(1 - \frac{w}{P \cdot x}\right), w_c = w_i = w;$$

profit share (h) can remain constant only if *money* wage rate (w) and *nominal* labour productivity (Px) rises at the same percentage rate i.e.,

$$h = h_{\text{const}} \quad \text{if} \quad \frac{\Delta w}{w} = \frac{\Delta P}{P} + \frac{\Delta x}{x}$$

$$\text{or,} \quad \left(\frac{\Delta w}{w} - \frac{\Delta P}{P}\right) = \frac{\Delta w_r}{w_r} = \frac{\Delta x}{x} = q \tag{7.20}$$

where w_r is the *real* wage rate.

In other words, *neutrality* of technical progress that leaves the steady rate of growth undisturbed, also keeps the share of profit (h) constant by allowing *real* wage to rise at the same rate (q) as *physical* labour productivity (see (7.20)). Therefore, *steady* growth, with or without full employment, becomes possible only when technological progress is also 'neutral' to the class distribution of income.

It would now be realised that steady growth with full capacity utilisation as well as full employment, given by condition (7.19), is a mere *logical* possibility in a capitalist economy. Historically it is most implausible. This is emphasised by the fact that only as an *accident* of history can the '*right*' *initial conditions* hold with respect to the composition of the initial capital stock (see condition (7.17)) and the level of initial employment (see condition (7.19a)). Such 'right' initial conditions also signify that the economy must have been in equilibrium even in the very initial period. Thus, to continue along equilibrium growth, such equilibrium must have been attained already! The requirement of steady growth in a capitalist economy also robs technical progress of any possible *autonomy*; because only a certain type of 'neutral' technical progress was seen to be compatible with such steady growth.

Nevertheless, initial conditions that are *arbitrarily* inherited from history as well as the possibility of autonomous, non-neutral technical progress are essential prerequisites for studying capitalistic accumulation as an actual, historical process. From this point of view, accumulation at a steady rate must be recognised to be no more than a fiction. It is an analytical construct with no historical counterpart. The various conditions that need to be satisfied for such steady accumulation, as examined in this section, provide at best convenient points of reference for understanding actual processes of capitalistic accumulation. They also provide us with the negative knowledge that steady growth in a capitalist economy is almost a *mythical* concept, created for analytical convenience rather than for describing any actual phase in the history of capitalistic development.

B Relative Prices in the Steady State

The system of prices that would prevail along a path of steady accumulation must combine *three* distinct aspects. First, such prices must be consistent with the *short term* rule of industrial pricing which is based on fixed mark-up on the unit prime cost of business (see Chapter 3, Section B). Ignoring complications due to unprocessed, non-industrial raw materials, this implies a *constant*, proportional relation between prices and money wages, envisaged by the 'wage-unit' measure (see Chapter 3, Section A). Consequently, *class distribution of income*, represented by parameters such as h_i and h_c, remains *constant* along the steady growth path.

Secondly, prices under conditions of steady growth must satisfy the *long term* postulate of equilibrium, requiring the rate of return on investment (ζ) to be *uniform* in all lines of production (see (7.13)). Under conditions of free entry, the pattern of sectoral distribution of investment (λ) can remain constant only when the rate of return on investment is the same in all sectors. Otherwise, there would be a tendency for investment to be attracted to those lines of production which fetch a higher return while disinvestment through inadequate replacement would be encouraged in other lines that fetch lower return.

Finally, prices that rule along a path of steady accumulation must also *match demand with supply* in the case of each individual commodity. Indeed, under ideal conditions of steady growth examined in the last Section A, supply generated at full utilisation of capacity is matched by the corresponding level of effective demand so that the expanding size of the market presents no barrier to the realisation of surplus into profit in any sector of the economy (see conditions (7.6) and (7.8)). Such conditions would also ensure that the prices not only yield a uniform rate of return on investment (7.13), but also *realise* the rate of return expected by the capitalists along the path of full capacity growth (see (7.15)).

Ignoring complications caused by *unprocessed* raw materials (see Chapter 3, pp. 78–81), the *uniformity* of the rate of return on investment in (7.13) requires that the sector with a higher share of profit per unit of value added (h_i or h_c) must also have a correspondingly higher investment cost (v_i or v_c) per unit of value added, as given by (7.4a) and (7.4b). Thus, if for instance $h_c > h_i$, then $v_c > v_i$ by a corresponding proportion, to satisfy the postulate of the *uniformity* of the rate of return on investment given in (7.13).

When sectoral prices (P_i and P_c) are *explicitly* considered, the investment cost per unit of output in each sector is valued at the respective prices. Thus, we can write (7.4a) as,

$$v_c = \frac{\text{investment cost per unit of output of consumption goods}}{\text{price of a unit consumption goods}} = \frac{P_i b_c}{P_c} \qquad (7.21a)$$

and

$$v_i = \frac{\text{investment cost per unit of ouput of investment goods}}{\text{price of a unit of investment goods}} = \frac{P_i b_i}{P_i} = b_i \quad (7.21b)$$

where P_i is the price of investment goods, P_c is the price of consumption goods, b_c are the investment goods needed to create one additional unit of capacity in the consumption sector and b_i are the investment goods needed to create one additional unit of capacity in the investment sector.

Under equilibrium growth, all sectors have the *same* rate of return on investment (ζ) as defined by (7.13). We may also simplify by assuming that a *uniform* money wage rate (w) rules in all the sectors.[12] Using the definition of the share of profit (h_c of h_i) from (3.2) of Chapter 3, we then have for the consumption sector,

$$\zeta = \frac{h_c}{v_c} \quad \text{and} \quad h_c = 1 - \left(\frac{w}{P_c x_c}\right) \qquad (7.22a)$$

Similarly, for the investment sector,

$$\zeta = \frac{h_i}{v_i} \quad \text{and} \quad h_i = 1 - \left(\frac{w}{P_i x_i}\right) \tag{7.22b}$$

where ζ is the *uniform* rate of return on investment,[13] w is the *uniform* money wage rate ($= w_i = w_c$) and x_c and x_i are labour productivity in the consumption and in the investment sectors respectively.

Equations (7.21a) and (7.22a) define the *price equation for consumption goods* along the steady growth path as,

$$P_c = \frac{w}{x_c} + \zeta P_i b_c \tag{7.23a}$$

The *price equation for investment goods* is similarly defined from (7.21b) and (7.22b) as,

$$P_i = \frac{w}{x_i} + \zeta \cdot P_i b_i \tag{7.23b}$$

Equations (7.23a) and (7.23b) together define the *price system* ruling along an equilibrium growth path. Note that such a system of prices cover the wage cost per unit of output w/x_c or w/x_i, *plus* a uniform rate of return (ζ) on investment cost incurred per unit of output namely, $P_i b_c$ for the consumption and, $P_i b_i$ for the investment sector. In this sense, price equals average cost per unit of output in each sector, when decomposed on the right-hand side of (7.23a) and (7.23b) into wage cost *plus* return on investment cost per unit of output.

The price equation (7.23b) can be rearranged to yield the product wage rate in terms of investment goods (w/P_i) as,

$$\frac{w}{P_i} = x_i(1 - \zeta b_i) \tag{7.24}$$

which has a meaningful non-negative value only if,

$$\zeta \leqslant \frac{1}{b_i} \tag{7.25}$$

The above condition (7.25), imposes a *technological* ceiling to the *maximum possible* rate of return on investment. Its economic implication is evident from (7.21b) and (7.22b). By inserting (7.21b) into the expression for the rate of return (ζ) on investment given in (7.22b), we obtain, $\zeta = h_i/b_i$, i.e., $h_i = \zeta b_i$. This implies that the *share* of profit in the investment sector (h_i) would not exceed unity (i.e., $h_i < 1$) so long as (7.25) holds.

Dividing both sides of the price equation for consumption goods in (7.23a) by w and substituting for P_i/w from (7.24), we obtain, on simplification, an expression for the product wage in terms of consumption goods. This is also the *real* wage rate, given as,

$$\frac{w}{P_c} = \frac{x_c x_i (1 - \zeta b_i)}{x_i + \zeta(b_c x_c - b_i x_i)} \tag{7.26}$$

Further, dividing (7.26) by (7.24) we also obtain the *relative price* of investment goods in terms of consumption goods as,

$$P = \frac{P_i}{P_c} = \frac{x_c}{x_i + \zeta(b_c x_c - b_i x_i)} \tag{7.27}$$

There are *four important propositions* which the steady state price system (7.23a) and (7.23b) imply in terms of the algebraic relations (7.24) to (7.27).

Proposition 1. There is a *technologically implied maximum* $(1/b_i)$ *to the uniform rate of return* on investment (ζ). This follows directly from condition (7.25).

Proposition 2. The individual *product wage rates decrease as the rate of return* (ζ) *increases*, from zero to its maximum value $(1/b_i)$. From (7.24) and (7.26) it is clear that *each* product wage attains its maximum value of labour productivity in that sector when $\zeta = 0$, i.e.

$$\frac{w}{P_i} = x_i \quad \text{and} \quad \frac{w}{P_c} = x_c \qquad \text{at } \zeta = 0$$

Conversely,

$$\frac{w_i}{P_i} = \frac{w_c}{P_c} = 0 \qquad \text{at } \zeta = \frac{1}{b_i}$$

It can also be checked that for intermediate values of ζ in the range $(1/b_i \geqslant \zeta \geqslant 0)$, *each* product wage decreases as ζ increases. From (7.24)

$$\frac{d}{d\zeta}\left(\frac{w}{P_i}\right) = -x_i b_i < 0 \tag{7.24a}$$

and from (7.26),[14]

$$\frac{d}{d\zeta}\left(\frac{w}{P_c}\right) = \frac{-b_c x_i x_c^2}{[x_i + \zeta(b_c x_c - b_i x_i)]^2} < 0 \tag{7.26a}$$

Proposition 3. The *relative price system is not independent of the rate of return* (ζ) in general. The functional dependence of relative price $P = P_i/P_c$ on the rate of return (ζ) is shown in (7.27). Only when, either $\zeta = 0$ or $(b_c x_c - b_i x_i) = 0$, the price ratio in (7.27) becomes a technologically determined ratio, i.e.

$$P = \frac{P_i}{P_c} = \frac{x_c}{x_i} \qquad \text{if either } \zeta = 0 \text{ or } (b_c x_c - b_i x_i) = 0 \qquad (7.27a)$$

Since $1/x_i$ represents the amount of labour needed to produce a unit of investment goods output and, $1/x_c$ represents the amount of labour needed to produce a unit of consumption goods output, the price ratio in (7.27a) is determined by the ratio of labour requirement per unit of output in the respective sectors. In this sense, the Marxian *labour theory of value as a theory of relative prices* holds in (7.27a) if *either* the rate of return on investment, ζ is zero *or*

$$b_c x_c = b_i x_i \qquad (7.27b)$$

In this latter case of (7.27b), the amount of investment goods required *per unit of labour* (i.e., $b_c x_c$ or $b_i x_i$) is the same in *both* the sectors. This is the case of the '*equal organic composition of capital*' in all sectors postulated by Marx to ensure that prices are *proportional* to labour value embodied in a commodity (see (7.27a)). In this case, there is no '*problem of transformation*' of labour values into prices of production (given by (7.23a) and (7.23b)), as labour values are strictly proportional to prices in each sector so long as (7.27b) holds.

Proposition 4. *The system of prices operates with one degree of freedom.* Because, the two equations in (7.23a) and (7.23b) have *four* *unknown* variables (w, ζ, P_i and P_c) so that, even if we choose one of the variables as the numeraire or the 'measuring rod' of the system, e.g.

$$P_c = 1$$

the system is not *determinate*. Either the *real* wage rate (w/P_c) or the rate of return (ζ) has to be *exogenously* specified to determine the relative price system ($P = P_i/P_c$). This is also evident in the 'reduced equation' (7.27) where the *relative* price (P) is determined only for an *exogeneously* given value of ζ, except in the special case of (7.27a). Consequently, we would need *additional information* in general, to have a determinate system of relative prices.

Under conditions of steady growth that additional information is provided by the *profit realisation equation* (7.14a) which establishes a relation between the rate of growth (g_i^w) and the rate of return on investment (ζ^s). Along the steady growth path, the growth rate of investment (g_i^w) warranted by full utilisation of new capacity is such that the additional *supply* from new capacities is exactly matched by additional *demand* (see (7.6) and (7.8)). This means additional sales corresponding to full utilisation of new capacities are realised along such a growth path at the given profit margin (defined by h_c and h_i) per unit of sale. Given the profit margin and the investment costs per unit of sectoral outputs (see (7.4a) and (7.4b)), the rates of return on investment are defined at full capacity output (see (7.12a) and (7.12b)). Thus, with a *uniform* rate of return on investment, ensured by (7.13), the rate of growth of investment (g_i^w) uniquely defines the uniform rate of return (ζ^s) on investment shown by (7.14a). Inserting this value of the rate of return on investment from (7.14a) into (7.27), we are able to obtain a completely *determinate system of relative prices along the steady growth path* warranted by full utilisation of capacity.[15] Algebraically, (7.14a) yields,

$$\zeta = \zeta^s = \frac{g_i^w}{sp} \tag{7.28a}$$

which defines the relative price system from (7.27) as,

$$P^s = \frac{x_c}{x_i + \zeta^s \cdot (b_c x_c - b_i x^i)} \text{ at } \zeta = \zeta^s \tag{7.29}$$

In particular, if we postulate *full capacity* as well as *full employment* growth, then the rate of growth warranted by full utilisation of capacity (i.e., g_i^w) must also equal the *natural rate* of growth determined by growth in labour force (n) as well as in labour productivity (q). Thus, the earlier condition (7.19) must hold, where $g_i^w = (n + q)$. Consequently, the rate of return on investment would be defined at full employment growth by a relation,

$$\zeta = \zeta^s = \frac{(n+q)}{s_p}, \qquad g_i^w = (n+q) \text{ by assumption} \tag{7.28b}$$

Thus, inserting (7.28b) instead of (7.28a) in the relative price equation (7.27), a determinate set of relative prices that corresponds to full capacity (because $\zeta = \zeta^s$) as well as to full employment growth (because $\zeta = (n+q)/s_p$) is obtained along the steady growth path.

Despite the growth in labour productivity (x^i and x_c) at a steady rate

q, the Harrod-*neutrality of technical progress* leaves, by definition, the investment goods required per unit of sectoral output (b_i and b_c) constant at a constant rate of return ζ. Thus, in the relative price equation (7.27), such growth of labour productivity over time may be explicitly introduced to yield,

$$P = \frac{P_i}{P_c} = \frac{x_c(1+q)^t}{x_i(1+q)^t + \zeta[b_c x_c(1+q)^t - b_i x_i(1+q)^t]}, \qquad (7.30)$$

where $\dfrac{\Delta x_c}{x_c} = \dfrac{\Delta x_i}{x_i} = q$

By factoring out the term $(1+q)^t$ in both the numerator and in the denominator of (7.30), it is seen that the *relative price P* remains *invariant over time*, despite such growth in labour productivity due to neutral technical progress.

However, the *product* wage in terms of investment goods under growing labour productivity is given from (7.24) as,

$$\frac{w}{P_i} = (1+q)^t [x_i(1 - \zeta b_i)] \qquad (7.31a)$$

Similarly, from (7.26), the product (real) wage in terms of consumption goods is given as,

$$\frac{w}{P_c} = \frac{x_c(1+q)^t \cdot x_i(1+q)^t(1 - \zeta b_i)}{x_i(1+q)^t + \zeta[b_c x_c(1+q)^t - b_i x_i(1+q)^t]}$$

or, by factoring out $(1+q)^t$,

$$\frac{w}{P_c} = (1+q)^t \cdot \left[\frac{x_c x_i(1 - \zeta b_i)}{x_i + \zeta(b_c x_c - b_i x_i)} \right] \qquad (7.31b)$$

Thus, neutrality of technical progress, which raises *labour productivity at the same rate* (q) in *both* the sectors implies:

(a) A system of constant relative prices that remains invariant over time (see (7.30)).

(b) Percentage rise in *all the product wage rates* at the same rate as that of physical labour productivity (q), as demonstrated by (7.31a) and (7.31b). This also implies, as already noted in (7.20), that the pattern of distribution of income, given by profit *shares* h_i and h_c

in sectoral value added remains *unaffected* by neutral technical progress.

Note, these properties of constancy of (a) *relative* prices and (b) of profit *shares* are maintained only when labour productivity rises at the same rate $(\Delta x_c/x_c = \Delta x_i/x_i = q)$ in all sectors. Consequently, (Harrod-)neutrality of technical progress also entails the *same rate of growth in labour productivity in all sectors*, if it is to be compatible with steady growth.

When steady growth entails full utilisation, not only of *new*, i.e., additional capacities created through net investment (as in (7.6) and (7.8)), but also of all *existing* capacities, the *initial stock* of capital goods must be in the 'right' proportion to avoid any problem of realisation (see (7.17) and Figure 7.1). In such a case, the *entire* existing *stock* of capital goods are as fully utilised as the flow of new capital goods created during every period through net investment. Consequently, the accountants may be assumed (under such equilibrium conditions) to put a book value on the existing stock of capital goods which would yield an *average* rate of profit (γ) no different from the rate of return (ζ) on the current *flow* of investment. Thus, when the entire *stock* of capital goods is in its equilibrium configuration, we have,

$$\text{the } average \text{ rate of profit, } \gamma\left(= \frac{P}{K}\right) = \text{the rate of return on new investment, } \zeta\left(= \frac{\Delta R}{J}\right) \tag{7.32}$$

where R is the total profit *net* of replacement cost,[16] ΔR is the additional *net* profit, J is the *net* investment (see (7.2)) and K is the accountants' book valuation of the existing stock of capital goods.

It must, however, be realised that the *average* rate of profit (γ) on the book value of the existing *stock* of capital goods would be equal to the *marginal* rate of return (ζ) on new capital goods created through net *flow* of investment of each period, only when all the stocks, historically inherited from the past conform to the exact requirements of the steady growth path (see (7.17)). In other words, the economy must be fully settled in its equilibrium configuration with the 'right' proportions in terms of *both* the existing *stocks* and the new *flows* of capital goods of every period. Only in such a case, where both the stocks and the flows of capitals goods conform to the requirements of equilibrium growth, can we *interchange* the concept of the *average* rate of profit (γ) with the *marginal* rate of return (ζ) on investment, because all structural problems arising from historically inherited disproportionalities in stocks are ruled out by assumption under such a hypothetical equilibrium configuration of steady growth.

C Capitalistic Accumulation at a Sustainable Rate

Except as a matter of *historical* accident, capitalistic accumulation cannot be sustained at a steady pace with full utilisation of *all* the existing capacities and full employment of the *entire* labour force. The disproportionality inherent in an *arbitrary*, initial stock of capital goods would prevent the full capacity growth path from materialising in a capitalist economy (see Figure 7.1). Similarly, any significant initial unemployment would tend to upset the possibility of full employment growth (see (7.19a)).

Since only by chance could the *arbitrary* initial conditions coincide exactly with the requirements of such steady state growth (see (7.17) and (7.19a)), the free enterprise capitalist economy must depend on benevolent historical accidents, rather than on any intrinsic market-based mechanism, to sustain accumulation at a pace that ensures full utilisation of existing capacities and offers full employment to the labour force.

In this sense, steady state accumulation is a matter of chance and *not* of necessity in a capitalist economy. And, even that chance factor is extremely improbable, almost negligible, because not only must the initial conditions be 'right' but even *technical progress* must accidentally maintain its *neutral* character. Unless technical progress raises labour productivity at the *same* rate in *all* the sectors (see (7.30)) and the *product* wages rise at exactly the same rate as labour productivity (see (7.31a) and (7.31b)), the *bias* in technical change would tend to upset the pace of steady growth over time by altering the pattern of class distribution of income, captured by the value of the parameter h (see (7.20)). Once again, instead of being autonomous, technical progress must accidentally conform to the requirements of steady accumulation.

Such stringent conditons involving 'right' historical accidents are clearly most unlikely to obtain in reality. Consequently, capitalistic accumulation with full utilisation of capacity and full employment is *not* attainable in general. More important, however, is the fact that the capitalist class itself may not even be especially interested in sustaining such a growth path. It must be recognised that the expansion of capitalistic commodity production is based on the logic of profit realised in an expanding market. Capitalists, individually or collectively, are usually indirectly concerned about the level of employment or of capacity utilisation, only in so far as it affects their profit. So long as *realised* profit match their *expectations* along any *actual* growth path (g^a) the capitalists would be quite content to maintain that rate of growth, irrespective of whether it guarantees full employment or full utilisation of capacity. From this point of view, the logic of capitalistic commodity production dictates a rate of growth which is warranted *neither* by the requirements of full employment (see (7.19)) *nor* by that of full utilisation of capacity (see (7.11)). Instead, it is simply that rate of accumulation which would satisfy the profit expectations of the capitalists. This is also emphasised by our earlier condition (7.15), where the rate of return on investment which the capitalists *expect* (ζ^e) is assumed to coincide with the *realised* rate of return on investment (ζ^s) at full utilisation of new capacities. Unless this condition (7.15) is satisfied, there would be no reason for the capitalists to continue investing along the full capacity growth path (g_i^w).

Therefore, the very logic of capitalistic commodity production dictates that *any actual rate of growth* (g^a) becomes sustainable simply by virtue of the fact that it is desired by the capitalists (g^d),[17] and it is desired by the capitalists when it fulfils their profit expectation. Thus, the sustainability of *any* actual rate of growth (g^a) over time requires,

$$g^a = g^d \qquad \text{because } \zeta^a = \zeta^e \qquad (7.33)$$

where g^a is the *actual* (realised) rate of growth, g^d is the rate of growth *desired* by the capitalists, ζ^a is the *realised* (actual) rate of return on investment and ζ^e is the capitalists' *expected* rate of return on investment.

When capitalists *expect* to earn a rate of return on investment (ζ^e) which is *different* from that generated either by full utilisation of capacity $(\zeta^s$ in (7.14a)) or by full employment (see (7.28b)), growth at a steady pace with full capacity or full employment may even cease to be desirable from the point of view of the capitalists, because, such steady growth would then fail to satisfy their profit expectation (i.e., condition (7.15) is violated). This emphasises the fact that full utilisation of capacity or full employment are largely *extraneous* considerations in a process of capitalistic accumulation which is mainly guided by expectations of profits. It is precisely this dominant role of profit expectation by the capitalists as the prime mover of the system that is captured by equation (7.33).

Nevertheless, equation (7.33) has to be interpreted only as the *necessary condition* for any actual rate of growth (g^a) to be sustainable over time. The growth path characterised by (7.33) also has to be *stable* in the sense that any chance displacement from it would set up self-correcting adjustments to restore back the original growth path. Unless that *sufficient condition* ensuring the stability of the growth path is also satisfied, any chance displacement would make such a growth path unsustainable over time.

The nature of this stability condition deserves elaboration. Consider a case where *expectation formation* is of the simplest type. Capitalists extrapolate the *actual* rate of return (ζ^a) realised on current investment into the future, as their *expected* return (ζ^e). This yields a simple equation for 'static' expectation formation as,

$$\zeta^a = \zeta^e \tag{7.34}$$

It is also reasonable to assume that the rate of accumulation *desired* by the capitalists (g^d) is, in general, an *increasing* function of their expected rate of return (ζ^e) i.e.,

$$g^d = G(\zeta^e), \qquad G' > 0 \tag{7.35}$$

Inserting (7.34) in (7.35), the capitalists' *desired* rate of growth is obtained as an increasing function of the *actual* rate of return (ζ^a), i.e.,

$$g^d = G(\zeta^a), \qquad G' > 0 \tag{7.36}$$

However, along any actual growth path, the increment in *actual* (net) investment (ΔJ^a) is matched by increment in net savings from realised profits (ΔR^a) to yield,[18]

$$\Delta J^a = s_p \cdot \Delta R^a, \qquad 1 \geqslant s_p > 0$$

Or, dividing both sides by the level of actual (net) investment J^a,

$$g^a = s_p \zeta^a \tag{7.37}$$

where $\Delta J^a / J^a = g^a$ and $\zeta^a = \Delta R^a / J^a$, i.e., the actual rate of return. Note that the *actual* rate of return depends on the *degree of capacity utilisation* (*d*). Thus, by definition,

$$\zeta^a \equiv \frac{h \cdot \Delta Y^a}{J^a} \equiv h\left(\frac{\Delta Y^a}{\Delta Y^s}\right) \cdot \left(\frac{\Delta Y^s}{J^a}\right) = \frac{h \cdot d}{v},$$

$$1 \geqslant d \geqslant 0 \text{ and } h = \frac{\Delta R^a}{\Delta Y^a} \tag{7.38}$$

where ΔY^a and ΔY^s being increments in *actual* and *potential* output respectively, their ratio, $d = \Delta Y^a / \Delta Y^s$ defines the degree of utilisation of new capacity (*d*) created by each period's net investment. And, as before in (7.4a) or (7.4b), we define, $v = J^a / \Delta Y^s$, i.e., investment cost required to augment capacity, i.e., *potential* output by one additional unit to obtain (7.38).

It should be noted from (7.38) that the actual rate of return (ζ^a) depends on the actual degree of capacity utilisation *d*, (lying between 0 and 1) for given values of profit share (*h*) and investment cost per unit of capacity creation (*v*). Therefore, as (7.12a) or (7.12b) shows, the rate of return at full utilisation of capacity (ζ^s) is defined only at the *extreme* value of $d = 1$.

Using (7.36) and (7.37) in (7.33), we are now in a position to define an equilibrium rate of return ζ^*, at which the *desired* growth rate (g^d) equals the *actual* growth rate (g^a). This shown by point *E* in Figure 7.2 where the *GG* curve representing the desired growth rate in (7.36) intersects the ray through the origin *OA* representing the actual growth rate given by (7.37).[19] The *actual* rate of return $\zeta^* = OR$ at *E* is exactly what the capitalists *expect* at that equilibrium rate of accumulation $OB (= g^a = g^d)$.

Consider now a chance displacement from the initial equilibrium position at *E* in Figure 7.2. Suppose the actual rate of return is displaced for some reason from *OR* ($= \zeta^*$) to *OC*. At that rate of return *OC*, the *actual* rate of accumulation in the economy is CQ_1 (from equation (7.37)), but the capitalists would *desire* a higher rate of accumulation CP_1 (from equation (7.36)). Consequently, the actual rate of accumulation becomes $CP_1 (= DQ_2)$ in the next period which induces a correspondingly higher rate of return *OD*. This higher rate of return *OD* is realised through a *higher degree of capacity utilisation*, i.e., *d* rises in (7.38), while *h* and *v* are supposed to remain constant.[20] The higher *actual* rate of return *OD* in turn raises profit expectation (see (7.34)) and induces a still higher rate of accumulation DP_2 and so on, until the discrepancy between the desired and the actual rate of

Figure 7.2 *Adjustment between the actual and the capitalists' desired rate of accumulation. Curve GG represents the capitalists' desired rate of accumulation given by equation (7.36). Ray OA represents the actual rate of accumulation given by (7.37) and has a slope, tan AON = s_p.*

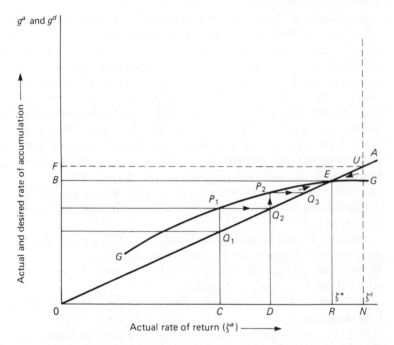

accumulation (shown for successive periods by $P_1 Q_1$, $P_2 Q_2$. etc.) is ultimately eliminated and equilibrium restored at E. Similarly, any displacement on the other side (e.g., $ON > OR = \zeta^*$) can also be shown to converge back to equilibrium at E.

A closer examination of Figure 7.2 shows that the *condition for stability* of the equilibrium position E is given by the fact that the *slope* of the GG curve at E must be *smaller* than the *slope* of the ray OA, i.e. GG must intersect OA from above for equilibrium to be stable at E. Therefore, for stability, slope of OA represented by (7.37) > slope at E of GG represented by (7.36), or algebraically,

$$s_p > G'(\zeta^a)|_{\zeta^a = \zeta^*} \tag{7.39}$$

Thus, the stability condition (7.39) requires variations in the actual rate of return (ζ^a) to have a *stronger impact* on saving than on the capitalists' desired rate of accumulation. This condition for stability bears a close resemblance to the stability condition derived earlier in (6.5) or (6.6) in Chapter 6, except for the fact that it is now set in the context of accumulation.

An actual growth path becomes *sustainable* over time when it not only fulfils the profit expectations of the capitalists (as shown by the *necessary* condition (7.33)) but it is also stable (shown by the *sufficient* condition (7.39)). Nevertheless, such a sustainable rate of actual growth, given by OB in Figure 7.2 need *not* ensure either full employment or full utilisation of capacity over time in a capitalist economy. This is also shown in Figure 7.2 by an exogeneously given *natural* rate of growth $OF = (n + q)$ from (7.19). When this *natural* rate is higher than the *sustained* actual rate of accumulation OB, BF per cent of the total growth rate in labour force is unable to find employment in every period. As a result, the *absolute* level of unemployed workers increases over time in the economy, although the capitalists continue to fulfil their profit expectations by sustaining the rate of growth at OB.

Similarly, the full capacity growth path may imply a rate of return on investment which is $ON = \zeta^s$ in (7.14a) implying $d = 1$ in (7.38). When the equilibrium rate of return $OR = \zeta^*$ is *less* than that rate of return ON at full utilisation of capacity (i.e., $\zeta^* < \zeta^s$), it means that new capacities created through net investment of each period are not being fully utilised along the steady growth rate OB. Instead, capitalists may expect a 'normal' degree of capacity utilisation along this growth rate OB, given by, $d = d_n < 1$. Although the rate of return associated with such 'normal' degree of capacity utilisation may be *lower* at OR (from (7.38)) compared with the full capacity rate of return ON, that rate of return (OR) is in conformity with what the capitalists expect. Consequently, the actual rate of growth is sustained at OB with 'normal' rather than full utilisation of capacity.[21]

The very exceptional set of circumstances which will make the *actual* rate of growth sustainable with *both* full employment and full utilisation of capacity (see (7.19)) is also shown in Figure 7.2. To start with, the *natural* rate of growth at $OF = (n + q)$ will intersect the ray OA at U to induce an actual rate of return ON. This rate of return ON has to coincide with the full capacity rate of return, $\zeta^s = (n + q)/sp$, as in (7.28b). Thus, the horizontal dotted line from F and the vertical dotted line from N intersect on the ray OA at U. In addition, the desired rate of accumulation by the capitalists at that rate of return $ON (= \zeta^s)$ must also be equal to OF, i.e., the GG curve must also pass through the point U (this is *not* shown in Figure 7.2). Unless the capitalists' *desired* rate of accumulation read from the GG curve at the full capacity rate of return $ON (= \zeta^s)$ happens to coincide with full employment rate of growth (OF) by accident, the *actual* rate of accumulation (OB) cannot be sustained with full utilisation of capacity and full employment.[22] In short, except in the most unlikely event where point E happens to coincide with point U, the utopian conditions for sustained accumulation with full employment and full utilisation of capacity are *not* fulfilled in a capitalist economy.

Despite its many unrealisms, our analysis therefore has an important message to convey. Any *actual* rate of growth may become *sustainable* in a capitalist economy only because it happens to fulfil the capitalists' expectations regarding profits (condition (7.33)) and satisfies the properties of a *stable* growth path (condition (7.39)). *Only* in this sense, the rate of growth desired or *warranted* by the capitalists' expectations regarding profits (see (7.35)) may have a tendency to adjust to the actual rate of growth of the economy, mostly through adjustment in capacity utilisation. However, this *neither* guarantees full employment *nor* full utilisation of capacities (see Figure 7.2). Indeed, there does *not* exist any viable mechanism in a capitalist economy to make any such *actual* rate of growth *sustained* by continuous fulfilment of profit expectations by the capitalists (as shown in (7.33)) coincide with either the *natural* rate of growth of the labour force or with full utilisation of capacities (see (7.19)). In addition, it must also be remembered that the *disproportionality* inherent in any arbitrary initial composition of the stock of capital goods (see Figure 7.1) makes full utilisation of *all* existing capacities only a *logical* possibility. It can never materialise in reality, unless by sheer accident the initial conditions cease to be *arbitrary* and coincide with the exact requirements of steady state growth with full capacity and full employment (recall conditions (7.17) and (7.19a)).

Such problems of initial conditions arbitrarily inherited from the past history of the economy that would prevent the full capacity growth path from ever materialising in a capitalist economy are often evaded by making artificial assumptions. For instance, a certain type of (neoclassical) growth theory takes recourse to the *artificial assumption of a perfectly malleable stock of capital goods*. This means that capacities can easily (i.e., without cost or time-lag) be transferred from one sector to another. Also, labour productivity can be instantaneously adjusted by selecting the optimum technique of production, not only for the *flow* of new capital goods created by investment but for the *entire* stock of capital goods. The usual *aggregate 'production function'* with labour and 'capital' as 'factors of production' implies such fantastic assumptions.

It is not always recognised that these are not merely simplifying assumptions essential for theoretical analysis. The strange assumption of malleable (or perfectly versatile) capital goods rules out all problems of disproportionality inherent in any *arbitrary* initial condition. The assumption that perfectly malleable capital goods can always maintain their 'right' sectoral proportions (as well as 'right' techniques of production) without cost or time-lag simply means that there can be *no persistence of errors* from past investment decisions. All errors either in sectoral capacity disproportions or in choosing techniques of production are instantaneously rectified without cost or time-lag, as the malleable stock of capital goods is *always* optimally adjusted. Naturally, the consequence of *falsified* expectations have little significance in such analysis, because errors from false expectations never persist, but are costlessly and instantaneously corrected due to the perfect malleability of the stock of capital goods. Thus, by banishing the problem of sectoral disproportionality, by ruling out all consequences of errors and incorrect expectations from the past, we are left with a totally artificial analysis of capitalistic accumulation which is devoid of all complications caused by time. This is, what in effect the assumption of malleability of capital goods implies. Naturally, it cannot serve the purpose of any serious historical analysis, where disproportionality of the initial conditions are the results of *past* errors which are inherited today, while presently held expectations may again turn out to be false to create disproportionalities for tomorrow. By employing the assumption of a *malleable* stock of capital goods, we not only evade these crucial problems of historical analysis; more sadly, we may even fail to recognise that such problems are at the heart of every historical process of accumulation.

Notes to Chapter 7

1. This has a mechanical analogy. It corresponds to the 'adiabatic case' in mechanics, where the dynamical properties of a mechanical system are examined by assigning equilibrium values to the more rapidly adjusting variables.

2. Note, algebraically 'Δ' represents the *forward* difference operator on a variable. Thus, $\Delta I(t) \equiv [I(t+1) - I(t)]$, while $\Delta I(t-1) \equiv [I(t) - I(t-1)]$. Similarly, $\Delta C^d(t) \equiv [C^d(t+1) - C^d(t)]$ and $\Delta C^d(t-1) \equiv [C^d(t) - C^d(t-1)]$. It would be economically more natural to think of variable C^d and I in (7.1) as relating *to time period* $(t-1)$, where t represents the current period. Thus, as a convention for reckoning with time, we assume variables represent their values at the *end* of the period. For instance, $\Delta C^d(t-1)$ in (7.1) represents the increase in demand for consumption goods between *end* of period $(t-1)$, i.e., $C^d(t-1)$ the *end* of period t, i.e., $C^d(t)$, implying increase in consumption demand *during* period t. Similarly, ΔI in (7.1) represents $\Delta I(t-1)$, i.e. increase in investment *during* period t. This convention for reckoning with time is followed throughout Chapter 7; but the time variable 't' is not explicitly shown to make notations simpler whenever there is no possibility of confusion.

3. We define investment *net* of *replacement* rather than of *depreciation*. Although the latter concept of depreciation is common in national income accounting (e.g., see (1.3) of Chapter 1), it is an accountant's concept. In a *growing* economy, replacement typically falls short of depreciation allowance made by accountants on a 'straight-line basis'. Such excess of depreciation funds can finance nearly *half* of net investment over replacement costs. On this point see, R. F. Harrod, 'Replacement, net investment, amortisation funds' (Harrod, 1970) and A. Bhaduri, 'Unwanted amortisation funds: a mathematical treatment' (Bhaduri, 1972).

4. v_c and v^i are known as the marginal or *incremental* 'capital output ratios'. Note J_c in (7.4a) or J^i in (7.4b) represents once-for-all construction or installment cost; hence it is a *stock* item. On the other hand, ΔC^s in (7.4a) or ΔI^s in (7.4b) represents the (annual) *flow* of additional (potential) output in the consumption or in the investment sector. Hence v^c or v^i is *a ratio of stock to flow having a time dimension*, e.g., if a 'machine' costs $2000 and gives an annual flow of consumption output (ΔC^s) worth $500, then v^c in (7.4a) is $4:1$ *per year*. If we took a six month period instead, the flow of six-monthly output may be assumed half its annual figure i.e. $250 so that v^c in (7.4a) is $8:1$ per six months. The value of the 'capital–output ratio' is therefore *not* independent of the length of the time period.

5. Note (7.4a) and (7.4b) imply one-period lag, e.g. $J_c(t-1)$ leads to an additional capacity in the consumption sector during period t because, $\Delta C^s(t-1)$ is definitionally, $[C^s(t) - C^s(t-1)]$ (see, Note 2 of this chapter). These lags are not explicitly shown to simplify notations in the text.

6. Similarly, (7.10) and (7.13) implies,

$$\lambda^* = \frac{v^i s_p h_c}{v^c} = s_p h_i, \text{ because } \frac{h_c}{v_c} = \frac{h_i}{v_i}$$

Hence, $s_p h_i$ represents the equilibrium distribution of investment between the sectors, when the rate of return on investment is *uniform* in both sectors.

7. Note that profit expectation relates here to the rate of return on *new* investment $(\Delta R/J)$ which is different from the rate of profit R/K, where K is the accountant's valuation of 'capital', i.e., the stock of means of production. Thus, return on investment is a *marginal* concept, while the rate of profit is an *average* concept. There is considerable confusion in economic theory in its failure to keep these two concepts distinct. We return to this problem in condition (7.32) of section B Chapter 7.

8. It bears a close analogy with the 'von Newmann proportion' for steady growth and the 'causal indeterminacy' of full capacity growth in the dynamic Leontief system, discussed at an elementary level, for example, by Dorfman, Samuelson and Solow, *Linear Programming and Economic Analysis* (Dorfman *et al.*, 1958), Chapters 11 and 12.

9. Note from (7.16b) that θ_R would be flexible to the extent that the profit shares (h^i and h_c) or the relative money wage structure (w_c/w_i) can be changed. This would 'rotate' the ray OR in Figure 7.1 in a manner already discussed in connection with Figure 2.4 of Chapter 2. In other words, the discrepancy between realisation and proportionality depends mainly on the inflexibility of the real wage rates for a given money wage structure.

10. Assuming *constant* profit shares h_i and h_c.

11. This defines the Harrod-neutral technical progress, where at a constant 'capital–output ratio', the rate of profit remains constant, despite technical progress. Joan Robinson, for capital-theoretic reasons (see Section B, Chapter 7), *inverted* this definition: for technical progress to be (Harrod) neutral, at a constant rate of profit, the *nominal* value of capital to output must remain constant. Our definition is analogous. See also, equations (7.30) to (7.31b) for further elaboration of the implications of (Harrod-) neutral technical progress.

12. We could also assume a *constant* structure of *money* wages, i.e., w_c/w_i = constant. Since it only contributes to algebraic complication without adding economic substance to the present argument, we simplify by assuming $w_c/w_i = 1$.

13. The uniform rate of return (ζ^s) in (7.13) corresponds to full utilisation of new capacities created through net investment. Here, we assume *any* uniform rate of return (ζ) by dropping the superscript 's'; we return again to the assumption of full utilisation of capacity in (7.28a).

14. Note that the product wage in terms of investment goods decreases *linearly* in (7.24a) as ζ increases. However, the product (real) wage in terms of consumptions goods decreases in a more complex, *non-linear* manner in (7.26a). In view of (7.25), positivity of the real wage rate (w/P_c) in (7.26) requires,

$$[x_i + \zeta(b_c x_c - b_i x_i)] > 0. \text{ Using this fact, it is easy to show from (7.26a)}$$

that, $\dfrac{d^2}{d\zeta^2}(w/P_c) < 0$, if $b_c x_c > b_i x_i$,

implying investment goods required per unit of labour is higher in the consumption than in the investment sector (see (7.27b)). Consequently, the *inverse* relation between the real wage rate (w/P_c) and the rate of return on investment (ζ) is *convex* (or concave) to the origin depending on whether the consumption (or the investment) sector requires more investment goods per unit of labour.

15. This is one of the *possible* ways of 'closing' the system of relative prices. Alternatively, one could assume, the *real* wage rate to be given either by subsistence requirements (as in Ricardo's and Malthus' view of the 'natural price' of labour) or by customary requirements (as in Marx's earlier writings). Broadly speaking, the 'classical' economists found a determinate system of relative prices -- 'the prices of production' in the classical system -- by assuming the *real* wage rate to be exogenously given. In our interpretation, a similar system of prices can be shown to rule along a path of steady state growth, by assuming the rate of return on investment to be determined by an exogenously given growth rate in investment (see (7.28a) and (7.28b)).

16. See (1.18) of Chapter 1 for the distinction between *gross* and *net* profit. Here we are assuming profit net of replacement rather than of depreciation cost. Also, there are no (unplanned) inventories of finished goods by the assumption of full capacity growth equilibrium. Further, the profit rate is assumed to be the same for all sectors, e.g.

$$\frac{R_c}{K_c} = \frac{R_i}{K_i} = \frac{R}{K}.$$

17. Strictly speaking, workers must also accept the real wage rate implied along a sustainable growth path. However, since the capitalists have the power to unilaterally decide on the rate of accumulation, their expectations are more crucial to the sustainability of the growth path, as assumed in (7.33) in the text.

18. We assume that *actual* investment (J^a) or profit (R^a) does *not* include unplanned accumulation of inventories (see (2.6) and (2.11) of Chapter 2). Instead, the degree of capacity utilisation is instantaneously adjusted as a short period variable to eliminate such unplanned changes in inventories. See in particular equation (7.38) that follows.

19. There may be more than one intersection implying multiple equilibria; or, there may be no intersection at all implying that no sustainable growth path exists. For simplicity of exposition, Figure 7.2 assumes a *unique, stable*, equilibrium.

20. By assuming adjustment only in the degree of capacity utilisation, we intend to focus exclusively on quantity rather than on price-adjustments.

21. Recall Section B of Chapter 3 (especially Figure 3.2) which suggests that cost-determined prices usually presume some degree of excess capacity. Excess capacity may mean lower return, but as Keynes observed, there is no reason why the game (of accumulation) should not be played for lower stakes once the players (i.e., the capitalists) are used to them [The *General Theory* (Keynes, 1936), p. 374].

22. Note that the conditions for sustained growth with full employment and full utilisation of capacity are even more stringent than those given in (7.19). The existence of an *autonomous investment function* by the capitalists in the form of the *GG*-curve in Figure 7.2 (i.e., equation (7.36))

was not taken into account in (7.19). When this is also taken into account, using (7.28a) in (7.36),

$$g^a = g_i^w = (n + q) = G\left(\frac{n+q}{s_p}\right)$$

where the function G in (7.36) represents the autonomous investment function.

Further Reading

Harrod's 'An essay in dynamic theory' (Harrod, 1939) initiated much of the modern discussion on capitalistic accumulation. It is more difficult, but richer in economic content than Domar's analysis, e.g., in 'Expansion and employment' in his *Essays in the Theory of Economic Growth* (Domar, 1957).

An otherwise exhaustive survey of growth models by Hahn and Matthews, 'The theory of economic growth: a survey' (Hahn and Matthews, 1964) shows little awareness of problems caused by historical disproportionality or relative prices outside the steady state. Solow's *Growth Theory* (Solow, 1970) lucidly summarises work done in the same (neo-classical) framework with financial assets.

Robinson's *The Accumulation of Capital* (Robinson, 1956) Book II, more cogently presented in her article 'A simple model of accumulation' in her *Essays in the Theory of Economic Growth* (Robinson, 1962) are important readings for understanding problems inherent in trying to analytically capture any historical process of accumulation. This is further elaborated in her 'History versus equilibrium' reprinted in *Collected Economic Papers* vol. 5 (Robinson, 1980) Hicks' *Capital and Growth* (Hicks, 1965) discusses a similar range of problems. Kaldor's 'A model of economic growth' reprinted in his *Essays on Stability and Growth* (Kaldor, 1960) sets out an interesting model of capitalistic accumulation, which he successively revised. Sraffa's *Production of Commodities by Means of Commodities* (Sraffa, 1960) derives all the properties of the relative price system and its implications for class distribution of income, barely touched upon in Section B. Although difficult, at least Part I of the book should be read.

The two sector, non-shiftable capital goods model used in the text owes its origin to the Feldman-Mahalanobis model, presented also in Domar's 'A Soviet model of growth' in his *Essays in the Theory of Economic Growth* (Domar, 1957).

8
Economic Policy and the Theory of the State

A The Market and the State

The view that the society is *simply* a collection of individuals has always held considerable attraction for the 'liberal' tradition in political philosophy (see Section A, Chapter 1). And yet, this liberal view has never been at ease in explaining the *economic relation between the Society and the State*. A collection of individuals comprising the society must exist as a notion which is logically as well as historically prior to the existence of the State. In this sense, a society should be able to function independently of the State. Therefore, it should also be possible to envisage economic interactions among individuals without assigning any definite role to the State. Indeed, this theoretical possibility has never ceased to excite the imagination of the liberal tradition in economics. Even today, it is evidenced by the preoccupation of many conservative and liberal economists with (Walrasian) models of 'general equilibrium' which propose to examine the consequences of economic interaction among *individual* agents, relegating as far as possible to the background the economic role of the State.

Nevertheless, it must be realised that by focusing on the nature of economic interaction among individual agents in the market, the initial question is almost imperceptibly *changed*. Instead of examining the broader question of the relation between the State and the *civil* society which has always been a central issue in political theory, the question is *converted* into one of the *relationship between the State and the market*. Since under *generalised* commodity production of capitalism, every product including labour power becomes a commodity bought and sold in the market (see Section B, Chapter 1), the market is presumed to reflect the economic aspect of the functioning of the capitalist society. From this point of view, analysing the role of the State in relation to the market also implies an analysis of the *economic* relation between the State and the society.

The historical significance of Adam Smith's writings stems precisely from this. He provided the major intellectual impetus to *reformulate* the broader political question of the relation between the State and the *civil* society into a somewhat narrower question of the role of the State in relation to the market. Smith (1723–90) was writing at a time when industrial capitalism was still in the process of being born. In that nascent phase of capitalism, Smith's arguments were primarily directed against the earlier mercantilist view which had curved out for the State a relatively large role, particularly in the management of foreign trade. Broadly speaking, Smith argued against the dominant economic role of the State in two rather distinct logical steps. First, he articulated the idea of *economic individualism* by asserting that the individual 'knows better' than the State:

> 'What is the species of domestic industry which his capital can employ, and of which the produce is likely to be of the greatest value, every individual, it is evident, can in his logical situation, judge much better than any statesman or lawgiver can do for him'.[1]

Second, Smith argued that the *individual interest coincides with the broader social interest* through the operation of the market mechanism. Thus, economic individualism guided by the 'invisible hand' of the market ensures the coincidence of individual and social interest leaving little scope for the State to play an economic role.

However, this assertion of economic individualism, counterposed against the active economic role of the State, has never been logically secure. As Smith himself candidly admits, a fundamental role of the State and of the civil government is to defend the privileges of *private property*. 'Civil government, as far as it is instituted for the security of property, is in reality instituted for the defence of the rich against the poor, or of those who have some property against those who have none at all.'[2] And, this coincided with Locke's earlier view (approvingly quoted by Smith) that 'the government has no other end but the preservation of property'. In essence, this provided the framework needed for economic liberalism: it envisages an economic organisation of the society where the State has the singular responsibility to enforce the rules and privileges of private property. This in turn defines the framework of the market within which economic individualism can have its free play. The market then *presupposes* the rules of private property enforced by the State.

It is essential to note that in its role as the defender of private property, the State or the civil government was *not assigned a neutral role*. The State was neutral only in so far as it did not have to interfere with the market mechanism based on private property rights. Because called 'the market', was recognised by Smith to be based on private property rights which the State was supposed to defend. This central point, so candidly stated by Smith (and by Locke), must never be lost sight of in the course of any discussion of the role of the State in relation to the market. The non-interference by the State in the working of the market mechanism does *not* imply a neutral State; but a State which defends and ensures the rule of private property in the market.

Indeed, the *distinction between conservatism and reformism* in the formulation of economic policies of the State that has become increasingly important in modern capitalist economies, can be seen to depend largely on this very *question of the neutrality of the State*. The essence of economic conservatism lies in openly accepting the non-neutrality of the State in its role as the defender of private property, while arguing at the same time that the State has no need to interfere with the market mechanism based on private property rights. Because interference with the market mechanism would imply State interference with the consequences of private property rights that express themselves through the market. Although economic reformism does not question this *fundamental* principle of the organisation of capitalistic markets on the basis of right to private property, it does emphasise the need to moderate, at least to some extent, the market outcomes of private property rights. The need for such moderating influence of the State on market outcomes is justified in the reformist ideology on two analytically distinct counts: (a) on grounds of *economic efficiency*, and (b) on grounds of *income distribution*.

That Smith's 'invisible hand' operating through the market mechanism may fail to reconcile *individual* with the *collective* interest of the society leading to gross economic inefficiencies in many instances was pointed out by the philosopher David Hume (1711–76), a rough contemporary of Smith himself. Hume drew special attention to situations where individuals motivated by their narrow self-interests may fail to co-ordinate decisions in providing adequate *public goods and services* that are of *mutual* benefit to all the members of the society. Starting with the example of how 'two neighbours may agree to drain a meadow, which they possess in common' but how it is impossible to imagine 'that a thousand persons should agree to any such decision', Hume goes on to add,

> 'bridges are built, harbours opened, ramparts raised, canals formed, fleets equipped and armies disciplined, everywhere by the care of government, which, though composed of men subject to all human infirmities, becomes, by one of the fine and most subtle inventions imaginable, a composition which is in some measure exempted from all these infirmities'.[3]

Thus, Hume not only provided a basic justification for State interference with the market mechanism for adequate provision of public goods, but his justification crucially rested on *the notion of a neutral State* run by a group of men exempted from the usual 'human infirmities'. This needs to be contrasted with Adam Smith's view of the civil government which, in defending property rights is necessarily on the side of 'those who have some property against those who have none at all'.

The subsequent development of the reformist view of economic policies had two distinguishing characteristics, both of which can be traced back to Hume's original analysis. First, it tried to analyse in greater detail the conditions under which the market may fail to function efficiently, so that State intervention would be justified. The so-called theory of welfare economics worked out with considerable precision various conditions for such market failure in terms of the criterion of efficient allocation of resources. Second, it was essential for the reformist ideology to assume the *neutrality* of the State, i.e., a State which would intervene for improving economic efficiency (as suggested by Hume) rather than in the interest of the propertied class (as presumed by Locke and Smith). Indeed, it has been a curious feature of this reformist tradition that it analyses the logical conditions for market failure, but has almost nothing to say about the nature of the State which is supposed to intervene in case of such market failures.

According to the so-called *fundamental theorem* of welfare economics, every competitive equilibrium can be shown to have 'Pareto optimal' properties in the sense that no producer or consumer can be made economically better off without someone else being worse off. And conversely, to every such conceivable Pareto optimum situation corresponds a set of prices which all the consumers and producers accept as given parameters for the characterisation of the competitive equilibrium position.[4] The fact that the equilibrium under perfect competition is a mythical state of affairs that never obtains in reality (somewhat like the steady state accumulation described in Section A of Chapter 7) provided economic reformism with a strong logical case for State intervention purely on grounds of economic efficiency. For instance, Hume's argument in terms of inadequate provision of public goods could be reinterpreted as a particular case of market failure due to *external economies or diseconomies* arising from interdependent decisions of individual participants in the market which the price mechanism may not be capable of handling even in an otherwise competitive market.

Further, intervention by the State in the market mechanism could be justified not only on grounds of economic *efficiency*, but for the more compelling practical reason of income *distribution*. Economic efficiency in the sense of Pareto merely means that, given the resources of the economy, not more of any good can be produced without producing less of some other goods. Although, in this sense, economic resources can be said to be efficiently allocated, such efficiency in production does *not* in any way ensure a socially acceptable pattern of income distribution among the individuals, because *prices not only have a resource-allocative but also an income-distributive role*. Since higher prices for some commodities make their suppliers economically better off but their consumers worse off, every set of (relative) prices also carries with it implications for the pattern of distribution of income. Consequently, even if (and it is a big 'if') the set of prices correspond to efficient allocation of resources in a Pareto-optimal competitive equilibrium, such 'optimality' would have little practical significance if the resulting pattern of income distribution is unacceptable. Fiscal intervention by the State in the form of (direct or indirect) taxes and subsidies thus becomes justifiable to improve the pattern of income distribution, even if it does not help in the efficient allocation of resources.

The fact that the Pareto criterion of efficiency pays no attention to the distribution of income also has serious implications for the *com-*

position of output produced in a market economy. The proverbial choice between the production of 'butter and guns' remains a matter of indifference to such a criterion of efficiency. Under capitalistic commodity production, that choice between 'butter and guns' must be decided by the market. And, if the gun-lovers have more income than the butter-lovers, the resources would be efficiently allocated by the competitive market to produce more guns.

The fact that the composition of output, i.e., *which* goods to produce is a matter of indifference to the criterion of efficient resource allocation follows directly from the commodity producing character of capitalism. *The market-place operates like an undemocratic voting system*, where the rich have more 'votes' in terms of their purchasing power in the market than the poor in deciding on the composition of commodities that are produced. To insist on a *more equal distribution of income* or purchasing power is then tantamount to asking for a more democratic system of 'voting' in the market-place in deciding on the composition of goods to be produced under capitalistic commodity production. The fact that the efficiency criterion ignores all consideration of income distribution boils down to its accepting an undemocratic system characterised by unequal voting power in the market-place.

It follows that unregulated market outcomes can lead to a serious *conflict* between *political democracy* based on the principle of 'one man, one vote' and the corresponding lack of *economic democracy* arising from an unequal distribution of purchasing power in the market-place. Naturally, the more unequal is the distribution of income and wealth in a political democracy, the more acute would be such conflict. It is a distinguishing feature of convervatism in economic policy that it emphasises the importance of *political* democracy and of consumers' sovereignty in the free market, while conveniently forgetting its uncomfortable implications in terms of *economic* democracy. On the other hand, the ideology of economic reformism may be differentiated in its various shades depending on the degree of importance that it also attaches to the attainment of such economic democracy. In its relatively moderate form, only progressive *income* taxes (and some subsidies) may be relied upon to reform the pattern of post-tax income distribution. In such a case, the State tries to moderate the consequences of private property resulting in an unacceptable pattern of income distribution without confronting the main cause, namely the right to income from private property itself.

Direct tax on wealth and its inheritence (e.g., death duties, gift tax, etc.) can be seen to go a step further, in so far as it taxes property as a source of private income. The argument in favour of significant *public ownership* of property also follows from similar considerations. The role of the public sector may be enlarged to restrict the scope of private property. Further, it is helpful in coping with Hume's original problem of adequate provision of public goods and also in letting the government have a *direct* influence on the composition of output produced in a market economy, independently of the pattern of distribution of income.

Such attempts to bring closer the *political* and *economic* aspects of a democratic system through measures ranging from progressive taxes on income and wealth to increased share of the public sector, have been at the basis of the Social Democratic tradition. Its modern expression is the Welfare State, where precisely through these measures the State is expected to maintain a tolerably equitable pattern of distribution of personal consumption through a system of social securities. Nevertheless, it is seldom emphasised that the efficacy of the Social Democratic model depends on the crucial and *fundamental assumption of a neutral State*. Because only a State which impartially pursues the overall democratic objective of bringing closer the political and economic aspects of democracy through continuous redistribution of economic power from the propertied to the propertyless, can hope to make the 'voting system' of the market-place in terms of purchasing power, somewhat more democratic.

This assumption of the neutrality of the State, distinguishes reformism in the ultimate analysis from the more radical, Marxist tradition. Locke's or Smith's candid view that the civil government is instituted primarily in the defence of private property finds an echo here. A capitalist State, whose ultimate function is to defend the rule of private property, cannot curb the economic power of private property beyond a point without contradicting the very reason for its own existence. The conventional Marxist view of the State as an organ of class power, even though oversimplied in some important respects, has an essential element of truth. The role of the capitalist State in curbing the power and privilege of private property must be severely limited by the logic of its own existence. The reformist ideal of the State as the impartial mediator among the classes in its pursuit of economic democracy is at best realisable only in a limited sense.

From this point of view, it was a major *political achievement of the*

Keynesian policies of 'demand management' to have shown that, special historical circumstances do occasionally permit even the capitalist State to act successfully as a neutral mediator among the classes. A higher level of public investment in an economic depression not only provides more jobs to the workers (and therefore, a higher wage bill), but it also helps the capitalists to realise a higher level of profit in an expanded market. Indeed, the theory of the multiplier based on quantity-adjustment with a *constant* class distribution of income (presumed in Keynes' 'wage-unit' measure, see Chapter 3, Section A) was an analytical demonstration of this very possibility. It showed how the economic interests of the classes could be *reconciled*, at least temporarily, through intervention by the State in managing the level of effective demand. It can hardly be doubted that the wide *political acceptability* of Keynesian policies at that time was precisely the result of its ability to *temporarily* reconcile the economic interests of the major contending classes in a capitalist economy.

Nevertheless, such an impartial economic role for the capitalist State which acts to the mutual benefit of all the major classes can only be the product of special and passing historical circumstances. Already in 1943, Kalecki was emphasising the *political aspects of full employment* and the possibility of *political business cycles.*[5] He emphasised that continuous maintenance of full employment, although possible in principle through the redistribution of income from profit to wage (i.e., higher *real* wage rate) to stimulate the level of effective demand, can never be politically accepted as the viable way to full employment in a capitalist economy, because such policies of *demand management through redistribution* have an obvious bias against the capitalists which no capitalist state is likely to pursue for long. On the other hand, if private investment cannot always be stimulated sufficiently to maintain continuous full employment, then demand management through adequate public investment financed through government budget deficit (borrowing) remains the only viable way to full employment. However, even full employment maintained through such government spending is likely to falter on account of political business cycles. In a slump, an effort may be made by the government to reduce unemployment through increased public spending. However, in a boom the government would return to more orthodox fiscal policies aimed at reducing deficit spending and even creating unemployment, because continuous full employment would destroy the 'discipline of the market-place' as workers 'get out of hand' in their demand for higher wages. The 'captains of industry' therefore have a fundamental reason to oppose *continuous* full employment that destroys 'the discipline of the workers'. Consequently, the policies of demand management through public spending would be only *temporarily* acceptable to the capitalists in so far as stimulation of effective demand in a slump not only creates jobs but also guarantees higher profits for the capitalists. And, *the political business cycle emerges in this analysis as a regular pattern in which the capitalist State appears to act in the interest of both the classes in a slump, but has to side with the capitalists as the economic boom continues for some time.*

Kalecki's analysis of political business cycles, like Keynesian policies for demand management, was set in the context of a closed economy. It analysed fluctuations in the level of economic activity caused entirely by the *political* requirements of the domestic capitalist class, insulated from external pressures of international trade. In this respect, it was an over-simplification; it failed to point out that the very *autonomy* of most capitalist States in regulating the level of demand has become severely *restricted* due to considerations of the *balance of payment position*. The importance of this fact became increasingly evident in what are nowadays described as the '*stop-go*' *cycles*. Thus, large government spending in a slump may create demand that spills over as higher import to create deficit in the balance of payment, obliging governments to 'stop' their expansionary policies. The subsequent reduction in public spending deflates demand and helps to improve the balance of payment position at the cost of higher unemployment. The improved international payment position permits the government to 'go' for another round of expansionary policies, until large payment deficits forces such policies to be 'stopped' again.[6] Although Kalecki's original formulation of the political business cycles ignored this now familiar patter of 'stop-go' cycles induced by considerations of the balance of payment position, it had the foresight of emphasising the contradiction inherent in the capitalist State trying to maintain its neutral posture as a mediator between the classes in pursuing the objective of full employment over time.

That contradiction surfaced unmistakably after almost a quarter century of near-full employment in capitalist economies since the Second World War. Unionised workers under conditions of full employment could set up 'inflationary barriers', where they refused to accept any significant redistribution of income against them (see Chapter 6, p. 193). From the point of view of the capitalists, this meant a break-down in the 'normal discipline of the market-place' due to long years of full employment. In such a situation even the *fiscal role* of the State could become ineffective either in regulating demand or in redistributing income. A progressive tax system, for instance, could lead to accelerating inflation as both the classes shifted the burden of higher taxes through rising prices and money wages (see, in particular equations (6.24) to (6.30) in Chapter 6, pp. 190–3). The Social Democratic ideal of a neutral State pursuing economic policies to the advantage of *both* the classes had to be abandoned. The time for a counter-revolution in political ideology was ripe. It is not surprising that the posture of a neutral State was abandoned and, in many Western democracies the State sided openly with the capitalist class to curb the organised economic power of the trade unions. The intellectual apology for this was provided by a plethora of 'new' economic theories – 'monetarism' which justified a 'natural rate' of unemployment, 'supply-side economics' which argued for reduced public investment in the hope of stimulating private investment through incentives such as tax reduction and finally, the artificial construct of 'rational expectation' models that wanted us to return to Adam Smith's 'economic individualism'. It argued that individual economic agents efficiently process all available information and adopt the predictions of the 'relevant' economic theory as their subjective expectations. Since by such an *assumption* of 'rational expectation', the State can never out-perform the economic predictions of the individual agent, the very basis of State intervention was questioned. Such sophistry was intended at justifying Adam Smith's assertation that 'every individual, it is evident, can in his logical situation judge much better than any statesman or lawgiver can do for him'.

The 'new' theories need neither have convincing logic nor empirical evidence to sustain them. They are certain to find a ready audience among politicians and economic policy-makers alike because of the political purpose they ultimately serve. Such theories became politically acceptable at a particular historical juncture when the capitalist State was finding it increasingly difficult to maintain its social democratic posture of an impartial mediator among the major contending classes after a quarter century of near-full employment. Those long years of continuous high employment had bestowed on the unionised workers an extent of economic power which was simply incompatible with the 'discipline of the market-place'. Breaking the full employment boom became a political necessity for the 'captains of industry' and an economic slump could be conveniently precipitated in the name of controlling inflation. The 'new' theories resurrected old-fashioned *laissez-faire* policies to justify unemployment as 'natural'. And, the ready political acceptance of such theoretical constructs only shows that political business cycles are a necessity for contemporary capitalism. And, apologetic theories would never be lacking to justify such politically motivated cycles.

B The Theory and Practice of Economic Policy

Almost from the time that Adam Smith asserted that the collective interest of the society is best served by pursuing individual self-interest through the 'invisible hand' of the market mechanism, there has persisted a *dichotomy* between the theory and the practice of economic policy. At the level of theory, the dominant tendency has been to discuss the *desirability* of State intervention to influence market outcomes. In practice, a modern State without an important economic role has long been inconceivable. Nor is this gap between theory and practice narrowed by maintaining that the State should only have a minimum economic role. This merely begs the question in so far as it needs to be theoretically explained how that 'minimum role' is to be defined.

The old, *pre-Keynesian orthodoxy* wanted to deny the State an active economic role by insisting that market outcomes are usually optimal. Indeed, the myth of perfect competition was created and later logically refined to show how market outcomes would have such optimal properties. The so-called fundamental theorem of welfare economics claiming every competitive equilibrium to be Pareto optimal (and vice versa) summarises this position. Nevertheless, with these logical refinements also came the recognition that hopelessly unrealistic conditions would have to be satisfied to ensure the attainment of any such competitive equilibrium. It therefore followed that in most realistic situations, economic intervention by the government would be theoretically justified, even on grounds of allocative efficiency. In addition, the fact that there are many possible competitive equilibria, each corresponding to a *different* pattern of personal distribution of income, left *open* the entire question of the desirability of market outcome in terms of income distribution. In short, the case for the allocative efficiency of the market was *not* proved outside the mythical world of perfect competition. Even under perfect competition, the question of a socially acceptable pattern of income distribution remained unresolved (see pp. 241–5, Chapter 8).

Although the orthodox view continued to argue in favour of the efficiency of the market mechanism in allocating 'scarce resources among alternative ends', the practical experience of severe economic depression demonstrated the absurdity of this view. Surrounded by the massive unemployment and under-utilisation of capacity during the 1930s, which also meant massive loss in potentially producible output, it was absurd to maintain that the market allocates resources efficiently. Conventional academic wisdom tried to wish away the problem by talking of 'voluntary' unemployment which could be cured by the market only if the workers accepted lower *real* wages (see Chapter 3, pp. 70–3 on the 'wage-cut controversy'). It was in this context that the Keynesian *policies of demand management* powerfully demonstrated how the market outcome in the form of massive unemployment could be rectified through the economic policies of the government. Politically, it established the validity of the assumption that suitable government intervention can improve upon the outcome of the *laissez-faire* market system. Demand management, Keynes also argued, might require reliance on *fiscal policies* directed at higher *public* investment, rather than on *monetary policies* directed at stimulating *private* investment, through lowering the cost of borrowing finance (i.e., the lending rates of the banks). Because, monetary policies may simply be ineffective in lowering the interest rates sufficiently, as was theoretically demonstrated in the case of the 'liquidity trap' (see Chapter 4, p. 100).

Although running contrary to the economic orthodoxy of its time, the Keynesian policies for regulating the level of effective demand through government spending, which also meant an enlarged role for the public sector, found *political acceptance* in a wide circle. Because, such policies were fundamentally rooted in a view of co-operative capitalism: larger public investment not only reduced unemployment but it also increased profit through higher capacity utilisation. Under these circumstances, the capitalist State could maintain its *posture of neutrality*, as an impartial mediator among the major contending classes.

However, the Keynesian prescription of demand management

through active State intervention had more radical implications, going beyond the comfortable view of co-operative capitalism. It indicated the possibility of maintaining an adequate level of effective demand through *redistribution of income* among the classes. So long as wage earners spend more than capitalists, redistribution of income from profit to wage would tend to stimulate the level of effective demand due to higher *real* wages (see pp. 53–4, especially Figure 2.4 of Chapter 2). This argument lay at the heart of the 'wage-cut controversy' and explains the passion it generated on both sides of the debate. Nevertheless, in so far as higher *real* (and product) wages also meant lower *profit margin* per unit of sale, it could be validly argued that under certain circumstances, *private* investment would be discouraged. In turn, this reduces effective demand as a result of such redistributive policies from profit to wage. Therefore, the central issue becomes the *lower profitability of private investment* (per unit of sale) *versus a larger market* for profit realisation created through a higher level of *real* wages (see also Chapter 3, Section A).[7]

A radical implication emerges in so far as public investment can compensate for such shortfalls in private investment due to its reduced profitability. This, of course, goes against the spirit of 'free-enterprise capitalism', which must oppose all such policies that lower profit. An alternative to this could be sought in the Social Democratic tradition of the Welfare State which argued for higher *social wages*. Because, higher social wages would not reduce the profitability of private investment. This also meant a wider network of *social securities including unemployment benefits* which could act as *built-in-stabilisers* in regulating the level of effective demand. Thus, even when the level of unemployment is high, such subsidies and transfers from the State to the unemployed would prevent their consumption level from falling drastically to stabilise the level of effective demand. Such welfare policies of the State again appeared to evoke a spirit of *co-operative* capitalism, in so far as it combined the objectives of demand management with some redistribution through higher social wages and social securities. The unprecedented boom in post-war capitalism for nearly a quarter century seems to owe a lot to such co-operative management of demand through a widening role for the State in pursuing welfare policies.

However, this politically comfortable position based on a co-operative view of capitalism was inevitably undermined by its own logic. The maintenance of continuously high employment coupled with the safety net of social securities blunted the economic threat of being unemployed. It also gradually increased the bargaining power of the workers. As the balance of power began to shift in favour of the workers, the very 'discipline' of the capitalist market-place, based on the rule of property, was partly undermined through the organised power of trade unions. The Keynesian model of co-operative capitalism mediated by a neutral State began to disintegrate under the force of changing balance of class power.

At first, this change in political circumstances showed itself as *conflicting objectives of economic policies*. Within the prevalent policy framework of co-operative capitalism, it appeared as conflict in national objectives which the State in its role as an impartial mediator was supposed to reconcile. For instance, the empirical evidence of the Phillips' curve (see p. 194, Chapter 6) was interpreted to exhibit a choice between price stability (i.e. stability in money wages) and full employment. The State as a neutral agent could *trade off* some employment for a greater degree of stability in prices. Similarly, there was a choice between external and internal balance; the *'stop-go'* *cycles* induced by balance of payments considerations were expressions of such choices actually made over time (see Chapter 8, p. 247).

Within this policy framework of partly trading off one economic objective for the partial attainment of another, it appeared analytically useful to distinguish macroeconomic variables as *targets and instruments of economic policy*. The latter set of variables are the instruments of policy which the State is assumed to have at its disposal in the form of various fiscal and monetary measures (e.g., changes in taxes and subsidies, the government budget and the level of public investment, the Bank rate of interest, etc.). The policy-makers for the State could be assumed to choose values for these instrument variables in their pursuit of the *preassigned* values for the target variables, representing quantified economic objectives (e.g., the degree of price stability, the level of employment, the balance of payment position etc.).[8] In this evidently technocratic scheme for designing economic policies, not only the relevant target and instrument variables are assumed to be precisely quantifiable, but even the macroeconomic relations governing them are assumed to be quantifiable functional relationships. Thus, if there are m target variables, $T_1, T_2, \ldots, T_m$ and n instrument variables, $d_1, d_2, \ldots, d_n$, then a first formal requirement for designing economic policies is to express the target variables as functions of the instruments variables, i.e.

$$
\left.
\begin{aligned}
T_1 &= f_1\,(d_1, \ldots, d_n) \\
T_2 &= f_2\,(d_1, \ldots, d_n) \\
T_m &= f_m\,(d_1, \ldots, d_n)
\end{aligned}
\right\} \tag{8.1}
$$

where T_j is the target variable j ($j = 1, \ldots, m$) and d_k is the instrument variable k ($k = 1, \ldots, n$).

As shown by the above system of equations (8.1), there are n instruments $(d_1, \ldots, d_n)$ whose values have to be determined by economic policies to obtain m preassigned target values $(\overline{T}_1, \overline{T}_2, \ldots, \overline{T}_m)$. In general, this is not possible. In the special case where the above system (8.1) can be represented by m *independent, linear* equations, the system is either over- or under-determined. In the more usual case the system is likely to be *over-determined* with too few instruments available to achieve too many targets (i.e., $m > n$). In such a case, either the number of instruments (n) must be increased (until, $m = n$), or the *scope* of economic policy must become less ambitious by reducing the number of targets (again, until $m = n$). In the more fortunate, but less likely, case the number of instrument variables may exceed the number of targets (i.e., $m < n$) to yield an under-determined system. The policy-makers would then have the choice of leaving some *potential* instruments unused or of widening the scope of economic policy by adding to the number of targets (again, until $m = n$). Thus, designing of *consistent economic policies* would generally require the number of targest (m) to be *equal* to the number of instrument variables (n), i.e., $m = n$, as a general rule for *consistency* in formulating economic policies.

However, it must be recognised that *matching* the number of targets with the number of instruments is *formally* neither a necessary nor a sufficient condition for attaining such consistency in the formulation of economic policies. At best it indicates a way of thinking about economic policies without being over- or under-ambitious about the general scope for such policies. In a case where the macroeconomic relations underlying the system of equations (8.1) turn out to be a *non-linear* system (recall, for instance, the Phillips' curve is usually a non-linear empirical relation), *counting* the number of equations (m) and the number of unknown instrument values (n) is in no way adequate to guarantee the consistency of the system. But even apart from such technical difficulties, there is a basic problem of *political ambiguity* in the proposed separation of macroeconomic variables into 'targets, and 'instruments'. A simple example illustrates the point: suppose a reasonable degree of price stability is assumed to be a stated objective specifying the value of the relevant target variable. Also suppose, the government rightly or wrongly believes in a macroeconomic relationship where such price stability can only be achieved by increasing the rate of unemployment. In this context, is the level of employment to be treated as a 'target' or as an 'instrument' variable? Formally, this means that 'targets', e.g., price stability and employment level in this case, often have *interdependent* values. So the government cannot *independently* choose the values of each target *separately*, unlike in the simple case shown by (8.1). Although, it is *formally* possible to introduce additional constraints to show such interdependence among target values, e.g. 'targets' T_1 and T_2 may be related by,

$$T_1 = F(T_2) \tag{8.2}$$

such interdependence spoils the conceptual clarity of the separation shown in (8.1).[9] Because, it is no longer clear why T_2 should be treated as a 'target' variable, and not as an 'instrument' variable influencing T_1. The lesson to be drawn is that the *separation* of macroeconomic variables into 'targets' and 'instruments' *presupposes* prior political considerations which not even a technocratic scheme for designing economic policy can meaningfully avoid.

The notion of trade-off among conflicting economic objectives emphasised precisely such interdependence in economic targets (as shown by (8.2), with $F' < 0$). It intended to show that politically unpleasant choices have usually to be made in setting the target values. Nevertheless, actual experience suggests that governments in industrial democracies usually find it imprudent in terms of electoral politics to make explicit such choices. Thus, elected governments often try to attain *one target at a time*, i.e., economic targets are set *sequentially* rather than *simultaneously* in executing economic policies. This means directing most, if not all, the relevant policy instruments at the command of the government towards satisfying a single objective at a time and then, moving on to another objective with again most instruments directed towards it.[10] The experience of the 'stop-go' cycles (see Section A, Chapter 8) illustrates the plausibility of this view. A government may direct most or all of its policy instruments to cope with the employment problem at the temporary neglect of the balance of payments position. And, only when a serious payments 'crisis' develops, it may 'stop' all its expansionary policies and redirect the instruments to tackle the balance of payments situation, while employment is allowed to deteriorate to a 'crisis' level, requiring the government to return again to its employment objective at a later point of time. In short, it may appear as some sort of *sequential* management of economic 'crisis' over time.

Although it might appear short-sighted and inconsistent to move sequentially in this manner from one economic objective to another, it has an intrinsic *political* logic to it. So long as the State tries to maintain its posture of neutrality, it may not be able to *openly* trade off among major economic objectives without seriously tarnishing its image of neutrality. Such inconsistencies in economic policy over time therefore arise from the political prudence of maintaining a neutral posture when the State is confronted with conflicting objectives.

This emphasises the fundamental point that a *neutral*, economic posture by the State in formulating economic policies is compatible only with an underlying model of *co-operative* capitalism. Both the earlier success and the later failure of Keynesian policy stem from the fact that it based itself all along on this co-operative view of capitalism, which became increasingly untenable under post-war full employment conditions. Under these changed circumstances, there developed economic compulsions for the State to choose among conflicting objectives; but the logic of electoral politics tended to act as a barrier to exercising such choice. This is most clearly illustrated by the notion of an *incomes policy*, where the State is supposed to act as the mediator in settling income claims by the contending classes. And yet, such incomes policy usually works only under conditions of reasonable economic growth so that, the incomes of *all* the classes can be permitted to rise simultaneously. Otherwise, such income claims have a tendency to degenerate into an inflationary process in which the State itself ultimately becomes involved (see Chapter 6, Section B).

The fact that the *co-operative* model of capitalism is valid only under *special* circumstances, while capitalism in *general* is rooted in economic *conflict* among the contending classes, became apparent in the inflation of the 1970s. It also created the political climate for a 'new' economic orthodoxy to emerge. This *post-Keynesian orthodoxy* in economic theory, initially led by the Monetarist view of economic management, differed in one significant respect from the earlier, *pre-*

Keynesian orthodoxy. Instead of arguing that the market outcomes are necessarily 'optimal', it took the view that market outcomes are a 'natural' order of things, which cannot be improved upon 'in the longer run' through intervention by the State. It talked of a 'natural' rate of unemployment which the government cannot alter in the long run (see equations (6.34a) and (6.34b), Chapter 6). This ideology found its culmination in arguments based on 'rational expectations'. It attributes to the individual such extraordinary power of collecting and processing economic information that, by assumption, the State could never improve upon the performance of such individuals in the market in the longer run.

In practice, this new orthodoxy is a *reaction* to the welfare role that the State gradually came to assume through its role as a mediator among the classes, based on a model of co-operative capitalism. Thus, at the level of policy prescription, monetarist discipline usually means restriction on public sector borrowing. Public investment is opposed as it is supposed to 'crowd out' private investment (see also p. 58 and p. 127). Emphasising the 'supply side' usually means restricting taxes and government revenue as it blunts incentives to thwart the initiatives of private business. Even unemployment benefits and other social securities are supposed to have only detrimental effects on the 'supply side'; because, they are financed through higher taxes which reduce profit-incentives of private business, while providing wrong incentives to (lazy) workers to stay away from work. And finally, by virtue of the assumption of 'rational expectations', some members of the new orthodoxy found *any* economic role for the government unjustified in their world inhabited by such 'rational individuals'.

This glorification of market outcomes as 'natural' and therefore unalterable (in the long run) by government policies could prosper at a time when the economic role of the State as a mediator among the classes had been thoroughly discredited. With the Keynesian model of *co-operative* capitalism increasingly giving way to a situation of economic *conflict* among the classes, the political posture of a neutral State no longer worked. The model of a welfare State was increasingly in difficulty. The capitalist State was torn between its natural inclination to 'discipline' workers through *political* business cycles on the one hand (see p. 246, Chapter 8) and the compulsion of electoral politics to maintain its neutral image on the other. Arguments that market outcomes are 'natural' proved most convenient at this juncture. In the name of monetary discipline and control of inflation, a *political* business cycle was precipitated. But it was justified as the 'natural' rate of unemployment which according to the new orthodoxy, the State cannot alter anyway. Thus, unemployment rules. The State maintains a 'neutral' posture of non-interference with the market outcome.

The 'new' orthodoxy in economic theory justifies it as the 'natural' outcome of the market. However, the question remains, why must the working class accept such market institutions whose 'natural' outcome is heavy unemployment? The industrial democracies cannot escape this question.

Notes to Chapter 8

1. Adam Smith, *An Enquiry into the Nature and Causes of the Wealth of Nations* (Smith, 1961), vol. I, p. 478.
2. *Ibid.*, p. 236.
3. David Hume, *A Treatise on Human Nature* (Hume, 1948), vol. II, pp. 238–9.
4. For a modern, but mathematically less advanced exposition of these propositions, see Dorfman, Samuelson and Solow, *Linear Programming and Economic Analysis* (Dorfman *et al.*, 1958), especially Chapters 13 and 14.
5. See 'Political aspects of full employment', in M. Kalecki, *Selected Essays* (Kalecki, 1971).
6. It may be recalled here that the Keynes Plan for an International Clearing Union aimed to insulate domestic full employment policies from such international payments problems (see Chapter 5, Section B, pp. 156–7).
7. E. Malinvaud in *'Wages and Unemployment'* (Malinvaud, 1982) attempts such an analysis. However, his distinction between 'Classical Unemployment' caused by high *real* wage and 'Keynesian Unemployment' caused by lack of effective demand is not logically acceptable as argued by Bhaduri, 'Multimarket classification of unemployment: a sceptical note' (Bhaduri, 1983). See also Rowthorn, 'Demand, real wage and economic growth' (Rowthorn, 1981) for a clear presentation of the analytical issues involved in the context of a one-sector model.
8. This view was analytically expressed by J. Tinbergen, *On the Theory of Economic Policy* (Tinbergen, 1952).
9. Similarly, instrument values may not be independent, e.g., the rates of interest and the money supply may be *interdependent* instrument variables, in which case ambiguity again arises regarding the meaning of an 'instrument' variable.
10. See P. Mosley, 'Towards a "satisficing" theory of economic policy' (Mosley, 1976) for an empirical analysis of the British economy along these lines.

Further Reading

The relation between economic policy and the nature of the State is a largely unexplored area. A good introduction to the political aspect of the problem is Miliband's *The State in Capitalist Society* (Miliband, 1969), while Lenin's *State and Revolution* (Lenin, 1943) is a Marxist classic. O'Conner's *The Fiscal Crisis of the State* (O'Conner, 1973) deals with some of the specific fiscal problems in the United States.

Kalecki's Political aspects of full employment', reprinted in his *Selected Essays on the Dynamics of the Capitalist Economy* (Kalecki, 1971) may be supplemented by Alexander's 'Opposition to deficit spending for the prevention of unemployment' in *Income, Employment and Public Policy* (1948). Goodwin's elegant, but mathematically advanced analysis of 'Growth cycles' in *Socialism, Capitalism and Economic Growth* (Feinstein, 1967) discusses economic mechanisms bearing some resemblance to political cycles.

On so-called 'welfare economics' as the basis for policy, Graaf's *Theoretical Welfare Economics* (Graaf, 1957) provides an insightful introduction. Koopmans' *Three Essays on the State of Economic Science* (Koopmans, 1957), essay 1 elegantly outlines the optimal properties of perfect competition.

References

Alexander, S. S. (1948) 'Opposition to deficit spending for the prevention of unemployment' in *Income, Employment and Public Policy*, Essays in honour of Alvin H. Hansen, Norton and Co., New York.

American Economic Association (1951) *Readings in the Theory of Income Distribution*, Blakiston, Philadelphia.

Bain, A. C. (1976) *The Control of Money Supply*, Penguin Modern Economics, 2nd edn.

Baumol, W. (1952) 'The Transactions Demand for Cash: an Inventory Theoretic Approach', *Quarterly Journal of Economics*, November.

Bhaduri, A. (1972) 'Unwanted Amortisation Funds: a Mathematical Treatment', *Economic Journal*, June.

Bhaduri, A. (1983) 'Multimarket Classification of Unemployment: a Sceptical Note', *Cambridge Journal of Economics*, December.

Bhaduri, A. and Steindl, J (1983) 'The Rise of Monetarism as a Social Doctrine', *Thames Papers in Political Economy*, Autumn.

Braverman, H. (1974) *Labour and Monopoly Capital*, Monthly Review Press, New York.

Bronfenbrenner, M. and Holzman, F. D. (1963) 'A Survey of Inflation Theory', *American Economic Review*, September.

Committee on the Working of the Monetary System (1959) Radcliffe Report. Cmd 827, London, HMSO.

Cooper, R. N. and Lawrence, R. Z. (1975) 'The 1972–75 Commodity Boom', *Brookings Papers on Economic Activity*, No.3.

Coutts, K, Godley, W. and Nordhaus, W. (1978) *Industrial Pricing in the United Kingdom*, Cambridge University Press, Cambridge.

Cripps, F. (1977) 'The Money Supply, Wages and Inflation', *Cambridge Journal of Economics*, March.

Dicks-Mireau, L. A. and Dow, J. E. R. (1959) 'The Determinants of Wage Inflation: United Kingdom 1946–56', *Journal of the Royal Statistical Society*, Series A, Part II.

Domar, E. (1957) *Essays in the Theory of Economic Growth*, Oxford University Press, New York.

Dorfman, R., Samuelson, P. A. and Solow, R. M. (1958) *Linear Programming and Economic Analysis*, McGraw-Hill, New York (The Rand Series).

Dunlop, J. T. (1942) 'Wage Policies of Trade Unions', reprinted in *Readings in the Theory of Income Distribution*, Blakiston, Philadelphia.

Eatwell, J., Uewellyn, J. and Tarling, R. (1974) 'Money Wage Inflation in

Industrial Countries', *Review of Economic Studies*, October.

Feinstein, C. H. (ed.) (1967) *Socialism, Capitalism and Economic Growth*. Essays presented to Maurice Dobb, Cambridge University Press, Cambridge.

Fisher, I. (1911) *The Purchasing Power of Money*, Macmillan, New York (reprinted), Kelley, New York, (1963).

Friedman, M. (ed.) (1956) *Studies in the Quantity Theory of Money*, University of Chicago Press, Chicago.

Friedman, M. (1968) 'The Role of Monetary Policy', *American Economic Review*, March.

Friedman, M. (1975) *Unemployment versus Inflation*, Institute of Economic Affairs, London.

Friedman, M. and Schwartz, A. J. (1982) *Monetary Trends in the United States and the United Kingdom: Their Relation to Income, Prices and Interest Rates, 1867–1975*. National Bureau of Economic Research Monograph, University of Chicago Press, Chicago.

Goldfeld, S. M. (1973) 'The Demand for Money Revisited', Brookings' Papers on Economic Activity, No.3.

Goodhart, C. A. E. and Crockett, A. D. (1970) 'The Importance of Money', *Bank of England Quarterly Bulletin*, June.

Goodwin, R. M. (1949) 'The Multiplier as a Matrix', *Economic Journal*, December.

Goodwin, R. M. (1951) 'Non-linear Accelerator and the Persistence of the Business Cycle, *Econometrica*, January.

Goodwin, R. M. (1967) 'Growth cycles' in C. H. Feinstein (ed.) *Socialism, Capitalism and Economic Growth*, Essays presented to Maurice Dobb, Cambridge University Press, Cambridge.

Gordon, R. J. (1981) 'Output fluctuations and gradual price adjustment', *Journal of Economic Literature*, June.

Graaf, J de V. (1957) *Theoretical Welfare Economics*, Cambridge University Press, Cambridge.

Gurley, J. G. and Shaw, E. S. (1959) Money in a Theory of Finance, Brookings Institution, Washington D.C.

Haavelmo, T. (1960) *A Study in the Theory of Investment*, University of Chicago Press, Chicago.

Hahn, F. H. and Matthews, R. C. O. (1964) 'The Theory of Economic Growth: a Survey', *Economic Journal*, December.

Hall, R. L. and Hitch, C. J. (1939) 'Price Theory and Business Behaviour', *Oxford Economic Papers*, June.

Harrod, R. (1939) 'An Essay in Dynamic Theory', *Economic Journal*, March.

Harrod, R. (1970) 'Replacement, Net Investment, Amortization Funds', *Economic Journal*, March.

Hicks, J. R. (1937) 'Mr. Keynes and the Classics: a Suggested Interpretation', *Econometrica*, April.

Hicks, J. R. (1965) *Capital and Growth*, Clarendon Press, Oxford.

Hicks, J. R. (1977) *Economic Perspectives: Further Essays on Money and Growth*, Clarendon Press, Oxford.

Hobsbawm, E. (1972) *Industry and Empire*. The Pelican Economic History of Britain Series.

Hobson, J. A. (1938) *Imperialism: A Study*, George Allen and Unwin, London, 3rd edn.

Hume, D. (1948) *A Treatise on Human Nature*, Everyman, New York. (1948) *Income, Employment and Public Policy*. Essays in honour of Alvin H. Hansen, Norton and Co., New York.

Jackson, D., Turner, H. A. and Wilkinson, S. F. (1975) *Do Trade Unions Cause Inflation?* Cambridge University Press, Cambridge, 2nd edn.

Johnston, R. B. (1982)*The Economics of the Euro-Market: History,Theory and Policy*, Macmillan, London.

Kahn, R. F. (1972) *Selected Essays in Employment and Growth*, Cambridge University Press, Cambridge.

Kaldor, N. (1960) *Essays on Value and Distribution*, Duckworth and Co., London.

Kaldor, N. (1960) *Essays on Economic Stability and Growth*, Duckworth and Co., London.

Kaldor, N. (1970) 'The New Monetarism', *Lloyd's Bank Review*, July.

Kaldor, N. (1980) 'Monetarism and UK Monetary Policy', *Cambridge Journal of Economics*, December.

Kalecki, M. (1939) *Essays in the Theory of Economic Fluctuations*, Allen & Unwin, London.

Kalecki, M. (1971) *Selected Essays on the Dynamics of the Capitalist Economy*, Cambridge University Press, Cambridge.

Keynes, J. M. (1936)*The General Theory of Employment, Interest and Money*, Macmillan, London.

Keynes, J. M. (1937)'The General Theory: Fundamental Concepts and Ideas', *Quarterly Journal of Economics*, February.

Keynes, J. M. (1940) *How to Pay for the War*, Macmillan, London.

Kindleberger, C. P. (1958) *International Economics*, Richard Irwin Inc., Illinois. Revised edition.

Kindleberger, C. P. (1973) *The World in Depression*, 1929–39, University of California Press, Berkeley.

Kleiman, E. (1976) 'Trade and the Decline of Colonialism', *Economic Journal*, September.

Knox, A. D. (1952) 'The Acceleration Principle and the Theory of Investment: a Survey', *Economica*, August.

Koopmans, T. C. (1957) *Three Essays on the State of Economic Science*, McGraw-Hill, New York.

Kula, W. (1976) *An Economic Theory of the Feudal System.Towards a Model of the Polish Economy*, 1500–1800, New Left Books, London.

Lange, O. (1970) *Papers in Economics and Sociology* (translation edited by P. F. Knightsfield), Pergamon Press, Oxford.

Leijonhufvud, A. (1968) *On Keynesian Economics and the Economics of Keynes*, Oxford University Press, Oxford.

Lenin, V. I. (1979) *Imperialism, the Highest Stage of Capitalism: a popular outline*, International Publishers, New York.

Lenin, V. I. (1943) *State and Revolution*, International Publishers, New York.

Leontief, W. W. (1953) *Studies in the Structure of American Economy*, Oxford University Press, New York.

Lerner, A. P. (1939) 'The Relation Between Wage Policies and Price Policies', reprinted in *Readings in the Theory of Income Distribution*, Blakiston, Philadelphia.

Lewis, W. A. (1977) *The Evolution of the International Economic Order* (Eliot Janeway Lectures on Historical Economics in honour of Josef Schumpeter), Princeton University Press, Princeton.

Maital, S. (1972) 'Inflation, Taxation and Equity: "How to Pay for the War" Revisited', *Economic Journal*, March.

Malinvaud, E. (1982) 'Wages and Unemployment', *Economic Journal*, March.

Marglin, S. A. (1974) 'What do the Bosses Do? The Origin and Function of Hierarchy in Capitalist Production', *Review of Radical Political Economy*, Spring.

Marx, K. (1904) *A Contribution to the Critique of Political Economy* (translated by N. I. Stone), Charles H. Kerr, Chicago.

Marx, K. (1969) *Wages, Price and Profit. Selected Works of Marx and Engels*, Progress, Moscow.

McCallum, J. (1983) 'Inflation and Social Consensus in the Seventies', *Economic Journal*, December.

Metzler, L. A. (1941) Nature and Stability of Inventory Cycles', *Review of Economic Studies*, August.

Metzler, L. A. (1942) 'Underemployment Equilibrium in International Trade', *Econometrica*, April.

Miliband. R. (1969) *The State in Capitalist Society*, Weidenfeld & Nicolson, London.

Mosley, P. (1976) 'Towards a "Satisficing" Theory of Economic Policy', *Economic Journal*, March.

O'Conner, J. (1973) *The Fiscal Crisis of the State*, St. Martin's Press, New York.

Okun, A. M. (1981) *Prices and Quantities. A Macroeconomic Analysis*, The Brookings Institution, Washington D.C.

Pasinetti, L. L. (1974) *Growth and Income Distribution, Essays in Economic Theory*. Cambridge University Press, Cambridge.

Phillips, A. W. (1958) 'The Relation between Unemployment and the Rate of Change of Money Wage Rates in the United Kingdom, 1862–1957', *Economica*, November.

Reynolds, L. G. (1942) 'The Relation between Wage Rates, Costs, and Prices', reprinted in *Readings in the Theory of Income Distribution*, Blakiston, Philadelphia.

Robinson, J. (1956) *The Accumulation of Capital*, Macmillan, London.

Robinson, J. (1962) *Essays in the Theory of Economic Growth*, Macmillan, London.

Robinson, J. (1965) *Collected Economic Papers*, Volume 3, Basil Blackwell, Oxford.

Robinson, J. (1980) *Collected Economic Papers*, Volume 5, Basil Blackwell, Oxford.

Robinson, R. (1958) 'A Graphical Analysis of the Foreign Trade Multiplier', *Economic Journal*, September.

Rowthorn, B. (1980) *Capitalism, Conflict and Inflation*, Lawrence & Wishart, London.

Rowthorn, B. (1981) 'Demand, Real Wage and Economic Growth', *Thames Papers on Political Economy*, Autumn.

Samuelson, P. A. (1939) 'Interaction Between the Multiplier Analysis and the Principle of Acceleration', *Review of Economic Statistics*, May.

Samuelson, P. A. (1948) 'The Simple Mathematics of Income Determination' in *Income, Employment and Public Policy* Essays in honour of Alvin H. Hansen, Norton and Co., New York.

Scherer, F. M. (1970) *Industrial Market Structure and Economic Performance*, Rand McNally, Chicago.

Schumpeter, J. A. (1947) *Capitalism, Socialism and Democracy*, George Allen & Unwin, London.

Simon, H. A. (1979) 'Rational Decision-Making in Business Organization', *American Economic Review*, September.

Smith, A. (1961) *An Enquiry into the Nature and Causes of the Wealth of Nations* (first published in March, 1776) Vo. 1, edited by Edwin Cannan, Methuen, London.

Solow, R. M. (1970) *Growth Theory*, Oxford University Press, New York.

Sraffa, P. (1960) *Production of Commodities by Means of Commodities*, Prelude to a critique of economic theory. Cambridge University Press, Cambridge.

Stone, R. (1961) *Input-Output and National Accounts*, OECD, Paris.

Tarshis, L. (1939) 'Changes in real and money wages', reprinted in *Readings in the Theory of Income Distribution*, Balkiston, Philadelphia.

Tinbergen, J. (1952) *On the Theory of Economic Policy*, North-Holland, Amsterdam.

Tobin, J. (1956) 'The Interest-elasticity of Transaction Demand for Cash', *Review of Economics and Statistics*, August.

Tobin, J. (1958) 'Liquidity Preference as Behaviour Towards Risk', *Review of Economic Studies*, February.

Tobin, J. (1981) 'The Monetarist Counter-revolution Today: an Appraisal', *Economic Journal*, March.

Trevithick, J. A. (1975) 'Keynes, Inflation and Money Illusion', *Economic Journal*, March.

United Nations Organization (1948) *Proceedings and Documents of the United Nations Monetary and Financial Conference*, Vol. 2, Government Printing Office, Washington.

United Nations Organization (1973) *Input-Output Tables and Analysis* Studies in Methods, Series F, No.14, New York.

Van Arkadie, B. (1969) *Economic Accounting and Development Planning*, Oxford University Press, Oxford.

Author Index

Subject Index